More Praise For The Books Of Abigail Pogrebin

Stars of David

"Consistently engaging . . . Pogrebin says this book grew out of her efforts to clarify her own Jewish identity. But you don't need to be on such a quest to enjoy the wide range of experiences and feelings recorded here."

—*Publishers Weekly*

"Pogrebin, a former producer for Charlie Rose and *60 Minutes*, had the tools to push her interviewees beyond their comfort zone."

—*Jewish Journal of Greater Los Angeles*

"...a wide and interesting variety of stories about faith and the lack thereof, family memory, ritual, continuity, and the choices they have made."

—*The Jewish Week*

One and the Same

"An enchanting, fascinating book."

—Lesley Stahl, *60 Minutes*

"Spot on. An honest explanation of how multiples feel about the relationship into which they were born."

—*Newsweek*

"One and the Same is a touching, funny, smart book, written with considerable flair. Though it contains medical, social, political, and historical perspectives, it is at its core a book about love and intimacy."

—Andrew Solomon, author of *Far from the Tree*

"An immensely satisfying, enlightening read."

—*BookPage*

"This book about what it means to be a duplicate is smart and revealing and wise—and, well, singular."

—*The Daily Beast*

ABIGAIL POGREBIN

FOREWORD BY A. J. JACOBS

MY JEWISH YEAR

18 HOLIDAYS, ONE WONDERING JEW

FIG TREE
BOOKS

BEDFORD, NEW YORK

Bedford, New York

Copyright © 2017 by Abigail Pogrebin

All rights reserved.

Published in the United States by Fig Tree Books LLC, Bedford, New York

www.FigTreeBooks.net

Jacket design by Jenny Carrow
Interior design by Neuwirth & Associates, Inc.

Library of Congress Cataloging-in-Publication Data Available Upon Request

ISBN number 978-1-941493-20-5

Printed in the United States
Distributed by Publishers Group West

10 9 8 7 6 5 4 3 2 1

CONTENTS

FOREWORD

A. J. JACOBS

Abby Pogrebin subtitles her book *18 Holidays, One Wondering Jew.*

Which is an excellent way to describe it.

But let me break her year down a little further for you.

We're talking a year filled with:

- Fifty-one rabbis
- Six days of fasting
- Countless prayers
- One day without deodorant
- A couple of barrels of booze (Shabbat wine and Simchat Torah scotch among them)
- Untold amounts of revelation, joy, and, of course, guilt

In short, a *lot* of Judaism.

We're talking an Ironman triathlon of holiday observance (or so it seems to those of us not brought up Orthodox).

For most of her life, Abby was only loosely connected to her heritage. To borrow a phrase from my own book, Abby was Jewish in the same way the Olive Garden was Italian. Not very. (No offense to the Olive Garden. Great breadsticks.)

But she hungered for a more authentic taste of Judaism.

And this wonderful book is the result.

I'm impressed that Abby finished the year, with all its fasts and feasts, praying and partying. And I'm even more impressed that she produced this book—it's wise, thought-provoking, and funny.

I've known Abby since we were about the age when most of our friends were becoming *bar* or *bat mitzvah*. (Neither of us Olive Garden types went through the ritual ourselves at the time.)

Ever since, I've followed her career with a mix of *naches* (pleasure) and envy. I loved her work as a producer on *60 Minutes*. And her book *Stars of David*, where prominent Jews—from Ruth Bader Ginsburg to Larry King—reflect on their faith. And her book *One and the Same*, about her experience as an identical twin.

But this could be my favorite work Abby has ever done.

She achieves a beautiful balance—in many ways.

She balances passion and skepticism. Learning and memoir.

She balances humor and tragedy—which, as Abby points out, is a very Jewish thing to do. The holidays themselves career from celebrations to penance and remembrance. As Abby told me, "There's really no stretch of mourning and sadness that's not broken up by revelry. The calendar doesn't let you get too low without some dose of happiness."

She balances the modern impulse to rush around with the ancient imperative to slow down (a huge challenge for a Type A like Abby).

She balances her individuality with the demands of community. Because unlike Netflix, the Jewish calendar does not conform to your own schedule. You don't get to choose when to observe.

And she balances tradition with reinvention. She experiences the Orthodox route, but also experiments with ways to tweak the rituals ("For starters, I plan to add some games and quizzes to keep my kids engaged during Passover. Name the second plague? Frogs!").

Her book has changed the way I look at Jewish rituals, history, and the religion itself. She is a dogged investigator and frank witness. Obscure holidays suddenly made sense; the ones I thought I knew took surprising turns.

A few years ago, I wrote my own book about the Hebrew Scriptures—*The Year of Living Biblically*. Mine was a much different journey. I was trying to follow the written law, the hundreds of rules contained in the Bible itself. (Do not shave the corners of your beard; don't wear clothes made of mixed fibers.)

Abby's journey is very different. She followed both the written and the oral Torah. She took on both the Bible and the thousands of years of commentary and ritual. Her quest is more explicitly Jewish.

And yet I did recognize one common theme in our books: the head-to-toe immersion in a topic.

Before I embarked on my book, I was frankly quite anxious. I was nervous about how it would affect my day job as a magazine editor and my marriage (the beard alone would be a crucible for my wife). I was anxious about the public reaction. I knew it would be easy for detractors to slam my approach as misguided. Would observant folks condemn me as too irreverent? Would atheists slam me for being too gentle on the Bible? Would I be afflicted by boils?

So I went to breakfast with a rabbi friend of mine, Andy Bachman, then head of Brooklyn's Congregation Beth Elohim. And Rabbi Bachman told me a story (which I've written about before; but I figure Judaism is all about the repetition of stories, so maybe you'll forgive me).

The story is a legend from the *Midrash*, and it goes like this: when Moses was fleeing the Egyptians, he arrived at the Red Sea with his thousands of followers. Moses lifted up his staff, hoping for a miracle—but the sea did not part.

The Egyptian soldiers were closing in, and Moses and his followers were stuck at the shore. It was only a matter of time before every one of them would be slaughtered. Naturally, Moses and his followers were panicking. No one knew what to do.

And then, just before the Egyptian army caught up to them, a Hebrew named Nachshon did something unexpected. He simply walked into the Red Sea. He waded up to his ankles, then his knees, then his waist, then his shoulders. And right when the water was about to get up to his nostrils, it happened: the sea parted.

The point, said Rabbi Bachman, is that "sometimes miracles occur only when you jump in."

Thank you, Abby, for jumping in.

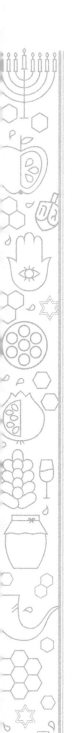
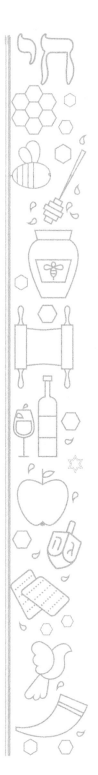

Rabbi David Ingber
ON THE JEWISH HOLIDAYS

Contrary to the other three hundred days of the year, when you're running and doing and building and constructing, the Jewish holidays provide a kind of in-built way to pause and to gather yourself and regenerate. . . . Our lives can become so full of activities and to-do tasks that, in some sense, the soul becomes overwhelmed. We need to defragment our souls. We can be pulled in so many different directions, but the holidays help that part of us that needs meaning and connection and great purpose. . . . Holiday rituals are ancient technologies that carry contemporary wisdom. Judaism works.

Rabbi Michael Strassfeld
ON THE HOLIDAYS

Judaism at its best—the ritually Jewish things—are things that help you pay attention. The holidays are not about doing the Jewishly Jewish things—the things that only Jews do. They are about awareness and mindfulness and paying attention. How do you live a life when you're paying attention?

INTRODUCTION
How Did I Get Here?

I T WAS A sure conversation-stopper: "This year I'll be researching, observing, and writing about every single Jewish holiday on the calendar."

My non-Jewish friends nodded politely: "That sounds really *interesting. . . .*"

Non-observant Jews looked puzzled: "Aren't there, like, a *thousand* of those. . . ? I guess you won't be doing much else this year."

Observant Jews shrugged, as if to say, "Welcome to our world; want a trophy?"

I'm exaggerating. Slightly.

But what everyone seemed to be asking was "Why?" and "Why now?"

Why, when my two kids were teenagers and well past their bar and bat mitzvah, when my husband of twenty years was content with our middling observance, when it was kind of late in the game to change the game, did I want to spend the next twelve months steeped in the Jewish calendar, interviewing rabbis about each holiday, reading entire books about one single prayer, attending temple services I didn't know existed, fasting six times instead of once?

All I knew was that something tugged at me, telling me there was more to feel than I'd felt, more to understand than I knew. It's hard to describe feeling full and yet lacking—entirely blessed with family, friendships, and work, and yet annoyed that I hadn't graduated much beyond the survey course when it came to Judaism.

I'm generally leery of "seekers" and the unceasing books about seeking a claim to offer a recipe for joy or insight. But here was a blueprint—thousands of years old—staring me in the face, and I'd never tested it. I'd already been drawn to Jewish life, but I hadn't fully lived one. Judaism's less-mainstream holidays seemed to separate the amateurs from the experts, and though I knew I'd never be fully observant, I also didn't want to be a neophyte forever.

I grew up celebrating Rosh Hashanah, Yom Kippur, Hanukkah, two Passover *seders*, and the sporadic Friday Shabbat. But those are a drop in the bucket compared to the total number of holidays that flood the Jewish calendar. I'd watched how observant families adhere to an annual system that organizes and anchors their lives. I envied not their certainty, but their literacy. I wanted to know what they knew. I had a hunch it would take me somewhere deeper.

My Jewish identity had previously been a given, not a pursuit. I lived in a Jewish town (New York City) in a Jewish neighborhood (the Upper West Side) with mostly Jewish friends, none of whom went to synagogue regularly.

My mother, Letty Cottin Pogrebin, had been raised in Queens by a mother who had emigrated from Hungary in cardboard shoes and never had an education, and a father who was a *macher* (big deal) in his synagogue and insisted—not because he was a feminist but because Mom was his third daughter and his only shot at raising "a Jewish boy"—that she receive religious schooling, despite how unusual it was for girls in the 1940s. She was a rare bat mitzvah for 1951.

When my mother was fifteen, her mother died of cancer, a rending loss that was compounded by the fact that she was not permitted to say Kaddish (the traditional mourner's prayer) for her own mother. My grandfather explained at the time that women didn't count in the necessary *minyan* (quorum of ten) required to recite this prayer. She wasn't "seen" as a Jew at the moment she needed Judaism the most. Stung and disillusioned, she turned her back on institutional practice for two decades. She ultimately came back to Judaism strongly, but my sister, brother, and I fell through the cracks during her estrangement. She didn't sign me up for Hebrew School nor suggest I become bat mitzvah. Feminism was her new religion. (She'd cofounded *Ms.* Magazine with Gloria Steinem and cocreated *Free to Be You and Me* with Marlo Thomas.)

Our Judaism was shaped by Friday night Shabbat candle-lighting when convenient, an epic Hanukkah party to counter the seductions of Christmas, and High Holy Day services twice a year—on Rosh Hashanah and Yom Kippur, because Mom still felt she couldn't be anywhere else on those days; their sanctity was in her DNA. When she eventually joined a synagogue again—B'nai Jeshurun on the Upper West Side—she was trying to replace something I'd never known well enough to miss.

My father, Bert Pogrebin, grew up as a "bagel Jew" in a small town in New Jersey. His father, who ran a fruit stand, died when Dad was twenty. His immigrant mom, Esther, one of five sisters, was more lefty than Jew. She wasn't sentimental. Yet Grandma Esther was a loving force in my life, cheering every tiny accomplishment, baking us *ruggelach* (Jewish crescent-shaped pastry), singing us Yiddish lullabies, and *kvetching* that we weren't staying longer the minute we arrived for a visit. My father doesn't believe in God the way Mom does. He loves Jewish discourse, the *Nation* and the *New York Review of Books*, reading every Bellow, Roth, and Malamud. But he isn't much for prayer. They share a love for the New York Philharmonic, new plays, cold vodka, and books. And when it comes to Judaism, they've had an effortless arrangement; Dad accompanies Mom to *shul* on the High Holy Days because she needs to be there and they prefer to do things in tandem. They have taken classes on Torah and Prophets together. But she didn't expect or ask him to pray or feel spiritual the way she does. She rediscovered faith in a way he couldn't. He never had it in the first place.

Every spring of my childhood, my parents, siblings, and I drove to two Passover seders on my mother's side of the family: the first at my uncle Danny's in Long Island, where, before the service began, my father and I imbibed peanuts from the bar bowl so we wouldn't be starving while we slogged through the Haggadah (the Passover liturgy). The second seder was always at my aunt Betty's in Larchmont, where we inverted the salt shaker into the matzah ball soup so it would have some flavor.

I loved these family seders because of the squeezes of my aunts and uncles, the din of politics competing with "Dayenu" (the central Passover anthem), the Barton's chocolate-covered macaroons. But I would have failed any test on the Exodus story. I was still missing the basics, having no clue that the majority of the Haggadah text isn't found in the Bible (the rabbis wrote it later) or why Moses is barely mentioned in the service despite his role in the Exodus escape (the rabbis wanted to emphasize God, not Moses, as the hero). I could never have explained why we drink four cups of wine (one for every iteration of deliverance in the Exodus text) or why Jews have two seders on consecutive nights, rereciting the same exact Haggadah both times. (The lunar calendar was less conclusive, so Diaspora Jews marked the holiday twice to cover their bases.)

Back in 1976, when I was an unhip eleven-year-old, Mom began taking my twin sister, Robin, and me to yet a third seder, the "Feminist Seder," a ritual that reimagined every segment of the service. It was conceived by four women, including Mom, who were fed up with the patriarch-focused Haggadah and the husband-recite-and-get-served seder meal. Writer Esther Broner created a text and tradition that honored women's sacrifices and the Bible's matriarchs.

I was giggly at the sight of a ceremony on the floor with bedsheets for the table, pillows for seats, and a potluck meal. I soaked up the stories of women's exclusion, centuries up until the present. Year after year, I heard poetic voices of strong women, including Gloria Steinem, whom I knew well from my regular visits to Mom's office at *Ms.*

magazine, and Bella Abzug, the firebrand congresswoman who always wore a wide-brimmed hat, and was the only seder participant to insist on an actual chair.

During the eight days of Hanukkah, my mother pulled out all the stops, set on creating a tradition to rival anyone's Christmas so that her kids would never feel deprived of the national frenzy. Every night, my sister, brother, and I lit the *menorah* and sang "Hanukkah, O Hanukkah" and "I Had a Little Dreidel"—the game in which a spinning top with four Hebrew letters, one on each side, was twirled. In our house, a gift was opened according to whose Hebrew letter landed faceup. The presents were modest (Billy Joel's *The Stranger* was a high point), but the thrill of eight wrapped boxes quickened a child's heart and felt Jewishly correct; we didn't gobble gifts as TV kids do around the Christmas tree. Our trinkets were meted out.

Mom hosted an annual Hanukkah party for about seventy-five people, buying a small present for every guest, asking every family to contribute some form of entertainment: song, poem, or skit. Who can forget Steinem tap-dancing in our living room, or *New York Times* editor Max Frankel delivering a lecture on the Maccabean revolt? My siblings and I wrote new Hanukkah-appropriate lyrics to a medley of Broadway show tunes. From *West Side Story*: "*When you're a Jew, you're a Jew all the way from your first little* bris, *to your bar mitzvah day. . . .*" From *Evita*: "*Don't cry for me, Antiochus . . . the truth is I burned the latkes. . . .*"

I loved these traditions—our crowded living room full of families I'd known forever and our more intimate nightly family powwow around the menorah. But Jewish identity, per se, wasn't at the forefront of my mind until I was twenty-four and it was tested. For a year, I'd been dating a Catholic named Michael who cared a lot about his Catholic heritage. Mom was sure I'd soon abandon the Jewish people and start baptizing my babies. She blamed herself; she'd failed to give me enough Jewish identity to want to preserve it. She cautioned that I'd end up caring later, more than I did in my twenties, a warning that felt unnerving. Despite her sadness, I moved to Palo Alto with Michael when he was admitted to Stanford Law School.

The relationship ended nine months later. In part, I began to feel the fault lines more than I'd expected or that I could explain to him. It wasn't just that when I took him to my aunt Judy's seder in Palo Alto, I realized that everything familiar to me was foreign to him; it was the ineffable gaps that reminded me that we didn't come from the same "stuff." He knew more about his faith than I did about mine, so it was hard for me to visualize our religious future together. How would I teach our children what I didn't know myself? Our conversations on the topic were strained. He thought I was overdramatizing our differences; I thought he wasn't being honest about how hard it could become.

I cried a lot when I packed my bags and flew back to New York, despite my parents' loving welcome. Walking back into my childhood bedroom with its Laura Ashley wallpaper felt like failure; I'd left less than a year ago with fanfare and a certain degree of courage, to strike out on another coast. Now I was home without an apartment or a job. I had also come up against an unfamiliar realization: my Judaism mattered. Or at least, I was being forced to decide whether it did. I could shrug off the question for a while longer, join a gym, schedule dinner with friends, job-hunt. But it would keep circling back, perching on my shoulder like an insistent parrot, *"You have to deal with me."*

Which is not to say that I truly dealt with it until 1997: the moment I was looking at my newborn son at his bris (circumcision). This necessitates a rewind to 1993, when I had a blind date with a wonderful Skokie native named David Shapiro and married him eight months later. I had never felt such an instantaneous certainty about knowing someone without knowing them, of looking forward to talking to someone for the rest of my life. He had a Midwestern genuineness, a keen sense of humor, a fascination with history, and a devotion to family. Our family parallels felt like no coincidence: we both had parents with strong, uncomplicated marriages; I'm an identical twin, and Dave has identical twin sisters. Dave is three years younger than his twin sisters, and Robin and I are three years older than my brother, David. We had an instant shorthand and ease together.

On a sunny October morning, Dave proposed to me at the Lincoln Center fountain, pouring champagne from a bottle into two flutes, playing our favorite song on a portable CD player: "I Could Write a Book," by Rodgers and Hart.

David wanted a small wedding, so we culled the guest list to the bare minimum (not easy—I have regrets), picked a pre-high-season date with lower airfare to St. Lucia, and asked my Yale classmate Mychal Springer, by then an ordained rabbi, to come marry us. We exchanged vows on a mountain so windy, I thought I might blow off. Mom had requested a wedding canopy, and the island resort seemed to enjoy creating its first "hooper," as the St. Lucians referred to it— the *huppah* (canopy for weddings). It was important to me to be under one; all my ancestors had been, and I wanted to relive the *Fiddler on the Roof* wedding scene, having watched every Broadway iteration since 1969, memorized the movie, and played Chava (the rejected daughter) in a college production.

When our first child, Benjamin, arrived in all of his robust nine pounds, twelve ounces, something powerful reared its head as I watched his swaddled self, capped in a miniature *yarmulke*, held aloft by the *mohel* who performed the "surgery," Phil Sherman. (Phil is famously theatrical but he gets the job done fast, with an improvised pacifier of sweet wine for the infant, minimal baby-wailing, and plenty of *shtick*). I'll never forget the questions that echoed in my head as Ben was being blessed: *"Do you really understand why you're doing this? Does this mark the start of your Jewish family, or are you just checking the box?"*

The bris conveyed a decision I'd never made. We scheduled the ceremony because that's what Jews do: host a bris on the eighth day of a boy's birth, invite friends and family to come witness, bless, and then eat. I cried that morning because I was hormonal, true, but also because Ben was the newest tiny Jew, joining a tenacious people that many were determined to eliminate. And I cried at my deficits: how little I knew, and how late I'd have to learn it if I chose to start now.

This was the moment that led me to write my first book, *Stars of David: Prominent Jews Talk About Being Jewish*, an anthology of face-to-face interviews with Jewish celebrities about whether they cared about Judaism. Sure enough, these public figures had wrestled with similar vacillation—discarding what was inherited; feeling part of a tribe or indifferent to it; owning or abandoning tradition; mastering rituals or never learning them; navigating the patchiness of observance, the shame in stereotypes, the riddle of Israel.

No fewer than sixty-two people agreed to talk to me for the book, including both Jewish Supreme Court justices at the time, Ruth Bader Ginsburg and Stephen Breyer; actor Dustin Hoffman; director Steven Spielberg; opera legend Beverly Sills; comedian Gene Wilder; writer and director Nora Ephron; *Star Trek*'s Jewish duo, Leonard Nimoy and William Shatner; Olympic medalist Mark Spitz; and three of my former bosses at *60 Minutes*: Mike Wallace, Morley Safer, and Executive Producer Don Hewitt.

In the midst of what proved to be intense, intimate conversations, I realized that I hadn't answered the questions I was posing: How much does being Jewish matter to you? Do you care what religion your children are? Do you feel a personal weight because of our hard history? Are you pro– or anti–*gefilte fish*?

Then I was jarred by my interview with Leon Wieseltier, the wild-haired, erudite writer, who grew up Orthodox and is fluent in Jewish scholarship. I sought him out because I know he's unapologetically opinionated and I didn't want my hand held. But as we sat on chairs opposite each other in his spare office, the bluntness of his message was still bracing. He was entirely unsympathetic to the idea that I, and many of my interviewees, might be unmoved by, and uncommitted to, Judaism:

"The problem is that most American Jews make their decisions about their Jewish identity knowing nothing or next to nothing about the tradition that they are accepting or rejecting. We have no right to allow our passivity to destroy this tradition that miraculously has made it across two thousand years of hardship right into our laps. I think we have no right to do that. Like it or not, we are stewards of something precious."

I left this interview feeling both depleted and energized. I picked up Wieseltier's book *Kaddish* and underlined a line I've kept with me:

"Do not overthrow the customs that have made it all the way to you."
The proverbial lightbulb went off.

I began weekly Torah learning with a young rabbi, Jennifer Krause,
who had taught my parents' study group and who hails from Tucson.
It soon became a highlight of my week as I began to understand how
random Bible stories connected, how family dysfunction was timeless,
how right and wrong was clarified in our ancestors' mistakes. Torah
references suddenly popped up everywhere: novels, political speeches,
movie scripts, poems.

Ultimately Jennifer nudged me to cross the Rubicon—to become a
bat mitzvah at the tender age of forty. I fought her at first, because it felt
like much ado about not much, and I didn't want to celebrate myself for
such a belated milestone. A bat or bar mitzvah (literally: "daughter [bat]
or son [bar] of commandment"), typically marked at age twelve or thirteen, is the turning point of a Jew's life—as other religions have their
rites of passage—so I was hesitant, twenty-eight years late, to ask
friends and family to save the date, to rent out a defunct synagogue
since I still didn't belong to one, to reserve a restaurant space for lunch.
Jen told me to stop angst-ing; this wasn't about a party, but a promise.
I was signing up for Judaism, and that was worth a catered meal.

I gave in and soon found myself on the subway memorizing my
parsha (Torah section) with earphones every day, pressing stop and
rewind to make sure I knew the chant. As the date neared, I became
single-minded, going over the prayers and feeling pulled toward the
ceremony in some inexorable way.

I slept in my childhood bedroom the night before the service because my Chicago in-laws had kindly flown in and were bunking in
our apartment on various sofa beds and mattresses. I suspected that
I'd need a little separation and quiet to concentrate. Mom left a gift
on my old Laura Ashley comforter: a silver *Kiddush* cup (for wine
blessings on Shabbat and holidays) with my name engraved and the
date of my bat mitzvah. "Better late," she wrote in her card. "I'm so
proud you chose this."

Jen was right: my Big Fat Belated Bat Mitzvah was unforgetta-
ble. Maybe it was watching Ben and Molly come up on "stage" to

recite by heart the blessings for the candles and *challah* (braided bread), or seeing them witness their mom officially join the Jewish people. Maybe it was that when I chanted Torah, the handwritten Hebrew letters were no longer swimming on the parchment, but recognizable. Maybe I was overwhelmed by reciting the same text that has been read and read and read by Jew after Jew after Jew for more than three thousand years—even when people had to do so in secret. Maybe it was watching my mother crying in the front row.

My Torah portion in Leviticus included the concept of *Karet*—being cut off from one's people. I realized that I was choosing not to be.

After the bat mitzvah, I became somewhat insatiable, downloading books and journals, listening to recorded sermons of rabbis I admired, reading the Jewish press. I convened a monthly Torah study group over wine in my living room with friends, led by the cheeky, affable Rabbi Burt Visotzky from the Jewish Theological Seminary, an expert on Midrash (Torah commentary). Burt suggested that we begin at the beginning, so we chose the book of Genesis and didn't stop till we'd completed it five years later.

But I was still a Jew without a synagogue, and I didn't look for one because, for all my Jewish awakening, I didn't view temple membership as lacking. Then I stumbled into my first real Jewish home, Central Synagogue, a Reform temple in Manhattan with Moorish Revival architecture, a dazzling rose window, and thousands of devoted congregants.

I happened to attend the bat mitzvah of my friend Pamela's daughter and was drawn in by the splendor of the sanctuary, the urgency of Rabbi Peter Rubinstein's sermon, and the expressive voice of Cantor Angela Buchdahl. It was love at first sound.

Outside, I phoned my husband: "We have to join this place."

Ever the realist, he said, "You spent ninety minutes there."

"I'm just telling you, Dave: *this is where we should be.*" I knew I wanted to keep listening to this clergy. I wanted to keep coming back to that room.

I signed us up the following Monday. Dave trusted my gut and went along.

Central draws people in quickly. Suddenly, I was safeguarding Friday evenings to attend services—Central's largest weekly gathering, which numbers hundreds and feels ebullient and sacred. The music penetrated, the spoken prayers felt unforced.

I enrolled my children in the weekly religious school and delighted in watching them bow during their abbreviated *tefilah* (prayer) service and learn Hebrew alongside their new friends. For Ben's "mitzvah project" (community service), he chose to visit regularly with a Holocaust survivor and was affected by his stories.

But then Ben hit a roadblock, when he was saddled by severe anxiety in the seventh grade—a discomfort that was compounded by the loss of his friend Jacob, age ten, to brain cancer. Ben told us that he saw no point in a bar mitzvah or praying to a God who could let a ten-year-old die. I wrote to Senior Rabbi Peter Rubinstein, asking sincerely for help; I had no clue how to parent this moment.

Peter suggested that Ben stop by his office, and one meeting changed everything. Peter managed to connect with Ben in a way that no teacher or therapist had. Over the next few months, Peter talked Ben through his sense of religion's futility. One day, out of the blue, Ben told us he wanted a bar mitzvah after all.

Ben and Molly became bar and bat mitzvah two years apart in ceremonies that seized my heart. During each service, I felt my children uplifted by a ritual that conveyed, *This is about you and also beyond you. None of this lasts without you.* I cried at the same two moments: when the rabbi passed the Torah scroll from the two pairs of grandparents to

Dave and me and then to our child—a physical passing of the tradition—and also when they received a private blessing from the rabbi in front of the ark. I don't say this lightly: it felt as if God was close by that day. Central Synagogue brought home the idea that my mother had predicted years ago: Judaism is a train that circles back to pick you up.

So with all this newfound connection, why did I feel compelled to go further? I think because the more I did grasp, the more I saw what I didn't. It bothered me that I had never lived the entire Jewish calendar. I couldn't explain Shemini Atzeret. I wanted to fill in the gaps, not just asking what Tu B'Shvat means but why it began and its relevance today.

One rabbi, Irwin Kula, posed two questions that guided me throughout my yearlong undertaking: *"What do we hire a holiday to do for us? What is the yearning to which the holiday is a response?"*

I wanted to know what each holiday does. Not that I would sit back, fold my arms, and expect fairy dust; I'd do my part, leave my skepticism at the door, be as active and open as possible. I hoped to be taken somewhere. The land of the holiday-knowers looked compelling, grounding.

Of course, multitudes of Orthodox Jews follow every holiday as a matter of course, but most Jews in the United States are not living by the Jewish clock, nor even aware of what happens when. (The holiday dates change every year according to the Hebrew calendar, which is tied to the moon's cycles and is impossible to memorize; many holidays officially begin at sundown the night before, often lasting more than one day depending on the holiday: Rosh Hashanah is two days; Sukkot is eight or nine, depending on whom you ask.)

I wanted to understand what we non-Orthodox Jews are missing. Not just the facts and figures of Judaism, but their expression in real life. I wanted more of the intensity that I'd observed other people feeling.

The much-dissected Pew Research Center study of 2013 revealed that most Jews do not connect their Jewish identity to Judaism. I wanted to find out if that's because we haven't really looked there.

✡

So I took the leap. I began a column for the *Forward* newspaper, called "18 Holidays; One Wondering Jew," a journey generously shepherded and supported by the *Forward* and then expanded considerably for this book. I promised readers I'd dissect and digest every single Jewish holiday, no matter how obscure, promising to write *before and after* each major one—to share my preparation first, my experience afterwards. (For the less famous holidays, one chapter seemed sufficient.) I aimed to climb the scaffolding of a more rigorous Jewish life without knowing the outcome.

Yes, I could predict all the roadblocks:

1. Judaism's schedule is a bear. I committed to writing about eighteen holidays because when I started counting them, I came up with between eighteen and twenty, depending on how one tallies the major and minor festivals and fasts. I leaned toward a clean eighteen since it's a significant Jewish number: every Hebrew letter has a numerical value and the word *chai* (life) adds up to eighteen. Chai also means "raw" or "uncooked," an apt adjective since I considered myself an unbaked Jew.

2. The Sabbath is considered the most important holiday of all, but I thought I'd lose my audience if I wrote about all fifty-two. I wrote about two, without counting them in the total eighteen.

3. I like eating. The idea of graduating from one difficult fast (Yom Kippur) to six didn't electrify me.

4. Synagogue services are typically long, and, let's be frank, not always riveting. I decided to research and visit different temples and independent prayer groups across denominations, which would mean significant pew time.

5. My kids and husband didn't sign on for this. Now, not only did they have to participate (at least a little), but they'd have to hear about it (a lot). They said that they were game, but I wasn't so sure. I apologized in advance because I'd be absent at odd times (one penitential service, Selichot, began at midnight; on Shavuot [the giving of the Torah], people study all night till sunrise).

6. I apologized to my Central clergy because I'd be peripatetic for a year. I apologized to my husband because I'd be running off to spend hours without him, sitting in other shuls on the High Holy Days when we normally sit side by side.

7. I realized my method might appear quirky or hypocritical: I would be observing Jewish holidays without being observant, eating ritual foods without keeping kosher, designing a personal seminary without getting a degree. This would be an expedition, not a conversion. *I* was clear, but others might not be.

8. I worried that I'd be perceived by the Orthodox as a tourist or trespasser in what adds up to their way of life. Even though, even in Orthodoxy, there is no *one way*. I've met observant Jews who don't keep every fast, who parse kosher rules very personally, who discard one rite but wouldn't skip another. Judaism has become highly customized, and the labels of Reform, Reconstructionist, Conservative, and Orthodox are all moving targets.

9. My Hebrew is pathetic. I first learned the language in college (taught by a dynamic professor who used the Israeli Top-40 pop countdown to drill vocabulary), then promptly

forgot everything I'd mastered because I stopped using it, then relearned enough to chant my Torah portion, then recently went on Craigslist to find a tutor and found Joel Goldman, a very sage, very Orthodox instructor who looks anxious for the Jewish future every time I read aloud.

10. Okay, *The Year of Living Biblically* by A. J. Jacobs was a brilliant book. I went to high school with A.J., I know A.J., A.J. is a friend of mine. But he and I agreed that my voyage would be different—A.J. followed the Bible's scriptures, I'd be the holiday pilgrim. He gave me his blessing. And he kindly wrote the Foreword to this book. So everyone can stop bringing up A.J. already.

I noted the hurdles and then pressed ahead:

I printed out a Jewish calendar and taped it to my fridge.

I ordered a *shofar* (ram's horn) on Amazon.com. (FYI, they can be malodorous.)

I picked out white clothes for Yom Kippur. (We're supposed to dress in the white of our burial shroud.)

I polished my candlesticks and found a recipe for *hamantaschen* (the Purim pastry).

I researched a place to go for Selichot (penitence before the High Holy Days—who knew we atone before we atone?) and a place to observe Yom HaShoah (Holocaust remembrance). I was drawn to places where a holiday would be highlighted; not all synagogues program every holiday.

"Most American Jews don't see identity as an enterprise of labor, a matter of toil," Wieseltier told me. "So in America now it is possible to be a Jew with a Jewish identity that one can defend, and that gives one pleasure—and for that identity to have painfully little Jewish substance." I wanted my Jewish identity to have Jewish substance. I wanted more "toil." Wieseltier's prescription for Jewish meaning—a resonance I craved—was to "get into the fight." It was time.

First stop: Rosh Hashanah.

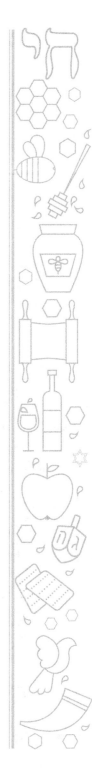

Rabbi Michael Strassfeld
ON ROSH HASHANAH

Rosh Hashanah is about possibilities and births, new beginnings. In some ways that's the potential of cyclical time. You think you're just a year older, but you can start again.

Jonathan Blake
ON ROSH HASHANAH

It's like you're on cruise control, mindlessly going down the highway, when suddenly you're confronted with lights and sirens and you have to think fast and take control of the pedals or you're going to end up part of the emergency situation up ahead.

That's Rosh Hashanah to me: Yes, it's a sweet time, a time for apples and honey, but even more it's alarm-clock time: the piercing wail of the shofar that shakes us out of the stupor of the daily routine. We understandably crave comfort and convenience: the chaos of the world around us practically demands that we insulate ourselves with regimen and regularity. Rosh Hashanah bolts us awake. It says: "Life doesn't have to be like this." You can change. Your hurting relationships can be better. Your unfounded anxieties and petty fixations need not strangle you forever in their grip. Your accumulated, tough scar tissue need not keep you from feeling. Your life holds possibilities—beautiful opportunities—some of which you've falsely assumed out of your reach, some of which you haven't even dared to dream up. That's Rosh Hashanah to me, a blast of the possible.

1

PREPPING ROSH HASHANAH
Self-Flagellation in Summer
9.22.14

T HE INSTRUCTION MANUAL from the Israeli company that shipped my shofar (the trumpet made from a ram's horn, blasted during the Jewish New Year) says the blowing technique can be learned by "filling your mouth with water. You then make a small opening at the right side of your mouth, and blow out the water with a strong pressure. You must practice this again and again until you can blow the water about four feet away."

Rosh Hashanah (literally "head of the year") marks the Jewish new year, the anniversary of Creation, and requires the shofar blast to alert the world to the new beginning—the moment we're supposed to "wake up" to who we've been in the last year and who we aim to become in the next one. The horn is notoriously impossible to blow, especially with its prescribed cadence and strength. Try it some time: it's really hard. Synagogues troll for the brave souls who can actually pull it off without making the congregation cringe at the sad attempts that emit tense toots or dying wails.

This year, I'm committed to fulfilling the commandment of hearing the shofar blast not only on the new year itself, but on nearly every morning of the Hebrew month of Elul, the weeks of self-examination that begin before Rosh Hashanah and end on Yom Kippur (the Day of Atonement).

So I'm standing at the kitchen sink, spewing tap water ineptly as my children look at me askance. My seventeen-year-old son, Ben, picks up the tawny plastic horn. "Let me try."

He kills it.

I hit on an idea. "I need you to be my blower every morning for the next thirty days."

"Sure," Ben answers blithely, despite the fact that he can't be roused before noon during the summer.

Before this project, I didn't know that the shofar gets blown daily for thirty days before the Jewish new year. (It's actually fewer, because the horn can't be honked on Shabbat nor the day before Rosh Hashanah.) Elul is the month prior to Rosh Hashanah and leads into the Days of Awe—the ten days between Rosh Hashanah and Yom Kippur.

Elul begins a forty-day period of repentance, judgment, and forgiveness. These forty days recall the weeks that Moses prayed for God's forgiveness on behalf of the Israelites who had sinned by building a forbidden idol—a golden calf. During this period of Elul, we ask forgiveness for that first, faithless idolatry and for our countless modern missteps.

This is new to me: starting the path to repentance in August's eighty-degree weather. I'd previously thought that self-abnegation was a one-day affair—the Yom Kippur Cleanse. And that was plenty; twelve hours in synagogue without eating has always felt to me like ample penitence. But now I'm learning a new rhythm. Contrition starts daily, early, forty days before the mother lode, spurred nearly every morning by a noise one can't ignore.

It's immediately obvious that there's no way I'm rousing Ben to blow the shofar for me. He's on Teenager Time. I'm on my own. The first day, I pick up the plastic trumpet and go into a room as far from my sleeping family as possible. I lift the horn to my mouth and try to follow the contradictory directions to simultaneously relax and purse the lips, whistling air into the mouthpiece. To my shock, out comes a blast. It's not pretty, but it's hardy. I keep my gaze out the window, thinking how bizarre this is and, at the same time, how visceral. The sound of the shofar is Judaism to me: raw, rousing, plaintive, adamant. I blow one more time, a little tentatively, because I don't want to disturb the house. I then sit down on the sofa to Google the twenty-seventh Psalm on my iPhone because I learned we're supposed to recite it aloud every morning from the first day of Elul until the end of Sukkot, the holiday that follows Yom Kippur. That's a lot of one psalm.

The verses are about God's protection, which we're going to need—Elul reminds us—during the upcoming days of judgment. I hear my voice saying the words, and they're oddly comforting—despite the motif of dread.

> The Lord is my light and my salvation; whom should I fear? The Lord
>   is the stronghold of my life; of whom shall I be afraid?
>
>   . . .
>
> Though a host should encamp against me, my heart shall not fear;
>   though war should rise up against me, even then will I be confident.

I then attempt the entire psalm in Hebrew, and manage to get through it. Slowly. But I'm proud of the fact that I can, in no small part thanks to Joel Goldman, my no-nonsense Hebrew tutor.

When my kids wake up, they inquire about my shofar debut. I tell them it felt poignant and pointless at the same time; I felt connected to something ancient, and yet foolish, standing in my pajamas, spitting through an ersatz ram's horn. Ben apologizes profusely for failing his assignment on the first day. I reassure him that I should be the one shouldering this ritual anyway; it's my Wondering Year, my obligation.

As the Elul days accumulate and become routine, I find myself actually looking forward to the new morning regimen—waking up ahead of my husband; turning on the coffee machine; grabbing my shofar and facing the window. My bleats are sometimes so solid, they surprise me, but more often they're jerky. I have to balance my desire to practice against alienating my family. "Cut the shofar!" my husband shouts from the next room.

The Medieval philosopher Maimonides described the blowing custom as "a wake-up call to sleepers, designed to rouse us from our complacency." It forces me to ask myself: "Am I complacent?" About my behavior, my friendships, my parenting, my work? If complacency means, as the dictionary says, "a feeling of smug or uncritical satisfaction with oneself," the answer is actually no. Just ask my therapist. I offer her a weekly catalogue of self-reproach. But the fact is, I don't scrutinize myself as comprehensively as I could when it comes to my character. Really, really truthfully: What kind of person am I, and how do I assess my pettiness, apathy, self-interest? The shofar should derail our rationalizations.

Rabbi Irving (Yitz) Greenberg, author of one of the classic guides to the holidays, *The Jewish Way*, explains that Elul is a time for "accounting for the soul," or *cheshbon hanefesh* (a reckoning with one's self). Yitz, eighty-two, a friend of my parents (which is why I call him Yitz), who is tall, slim, and somehow ethereal in his erudition, radiates placidity. If I could spend more time with Yitz, I'm convinced I'd be calmer, not to mention smarter. "Just as the month before the summer is the time when Americans go on crash diets, fearing how their bodies will look on the beach," he writes in his book, "so Elul, the month before Rosh Hashanah, became the time when Jews went on crash spiritual regimens, fearing how their souls would look when they stood naked before God."

I ask some other trusted rabbis how they'd suggest going about this nakedness, this "accounting for the soul." They recommend choosing one trait a day and examining that one quality. In an attempt to find a list of traits, I Google "Elul exercises" and "Elul practices" and come up with a list of *middot* (traits or measurements) that will take me through all forty days. It's an alphabetical litany of optional characteristics suggested by a Toronto teacher named Modya Silver on his blog (since taken down):

CHOOSE ONE OF THESE 40 TRAITS FOR EACH DAY OF ELUL:

- Abstinence—*prishut*
- Alacrity/Zeal—*zerizut*
- Arrogance—*azut*
- Anger—*ka'as*

- Awe of G-d— *yirat hashem*
- Compassion—*rachamim*
- Courage—*ometz lev*

- Cruelty—*achzariut*
- Decisiveness—*paskanut*
- Envy—*kina*
- Equanimity—
  menuchat hanefesh
- Faith in G-d—*emunah*
- Forgiveness—*slicha*
- Generosity—*nedivut*
- Gratitude—*hoda'ah*
- Greed—*taavat betza*
- Hatred—*sina*
- Honor—*kavod*
- Humility—*anivut*
- Joy—*simcha*
- Laziness—*atzlut*
- Leadership—*hanhagah*
- Life force—*chiyut*
- Love—*ahava*
- Loving kindness—
  chesed
- Miserliness—*tza'yekanut*
- Modesty—*tzniut*
- Order—*seder*

- Patience—*sav'lanut*
- Presence—*hineni*
- Pride—*ga'ava*
- Regret—*charata*
- Recognizing good—
  hakarat hatov
- Repentance—*teshuva*
- Respect—*kavod*
- Restraint—*hitapkut*
- Righteousness—*tzedek*
- Shame—*busha*
- Silence—*shtika*
- Simplicity—*histapkut*
- Slander—*lashon hara*
- Strength—*gevurah*
- Truth—*emet*
- Trust in G-d—*bitachon*
- Watchfulness—*zehirut*
- Wealth—*osher*
- Willingness—*ratzon*
- Worry—*de'aga*
- Fear/awe—*yirah*

I print out the list and think about who will tackle it with me. My rabbi-guides told me to find a *chevruta* (study partner) to keep me on track and ensure a daily review. So I need someone who's going to be game and won't balk at the discipline, let alone the candor. My close friend Dr. Catherine Birndorf is the ideal candidate: an accomplished psychiatrist and a fellow stumbling Jew, her bracing directness and humor keep me on my toes. Over our staple breakfast of soft-boiled eggs and toast, she relishes excavating our obsessions and personal roadblocks. She's helped me through more false-alarm crises than I want to name. I describe my proposal to her in our favorite diner, and Catherine doesn't hesitate before saying yes, which makes me feel grateful because I didn't really have a Plan B. It's a lot to ask of someone—to do one penance per day—swapping confessions. Not everyone has the patience or the curiosity.

Our agreed protocol is this: we'll mull the trait-of-the-day to ourselves privately during daylight hours, then, at night, email each other frank reflections. To give Catherine some context for this Elul assignment, I send Yitz's quote to her—the one about "crash diets" in anticipation of the beach. She writes back: "I'm a little skeptical of the beach analogy and crash dieting since it rarely leads to lasting change. But you gotta' start somewhere. . . ."

Rabbi Burt Visotzky, a jocund expert in Midrash (rabbinic commentary on Torah) who happens to be another family friend (so I'll call him Burt) and has taught for more than thirty years at the Jewish Theological Seminary, tells me that daily scrutiny is necessary to upend our complacency. "When you go to the therapist, you don't just go once," Burt reminds me. "You keep going. The repetition of Elul allows you to open yourself—not all at once—to things you've closed off."

What have I closed off? The realization that I still haven't managed to turn compassion into action often enough. I spent a semester teaching memoir-writing to formerly incarcerated men (a powerful experience), but failed to find a way to stay in touch with them. I don't see my parents enough. My aunt and I haven't recovered from a rift four years ago. I still look at my phone too much in restaurants, though I hate when others do that. I tend to remind my son what he needs to finish, instead of just asking how he is.

I see the point of Elul, the necessary runway to spiritual liftoff. How can one start the new year without looking fully—exhaustively—at the one that came before? When else do we permit ourselves, or demand, a detailed self-analysis?

I ask Burt—in his book-filled office—how he'd respond to those who say forty days of navel-gazing is overkill before Yom Kippur. "You can't walk into synagogue cold," Burt fires back. "Let me use the shrink analogy again: you don't just go into your therapy session without thinking ahead to what you want to discuss." No one knows that better than Catherine, a therapist by profession.

We dive in. And the middot force me to zero in on pockets of myself I rarely turn inside out.

Anger: I get riled when I feel something is unjust. I need to pause before writing the curt email.

Courage: I both have it and lack it, and wish I had the guts to worry a little less about gaining consensus before doing what I think is right.

Cruelty: I don't believe I'm ever mean, at least not consciously.

Forgiveness: I don't forgive my own mistakes. I'm slow to forget affronts. I beat myself up for being poor at things I could have studied harder: cooking, Hebrew, golf.

The imperfections go on. About two weeks into my middot list, I'm preparing dinner on a Saturday night with my mother-in-law, Phyllis, who is visiting us with my father-in-law, Milton, from Chicago. Every time she asks me how my holiday-immersion is going, she poses the same question: "Do you think you're going to turn really religious?"

I'm chopping cucumbers as I try to explain that I have no plan other than to simply keep up with the calendar and see where it takes me. One thing at a time. For now, I just need to focus on the Elul reflections. Phyllis doesn't hide her skepticism: "Don't you think it's going to be hard spending forty days tearing yourself apart?" My answer surprises me. I tell Phyllis that the task is already giving me a strange stillness. Contrary to Yom Kippur, when my penance in synagogue is often sidetracked by hunger, it's a very different experience to critique oneself on a full stomach while moving through an average day. I'm less impatient with the exercise; I take my time. I might even be harsher on my flaws because, unlike in services, when the litany of sins comes fast and furious, Elul allows for a scrupulous accounting.

My nightly exchanges with Catherine become trinkets of candor, which I collect. We make our way through the list as summer folds into fall, and I find that the specificity of the list makes self-examination sharper, plainer. There's less room to skirt the truth.

And yet despite all the introspection, I'm wholly at sea when it comes to the next phase of the atonement marathon—*Selichot* (penitential prayers). We beg for mercy. Selichot starts the Saturday night before

Rosh Hashanah and lasts until Yom Kippur. The kickoff service is like going to the late show, scheduled between 10 P.M. and midnight—and includes poetry of contrition.

I learn that the centerpiece of the Selichot liturgy is the "Thirteen Attributes of Mercy." They are God's virtues—which, if recited, are our ticket to clemency.

The Israelites were given this list after they angered God by building the Golden Calf. According to the Talmud (commentary on the Torah), God basically told Moses: "If your people want me to forgive them, they should recite this list describing me."

I'll input the numbers—though they're not usually in the text—because otherwise you may be as confused as I was as to how one gets to thirteen traits:

1. Merciful God, 2. merciful God, 3. powerful God, 4. compassionate and 5. gracious, 6. slow to anger, and 7. abundant in kindness and 8. truth. 9. Preserver of kindness for thousands of generations, 10. forgiver of iniquity, 11. willful sin and 12. error, and 13. Who cleanses (Exodus 34:6–7).

Okay. I get the Thirteen Attributes of God . . . kind of. Truthfully, it seems oddly insecure of God to require thirteen compliments in exchange for mercy. But as I reread the prayer, I start to absorb a different message. Maybe God is saying, "These attributes of mine should also be yours. Emulate and live by them."

When I read the prayer that way, I love the list. They are traits I aspire to, even if I never thought to enumerate them. Ben Franklin did just that. He created a list of thirteen virtues and measured himself by them every week, including temperance, silence, frugality, and industry. Our Founding Father fashioned his own personalized Selichot.

Despite my epiphany about God and Ben Franklin, I'm not so keen on going to synagogue so late on a weekend night. But I've committed to push through my laziness, my excuses (and my comfort zone) to keep up and show up. Judaism has specific office hours.

I've picked a program that starts before midnight, because I'm a wimp about staying up late. I walk into the dignified Park Avenue Synagogue on Madison Avenue at 10 P.M. and feel like a party guest who's arrived too early. It's not crowded, not empty. This sanctuary always has a formality to it, but tonight there's extra pomp: the velvet-swathed Torah is adorned in pristine white garb for the impending High Holidays, like a child putting on a new birthday outfit. The music is majestic. Rabbi Elliot Cosgrove, whom I know and admire, is lacking his usual wry humor. Tonight is serious stuff.

> May my heart be open
> To every broken soul,
> To orphaned life,
> To every stumbler
> Wandering unknown
> And groping in the shadow.

I'm the stumbler, the wanderer, the groper in the shadow. That's why I started this project. I now realize it's a quintessential Jewish act: seeking, grappling. If you're reaching, it's because you believe there's something to grab hold of.

I can't stay till the end because I promised my friend Rabbi Elie Kaunfer I'd stop by his service way uptown. Cofounder of Mechon Hadar, an independent seminary, Elie taught my Torah study group and wrote me this email before the holiday: "Abby, You might like a more experiential *davening* (reciting prayers), even if you aren't able to understand or even follow every word."

I arrive late to the crowded room of young regulars on the second floor of the Fort Tryon Jewish Center in Washington Heights. They have run out of handouts and chairs, so I move to a corner of the dimly lit space, grab my iPhone, and quickly download the Selichot text Elie had sent me in advance. I steal a glance at the worshippers around me, making sure I'm not the only one relying on a handheld device. I'm not; this is the Y Generation. I manage to find where they are on the page, but can barely keep up, especially in the bad light.

It's clear, however, that no one cares what his or her neighbor is doing. When singing the *niggunim* (melodies without words), the full-throated, harmonizing voices somehow lift me up and carry me along. Elie's email comes back to me: "Prayer is not about a cognitive experience of the words."

Whenever we get to the "Thirteen Attributes of God"—which has a melody I somehow absorbed in Central's services—I can sing with the room, and that changes everything.

Adonai! Adonai! El rachum v'chanun / Erech apayim v'rav chesed ve-emet / Notzer chesed la-alafim / Nosey avon vafesha v'chata'ah v'nakeh!

It's revealing to watch Elie in this context and realize that a ritual like Selichot, with its raw pleading, can bring out someone's primal side. Usually a measured, scholarly presence, Elie is bowed in fervid prayer, his head tented with a tallis, his voice—more powerful than I knew it could be—rising and falling, driving the worship as if overtaken by some divine engine. I wish I could be that transported.

Each time we get to the Thirteen Attributes, the song gains in volume. We plead as one. *Hear me. Forgive me. Grant me another year.* It echoes the twenty-seventh Psalm I've been reciting daily. It could feel useless to repeat—day after day—verses that may (or may not) have been penned by King David. But just like the recurrent sound of the shofar each dawn, just like the recurrence of the Thirteen Attributes, I'm beginning to grasp the resonance in repetition. Each reprise offers another chance at meaning.

"Do not hide your face from me. . . . Do not forsake me, do not abandon me"—Psalm 27.

And repeat.

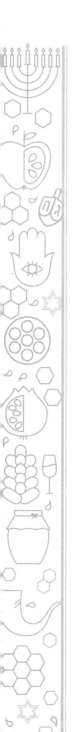
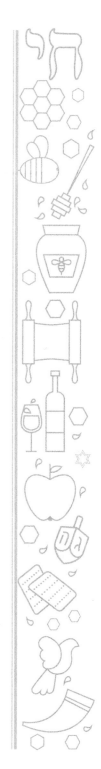

Rabbi Joanna Samuels
ON ROSH HASHANAH

"Today the world is born," we proclaim on Rosh Hashanah. A provocative Midrash teaches that Rosh Hashanah is not the anniversary of the *first* day of creation, but instead the *sixth* day of creation. On one long sixth day, God created Adam and Eve, who, in turn, loved, disobeyed, were banished from paradise, and learned that they would, eventually, die.

It is this sixth day that is the churning expanse of my *yoma arichta*—the "long day" that the sages called the two days of this holiday. I am intensely present to the miracle of being alive and yet frighteningly awake to the dark reality of mortality. I am optimistic that a new year could bring renewal to my soul and yet I confront my stubborn habits and long-standing failures. I am aware that I can—I must!—marshal my abilities in the service of making our world more just, and yet I am overwhelmed by how much seems unfixable.

Each and every Rosh Hashanah, as I seesaw from gratitude to fear, from possibility to narrowness, I consider the *yoma arichta* of Jewish history, the continuous narrative of a people, diverse and divergent, balancing on the same axis of optimism and fear. In the merit of all those whose lives make up the long years of our presence on earth, I commit to see possibility, to seek out repair, and to embrace the miracle of creation.

2

POST-ROSH HASHANAH

Tossing Flaws and Breadcrumbs

9.29.14

REMEMBER, AS A kid, feeling that the High Holy Day passage, *Unetaneh Tokef*—"Let us acknowledge the power [of the holiness of the day]"—which says that God is going to decide "Who will live and who will die," did not apply to me.

"Who by sword" seemed archaic; *"Who by water"* remote.

But that litany becomes alarmingly vivid as I get older. This year it feels as if every peril leaps off the page when I'm in Rosh Hashanah services.

"Who shall see ripe age and who shall not. . . ." My childhood friend Dan died a few weeks before the holiday while swimming in the ocean.

"Who shall perish by fire. . . ." Six members of a New Jersey family—related to Rhonda, who works the checkout counter where I get breakfast—died in a fire on Father's Day, three months earlier.

". . . and who by water." The *New York Times* just reported that global temperatures, left unchecked, will ultimately flood coastal cities.

"Who by sword. . . ." Steven Sotloff and James Foley were recently beheaded by ISIS.

". . . and who by beast. . . ." A twenty-two-year-old hiker was mauled by a bear.

"Who by earthquake. . . ." A main shock of 6.0 in Napa.

". . . and who by plague." The Ebola virus made headlines all summer.

The grim catalog rattles me when I read it in preparation for Rosh Hashanah—the day we'll recite the *Unetaneh Tokef* in morning services.

For now, the night before, I'm comforted by my congregation, Central Synagogue, packed into Avery Fisher Hall on the eve of the new year (our numbers require renting a larger space on the High Holidays). Looking out from the first-tier balcony, there's something symbolically powerful about rows and rows of yarmulkes and familiar families. Thousands are still here, not yet smote by water, fire, or sword. So many of us made it one more year.

Two self-evident facts are suddenly, atypically moving:

1. We've been given another chance to live—and to live better.
2. Look how many of us feel it's important enough to be in this room.

Whatever the sobering Pew Center Report of 2013 portended about synagogue attrition (in a nutshell: shuls are struggling and Jews don't find meaning there), there are still glowing pockets of connectivity. For my synagogue, there's an extra tenor of expectation on this *Erev* (eve of) Rosh Hashanah because just one week prior, Rabbi Angela Buchdahl, formerly Central's Senior Cantor, was installed as the new Senior Rabbi. Buchdahl is the first woman to hold the job in Central's 140-year history, inheriting the baton from the much-beloved Rabbi Peter J. Rubinstein, who led (and bolstered) the congregation for twenty-three years.

From the first words she utters, Buchdahl manages to shrink the grand auditorium to a hallowed sanctuary, addressing the multitudes with an intimacy that draws us in. When she later sermonizes about the Fifth Commandment (honor your mother and father), it reminds me of everything my parents are and how I haven't thanked them in a while. "It's precisely when parents are no longer critical in the primary sense," she says, "when we've done them out of a job, that we need to remember to honor them most."

When she pauses midway through the proceedings to acknowledge what was a painful summer (the 2014 war in Gaza) and to introduce the Hebrew prayer for Israel, "*Avinu Shebashamayim*" ("Our Father in Heaven"), I realize it's the first time since three teenage Israeli boys were kidnapped on their way home in June that I've stood alongside hundreds of fellow Jews, acknowledging, without speaking, the upheaval and disquiet we've all been feeling.

After the service ends and I greet synagogue friends whom I haven't seen all summer ("*Shana Tovah*"—"May you enjoy a good new year"), my family heads uptown to my sister's apartment for "the festive meal," which, in my family, might as well be called "the ravenous inhalation." This is the tradition I grew up with, the rituals my mother passed on to her twin daughters (my brother has yet to host a holiday meal, but there's still time): a beautifully set table; blessings over the candles; the round challah (for the cycle of the year and seasons); the bread sprinkled with honey (may the new year be a sweet one); the apples dipped in honey (we're supposed to eat a newly ripened fruit; more honey for sweetness). Saccharine as it may sound, the ease of my family at this table is sweetness itself. I'm keenly aware that we're lucky to be together on another Rosh Hashanah, healthy despite some medical hurdles for my parents. And I'm conscious that this new year is also new because I'm clocking it in a way I never have before.

On the following day—Rosh Hashanah itself—the petitionary song, "*Avinu Malkeinu*" ("Our Father, Our King"), feels unusually soul-wringing. Though the literal translation is somewhat distancing—formal and masculine—nevertheless the melody feels embedded in my DNA. I've heard it every year of my life.

Our father our king, hear our voice
Our father our king, we have sinned before you

Our father our king, Have compassion upon us and upon our children

I confess, not every section of this morning service comes alive for me. But I'm attuned, for the first time this year, to the three key themes of the day, which map the middle of the service:

God rules. *Malchuyot* (verses of sovereignty)
God remembers. *Zichronot* (verses of remembrance)
God redeems. *Shofarot* (verses of the *Shofar*)

I can hang my hat on that. Or at least, it gives me a sense of why there's so much God praise in this service: the tributes are for different things, not as redundant as I'd thought. It's too tidy to say that the God I believe in does rule, remember, and redeem. The "rule" part, at least, trips me up. Too authoritarian. And the "redeems" section suggests that we should rely too much on a higher being to do our heavy lifting. But my mind is firing differently now because I understand the framework: ruler, remembrance, and redemption.

That afternoon, the rain begins just as my fifteen-year-old daughter, Molly, and I walk to the East River with fellow congregants to observe Tashlich (casting off)—the ritual of throwing one's sins (aka hunks of challah) into a moving body of water. JTS professor Rabbi Visotzky hates Tashlich: "Throwing crumbs out of your pocket doesn't absolve you of your sins," he scoffs. "It's not the real work." But this is one rite I've done since the kids were small, and I have always found it to be profound in the simplest way. Maybe because it's a physicalized expiation instead of just atoning in our heads. Maybe because Tashlich has always made confession tangible for my children. Since they were little, I've taken them to the water to watch their faults float away.

I hesitate to confess what I threw into the East River this year, because it feels akin to revealing my birthday-candle wish—too sac-

rosanct, too risky. Suffice it to say that I have a pretty clear sense of
what needs fixing.

Friday morning, the second day of Rosh Hashanah (yes, there's a
second day, which most of my Reform friends don't observe, but the
Orthodox do, per the Hebrew calendar), I visit Romemu, a congregation on the Upper West Side, which draws from traditional and Eastern spiritual practices, and which strives to make every prayer feel not
just applicable but emotional.

Rabbi David Ingber, who maintains a kind of simmering concentration on the *bimah* (elevated platform), leads the service with Rabbi
Jessica Kate Meyer, who has a poetic presence. People clap or sway in
the pews around me, even, at times, lifting their arms in the air. Before each *aliyah* (call to the Torah), which precedes the reading of a
Torah portion, Ingber introduces an idea, or personal challenge, and
invites those for whom it resonates to come up for the blessing.

"Invite the Torah to say to you, 'Please find the places in your life
that you have yet to disclose, the places where privilege acts as a block
to more meaningful participation in the world, to making the world
a better place. If this speaks to you and you would like to stand for the
first aliyah this morning, I invite you to come forward.'"

I like the idea that a call to the Torah can be personalized. Ingber
offers an aliyah for those experiencing loss, for those who have felt
barren, for those who have had to make a sacrifice. He dramatizes
how current the Torah can be.

His choice of prayer book also underscores an insistence on relevance. Romemu's *machzor* (holiday prayer book) is fatter than any I've
ever seen, and far more captivating. I need to mention this volume
because it becomes my lifeboat throughout the morning. Without it,
I am unmoored. It's something I keep realizing in myself this year: I
need the facts in order to feel. The structure of this book provides a
running explanation of why each prayer is there and how it connects
to Torah or to the liturgy as a whole. Looking up the author's name

after the service, I am surprised to learn the book was compiled by a non-rabbi who was simply captivated by liturgy and eager to open it up for others. Joseph Rosenstein was raised Orthodox and teaches mathematics at Rutgers, my father's alma mater. I'm certain that if every bored Jew held this prayer book, they would never be bored again.

After services, I'm not quite finished with this holiday. It's time to experience a more modern *Tashlich*. I signed up for "Let it Go: A Tashlich Walk" near the theater district, conceived by the Lab/Shul, a self-described "Experimental Jewish Community" based in Tribeca, in collaboration with Elastic City, which organizes "participatory walks."

The self-selected group meets up near an open plaza in Hell's Kitchen, and I instantly feel shy among a group of thirty mostly younger strangers. What puts me at ease is our leader, Lab/Shul founder Amichai Lau-Lavie, a kinetic Israeli in jeans and baseball hat, sunglasses hanging on his shirt collar, whose obvious lack of self-consciousness makes me let go of mine. "Welcome, everybody!" he shouts over the city noise. "Let's get started."

We make a circle around the plaza's fountain, which includes four sculptural female figures representing the four seasons, all holding up the globe. Amichai directs us to stand near the season with which we identify most and to introduce ourselves to someone who's chosen the same season. I'm an autumn. I end up chatting with someone named Tony who works at Friends of the IDF (Israeli Defense Forces), an organization that ships supplies and care packages to soldiers in the Israeli army. Tony grew up in New York, and of course we know people in common, because that happens with Jews. He ends up being my buddy for this short *Tashlich* pilgrimage to the water.

We form a loose trail of wandering Jews following behind Amichai on the sidewalks of Hell's Kitchen. He pushes our group to make *Tashlich* urgent: "What are you holding on to?" he asks the group. "I invite you to find someone and confide what you are shedding today: skin, memories, iPhone apps."

What should I shed? (Where do I start?) An overconcern with others' opinions. My obsession with productivity. My inability to hide judgment. Fear of failure. Fear of cancer. Fear of cooking. Bad golf.

We make a stop to "shed" clothing donations at Housing Works (a thrift shop that supports AIDS patients), then pause in front of restaurants with names like "Gossip" and "Perdition"—apt stimuli for atonement. Amichai keeps demanding that we make this ritual real for us, that we don't cheat the expiation. It's not working if it's too easy. We make our way to the 46th Street footbridge that leads to the Hudson River, where we pause in a cluster, a communal confession. People verbally throw out the things they're discarding today: "Indecision." "Intolerance." "Guilt." I'm tempted to say, "I'm shedding my initial resistance to this event."

We cross over to the park by the river and Amichai gathers us in a large closing circle, holding hands once more, with the USS *Intrepid* aircraft carrier in view (more echoes of a summer of war). New Yorkers stroll by us, unfazed by the tambourine in Amichai's hand, the ram's horn jutting out of his jeans pocket, or our last flying breadcrumbs arcing into the Hudson. I'm struck by the unapologetic visibility of this faith: our big circle, the singing, the shofar, the bread lobs. Observance requires a certain boldness. Maybe today I've managed to shed a little of what keeps holding me back.

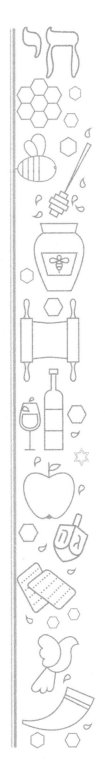

Rabba Sara Hurwitz

ON TZOM GEDALIAH (THE FAST OF GEDALIAH)

Although the Fast of Gedaliah memorializes the assassination of the Jewish governor by the same name, this fast day commemorates something far more tragic. The story of Gedaliah's death is recounted at the end of the book of Kings, which completes the narrative of the biblical story of the Jewish people. In other words, the story of the Jewish nation begins at the end of Genesis, with Jacob taking his family down to Egypt, after he learned his son Joseph was still alive and living there, and ends in the book of Kings, with the Jewish people fleeing back to Egypt after the First Temple is destroyed by the Babylonians. Seen in this light, we are fasting not only for the death of one person, but for the tragic cyclical story of our nation—one that began and ended in Egypt—the symbol of our people's destruction. But, just as the Jews were redeemed from Egypt the first time, each year, we pray for redemption: an everlasting, but ever-elusive, freedom from injustice and oppression.

3

THE FAST OF GEDALIAH

Lessons of a Slain Governor

9.28.14

HE FIRST FAST of the year falls two days later, and no, it's not Yom Kippur. The Fast of Gedaliah ("Tzom Gedaliah") is obscure, to say the least, and my having to honor some ancient assassinated governor feels like a major test of holiday stamina.

The story is dramatic: after the bloody destruction of the First Jerusalem Temple by the Babylonians in 586 B.C.E., most Jews fled The Judean kingdom (ancient southern Israel) to seek safety in Babylon. The cruel, conquering Babylonian king picked a kindhearted Jew named Gedaliah to govern those Jews who stayed behind. Gedaliah was murdered by a power-hungry rival—at a banquet, no less. The Fast of Gedaliah marks the assassination of one Jew by another and the destruction of the First Temple (the first of four nods we'll make this year to the losses of the First and Second Temples—our ancient, holy centers of worship).

It's safe to say that, until this year of living Jewishly, I never knew we had to fast before The Big Fast. And it's annoying. Especially because this fast happens mid-atonement, the day after Rosh Hashanah ends. (Except if the calendar drops Gedaliah on a Saturday, as it does this year, in which case the fast is delayed a day because fasts are prohibited on the Sabbath. Got that?) The upshot is that I'm fasting on a Sunday, September 28, 2014, six days before Yom Kippur.

This fast technically isn't as onerous as Yom Kippur's because it lasts from dawn to dusk instead of the full twenty-five hours (it's twenty-five because you have to wait about forty-five minutes after sundown on the day the holiday ends to make sure it's dark). But not eating or drinking is onerous at any stretch, at least for this Jew. Especially on a Sunday, when there's less to distract me.

My husband and kids choose not to join me in my starvation, though they apologize for the waft of toasted bagels. But my friend Jeremy from synagogue has offered to be my "Fast-Chum" in solidarity (I came up with that title since he's British), so that helps me feel less sorry for myself.

And what does Gedaliah have to do with Rosh Hashanah? It's a little fuzzy, but basically the Jews who chose to stay in Judea after the Temple's destruction were not sure whether to hang around after Gedaliah's murder. They awaited God's word, which would come through the prophet Jeremiah, who awaited divine guidance for ten days, around the time of Rosh Hashanah and Yom Kippur. (Jeremiah urged the people to stay; he was ignored and most fled.)

The Talmud (Torah commentary by ancient rabbis) says that we should fast for Gedaliah just as we fast for the Temple's ruin itself because "the death of the righteous is equivalent to the destruction" of the holy Temple. We fast to remind ourselves what happens when one Jew turns on another.

It reminds me of how ugly the divisions became months earlier, when every American Jew seemed to have an immovable opinion on the summer war in Gaza and an inability to listen to one another. Of course I understand dissent. But the discourse went beyond debate and turned vicious. Maybe this fast offers a way to be alert to that degeneration.

Steven M. Cohen, the droll, eminent sociologist who studies trends in Jewish identity, connectivity, and indifference, offers me an interesting tidbit: some peace activists have suggested that this holiday be updated to honor Yitzhak Rabin, the late Israeli prime minister who some pegged, like Gedaliah, to be a betrayer, and who was assassinated by a Jew in 1995. But during the fast itself, I'm more focused on hunger than infighting. Cohen explains to me that it's actually legal to eat breakfast before the sun comes up (technically seventy-two minutes before sunrise) so one can start the day on a full stomach, but I forget to set my alarm and I wake in the daylight, when the fasting-clock has already begun. My headache explodes from caffeine withdrawal as I kick myself for forgetting Cohen's advice.

But I have to admit that, whether or not Gedaliah's murder speaks to me, I remember I am a Jew today. All day. Hunger reminds me again and again of why I can't eat, why we give things up so that we don't repeat the errors of our ancestors, mistakes that are so easy to commit again. This people, to which I belong, doggedly replays history, however remote its events may be.

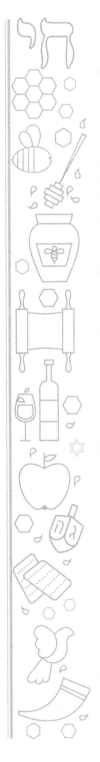

Rabbi Yitz Greenberg
ON YOM KIPPUR

This is the one time the Jewish religion really focuses on death and puts it before you. Yom Kippur is about failure and death. Stop and weigh your life. Have you lived on the side of dignity and what have you done wrong—not just to other people but to yourself? Did you respect your own life: or did you run it down? That's the dialectic. Celebrate life, but part of celebrating life is not to boast of it, but rather to look at your failures, look at your weaknesses, not in despair or in guilt, but as a corrector. . . . The Talmud says that if you overcome failure, if you try a second time with renewed effort, you'll reach a higher level than people who have never failed.

Yom Kippur is literally a ritual reenactment of your death. The Jewish version of what it is to die. You don't eat, you don't have sex, you're dead even if you're living. If your life were going to end tomorrow, where do you stand?

4

THE TRUTH ABOUT YOM KIPPUR

Death and More Death

10.2.14

HE FOCAL POINT of Yom Kippur is death? I thought it was All-Atonement-All-The-Time.

Your average Jew will tell you that Yom Kippur is the Day of Judgment, ten days after the new year, when we confess our sins in synagogue and feel somewhat pardoned because of it. Yet all you have to do is start talking to rabbis—or reading their books about preparing for Yom Kippur—and death takes center stage. Which upends my view of this holiday in a way that might finally make me more alert during the untold hours in synagogue.

When I say the rabbis focus on death, I don't mean death in the sense of a morbid fixation (cue the ominous organ music): it's death in the sense of a laser focus on life—how fragile it is, how unpredictable—which forces us to really ask ourselves, at any age: *If you knew you might not get another year, who would you be today?*

A friend tells me I absolutely *have to read* the 2003 dramatic book *This Is Real and You Are Completely Unprepared: The Days of Awe as a Journey of Transformation*, by the late rabbi Alan Lew, who had a pulpit in San Francisco and was often called "The Zen Rabbi" because he drew from both Buddhism and Judaism. I Google Rabbi Lew. It turns out that this pioneer of Jewish meditation died from a heart attack after—in tragic irony—a meditation session.

When I start reading his book, I'm surprised at how adamant and bleak he is about the stakes of the Ten Days of Awe between Rosh Hashanah and Yom Kippur. He says our very breath is in the balance. You. Could. Die. So how are you going to live? This perspective clears the nasal passages. It rattles but intrigues me.

> The Book of Life and the Book of Death are opened once again, and your name is written in one of them. But you don't know which one. The ten days that follow are fraught with meaning and dread. . . . For the next twenty-four hours you rehearse your own death. . . . You summon the desperate strength of life's last moments. . . . A fist beats against the wall of your heart relentlessly, until you are brokenhearted and confess to your great crime. You are a human being, guilty of every crime imaginable. . . . Then a chill grips you. The gate between heaven and earth has suddenly begun to close. . . . This is your last chance. Everyone has run out of time.

As I said: it's intense. In previous years, I hadn't grasped what Yom Kippur entailed, besides a lot of apologies. I'd put in my hours in synagogue, thinking: "This is sufficient. I'm here. I'm listening. I'm reciting. I'm starving. Dayenu." But Lew's writing grabs me and says: "That's bush-league. You have to work much, much harder than that."

"This is your last chance," Lew insists. *"Everyone has run out of time. Every heart has broken. The gate clangs shut. . . ."*

I suddenly want to know if Lew is an outlier, even a little *meshugenah* (nuts). Do other rabbis view the holiday as starkly?

"You do not have forever," writes Rabbi David Wolpe of Los Angeles in *Who By Fire, Who By Water*, a collection of essays edited by Lawrence Hoffman on the *Unetaneh Tokef* prayer (often referred to as "The Who Will Live, Who Will Die" prayer). "Repent now," Wolpe continues. "Repair now the broken relationships of your life. . . . There is little time to craft a self in this world before life is taken."

It's odd to admit I'm energized by this outlook, which turns out to be shared by many rabbis. Their unanimity begins to have a strong cumulative effect. I turn to the archived Yom Kippur sermons of another West Coast rabbi I admire, Sharon Brous. "STOP. EVERY-THING. NOW," she implores in her 2013 sermon. "And ask yourself: Who am I? Is this who you want to be in the world? I know how busy we all are, but High Holy Days come and say: 'Hit pause. This is the only life that you are given. If your narrative is choking you, or even just inhibiting you, do something about it.'"

I'm not sure what my narrative is, let alone whether it's choking me. But I do know what Brous is getting at: Worries that hold us back. Self-doubt that saps our courage. Self-involvement that obscures another person's pain. Anger that muddies what's actually worth getting mad about. Ask yourself, Brous demands, whether you want this one ephemeral life to be defined by what prevents you from being bold or being good.

As I listen to Brous on my headphones, I suddenly see that the Yom Kippur themes of death and atonement aren't as mutually exclusive as I'd first thought; they're intertwined. The threat of mortality moves us to atone: if we realized we might die in the coming year, we might act differently, see our blessings more clearly.

What I don't like is the notion that God will write us out of the Book of Life if we don't hit three marks: repentance, prayer, and charity. That quid pro quo is very explicit in the unsettling *Unetane Tokef* poem, which we also recite on Rosh Hashanah, and which is considered by many to be a peak of the service, though it appears nowhere in the Hebrew Bible or Talmud. It was added to the High Holy Day liturgy during the eleventh century and the author is unknown.

On Rosh Hashanah it is inscribed,
And on Yom Kippur it is sealed.
How many shall pass away and how many shall be born,
Who shall live and who shall die,
Who shall reach the end of his days and who shall not,

Who shall perish by fire and who by water,
Who by sword and who by wild beast,
Who by famine and who by thirst,
Who by earthquake and who by plague,
Who by strangulation and who by stoning. . . . *[The scary litany
continues a bit.]*
But repentance, prayer, and charity avert the severe decree.

It's hard to fathom that God, this week, is deciding who will die—depending on whether we've repented, prayed, or been sufficiently charitable. "I find that promise loathsome," writes British Reform Rabbi Tony Bayfield, in an essay in the *Who By Fire* anthology. "God has decided who will live and who will die and how they will die as well," he continues. "I may be scheduled for terminal cancer next November, and you may be scheduled for a car crash two weeks later. Do the right thing before the final gavel falls and neither the cancer nor the car crash will occur. All of my experience tells me that life doesn't work like that."

I'm on the fence. I refuse to believe God kills us if we sin, but I don't think it hurts to fear that possibility. I love how plainly Bayfield refuses to accept "an all-powerful Manipulator who has a level of control over our lives that defies credulity and morality." But I'd say a little anxiety about our fate can make us act more thoughtfully all year long.

As part of my atonement plunge, a few days before services, I attend a seminar about Yom Kippur given at Mechon Hadar, an independent learning institute cofounded by my Selichot guide, Rabbi Elie Kaunfer. Rabbi Shai Held, another cofounder and impassioned teacher, answers unhesitatingly when I ask him to tackle Yom Kippur's grim theme of the clock running out.

"I think it's hard—to the point of being impossible," he says, "to do what rabbis often say in High Holy sermons: 'We should live all the time with the realization that we might be killed in an hour.' You know what? I'll speak for myself: I would never get out of bed again. I mean that seriously. And by the way, if I thought that way about my *children*, I would lock my son and daughter in my apartment and they would never go outside. But, if we ignore that idea *all* the time, we do so at our own peril. And in some ways, Rosh Hashanah and Yom Kippur are about that: at least sometimes, we have to stop and realize we might not live until tonight. And what happens then? That's the tension, right? You can't live like that *all* the time. But you've got to live like that *some* of the time."

Live like you might die *some of the time*. That's my new Yom Kippur.

I already have practice because, without subjecting readers to all my demons, suffice it to say that I win the prize for Worst-Case-Scenario Catastrophic Thinking. I don't know if that's because I grew up with a mother who warned me not to walk under building scaffolding (it might collapse) and to avoid rock concerts (I could get trampled). She believed in the *Ayin Hara* (the evil eye), the idea that if things are too good, it will tempt the evil eye and something bad will be visited upon me. Mom would shoo that eye away with a spitting sound, "Tuh, tuh, tuh!" every time a misfortune was mentioned, as if to say, "God forbid that should happen to you."

Maybe some Jews are born to believe tragedy looms. Either way, this new Yom Kippur mind-set—you could die, so live better—keeps blessings in high relief.

Before we get too maudlin about this holiday, the rabbis tell us there's a happy coda: this rehearsal for death ends in resuscitation.

"Jews re-enact their own death," Yitz Greenberg writes, "only to be restored to life in the resolution of the day." It feels quintessentially Jewish to me: we collapse and then revive. We beat ourselves up and then get back in the ring. And Greenberg goes a step further on cleansing, offering a practical application: the *mikveh* (a bath, or a collection of water). Soul-refreshment, he writes, is sometimes reenacted *literally* by immersing one's self in the ritual tank. "The removal of ritual impurity," Greenberg writes, "is a symbolic statement of removing the stain of sin (death)."

The mikveh appears often in observant Jewish practice. Every Jewish conversion includes a body-dunking. Jewish funeral homes have a mikveh to purify the dead body. Orthodox women return to the bath after every menstruation or childbirth, though there has been feminist opposition to this ritual, because of its suggestion that women are unclean or impure. But in recent years, the mikveh has been reimagined by feminists as a powerful purge for any Jew at any time.

I make an appointment with ImmerseNYC—a pluralistic mikveh on the Upper West Side, which several people have recommended. Since renewal is epitomized by children, I invite my teenage daughter, Molly, and my niece, Maya (via text message, of course), to join me, explaining the bath's symbolism. They text me back instantly: "I'm there!" "Let's take the plunge."

ImmerseNYC was founded by Rabbi Sara Luria, who was spurred by her transformative experience at Mayyim Hayyim in Boston, a mikveh created by Anita Diamant, author of the best-selling book *The Red Tent*. "The mikveh is for you, just as you are," Luria tells me on the phone in calming tones before my appointment. "When you're naked, you are just as you are. There's nothing between you and the water. It's like the moment you were born. There are no barriers, no pretension. We tell you to bring yourself."

"Bringing myself" means bringing my reticence because I'm not big on nudity. I'm relieved to learn that I won't be naked in front of anyone else. When Sara outlines the three options—the girls and I can enter the bath chamber all together and watch each other, or we can turn our backs but be in the same room, or we can submerge separately—we agree to each go it alone.

The brownstone that holds the mikveh is hard to find. It looks like any nondescript ground-floor entrance of a walk-up in New York—not well lit, no signage. That's on purpose. There has historically been discretion-bordering-on-secrecy surrounding the mikveh: Orthodox women, who attend monthly, don't necessarily want to call attention to their cycles or personal hygiene.

The greeter at the desk is brusque but friendly, in that no-nonsense voice that sounds like my late aunt Helen. Her unceremonial approach reminds me that, for most people, this is not a spa, but a regular, practical stop in their routine.

We're led downstairs to a narrow hall with immaculate bathrooms sparkling with pearly-white tile and marble, each equipped with soap, toothpaste, mouthwash, shampoo, Q-Tips, cotton balls, comb, fresh towels, a white robe. We're instructed to remove all jewelry, nail polish, perfume, body lotion—anything that could come between us and the fresh rainwater. After using every cleanser in sight, I feel as if I've never been so scrubbed, so consciously stripped bare. Removing anything artificial from the body is an out-of-body experience: I feel lighter, childlike, distilled.

The ritualist—also named Sarah—has another soothing voice, and she offers me and the girls a choice of printed blessings to be recited while we sink. We sit side by side on a bench, reading through the options. I pick a passage from the Yom Kippur offerings:

"May I be open to the possibility of forgiveness. . . . May my entry into these waters mark my intention to forgive myself, forgive others, and ask others to forgive me."

It's finally my turn to go into the closed-off wet area with Sarah and disrobe. She holds a towel up between us so I can enter the tub unwatched. The small room looks like a mix between a hotel Jacuzzi and a physical-therapy whirlpool. As I descend the steps (seven of them, for the days of creation), I note the perfect temperature of the water and wonder if the womb felt like this.

Once enfolded by clear liquid, it's affecting to float without touching the bottom, feeling nothing but suspension, hearing nothing but the blessing I've selected as it's read aloud—though admittedly I don't hear it all when I go under. (The water is supposed to cover one's head.)

The three successive dunks don't take long, and I walk up the steps to retrieve my robe. When I reunite with the girls, their faces are rosy.

Maya announces, "I felt *seriously* cleansed." Molly adds, "It went too quickly. I should have stayed in it longer."

It all went unexpectedly fast. Though the guide didn't rush me, I can see that this ritual is efficient for the women who go monthly: you're basically in and out. I half-expected cymbals, or a certificate of some kind.

As I put on my clothes, I think about how I'll describe the whole thing to my husband when I get home. It will be hard to sum it up. I felt both inhibited and relieved. Alienated and alert. I was moved by the murmured blessings, but couldn't hear them all. I was hit hard by the tangible symbolism of a fresh start, but aware that, when it comes to the toil of atonement, this was a drop in the proverbial bucket (or bathtub). I felt recharged, not quite reborn.

V'al kulam, Eloha s'lichot, slach lanu, m'chal lanu, kapeir lanu. . . .
For all these sins, O God of forgiveness, forgive us, pardon us, grant us atonement.

Death spurs atonement. We rehearse our death on Yom Kippur. Then we get to come back to life.

Rabbi Elie Kaunfer
ON YOM KIPPUR

I remember the first time I saw people dancing on Yom Kippur. The fast had ended, the final shofar blast sounded, but instead of running for the exits, everyone broke out into spirited dancing. They were communicating with their feet: "The break-fast can wait." It was time to feel the joy. This was quite different from how I had previously experienced Yom Kippur: as a solemn day filled with apologies, existential questions, and acute experiences of mortality. The only joy, in fact, was in making it to the breakfast.

Yom Kippur as a day of joy dates back to the earliest rabbinic legal text, the Mishnah (Ta'anit 4:8): "R. Shimon ben Gamliel said: Israel had no better days than the 15th of Av and Yom Kippur." There is so much joy at the section of the service known as Avodah. It is the reenactment of the High Priest's encounter with God. It is also a moment when people sing and dance, remembering the ways in which we used to be so much closer to the Divine. Yom Kippur offers a glimpse of a pathway to return. It is a moment to enact—with joy—the possibility of a deeper connection with all that is holy. Isn't that reason to dance?

5

YOM KIPPUR LETDOWN

Maybe Next Year

10.6.14

VOTE TO BRING back the goat.

On Yom Kippur, the mighty Day of Atonement, in the days of the ancient Temple, all sins were symbolically heaped on an actual goat—the original "scapegoat"—which was then sent off to some undefined land called Azazel.

> "Thus the goat shall carry on it all their iniquities to an inaccessible region; and the goat shall be set free in the wilderness." Leviticus 16:21

I needed a cloven-hoofed animal to cart my sins away on Yom Kippur, because carrying them around in my head was taxing. Praying all day was hard for me. Pounding my heart with my fist in synagogue didn't break it open.

But I'm getting ahead of myself.

My Yom Kippur holiday begins at my dining room table with a big meal before commencing the fast at sundown, when the *Kol Nidre* service begins. Kol Nidre ("All Vows") is the name of the focal liturgy of the service that happens on erev (eve of) Yom Kippur.

I've set the placemats cheek by jowl to accommodate my family clan of thirteen and ordered food from a Turkish restaurant that makes dips and kebabs. I amassed desserts because the pre-fast meal is always a nice excuse to indulge in the treats I try to deny myself the rest of the year: banana pudding, cookies, cupcakes, and—my mother's favorite: brownies with walnuts.

Dinner is called for 4 P.M. since services start at 6 P.M. My husband, Dave, is home early from work to open the wine and help me finish setting up. Mom and Dad arrive on time; and my sister's and brothers' families rush in late from the office and school, apologizing for the stress they know they've added to the schedule. We always end up racing to say the blessings and scarf food before the sun sets and the urgent hour arrives when we have to start fasting as we clamber into cabs to get to Kol Nidre services.

The kebabs are laid out. The slivovitz is poured (Eastern European plum brandy, often compared to lighter fluid), two challahs crown the table. It's a typical year. Except that now I'm not just the dinner host, I'm "The Wondering Jew," who gets affectionate grief from my extended family, not to mention lots of questions as to how it's going.

"Are you keeping up?"

"Are you overwhelmed?"

"Do you feel yourself changing?"

"Are you turning Orthodox?"

Yes, yes, yes, and no.

I tell them I'm energized, I'm learning, I'm always looking forward to the next stop on the train. I tell them I find myself feeling a kind of suspense as to where the next holiday will take me. I explain my process so far—that I try to study as many texts and interview as many experts as possible before each holiday; but once I'm in the middle of one, I try to just be in it. But I also have to always be taking mental notes, so that I can remember what I was feeling when I process it later on my laptop.

I'm especially nervous about this big one. There's so much buildup to Yom Kippur. I've read and heard about what it's *supposed* to feel like, how we should be wrung dry, face the people we've wronged, come out renewed. I've been immersing myself—literally (mikveh) and figuratively (books, articles, interviews, sermons)—and I've Elul'ed for weeks. But who knows if I've prepared *enough*.

Hosting Kol Nidre dinner is something I at least know how to do. I inherited hostess duties from my mother back in 2004, when I was writing *Stars of David* and had started studying Torah. Before Yom Kippur that year, I suggested to Mom that instead of her trying to explain the holiday to the kids at the table, as she did using well-intentioned readings each year, it might be more effective to play a game with everyone, or do an exercise that requires participation. She loved the idea. I came up with a Yom Kippur Quiz with questions that taught and tested basic knowledge, such as, "How many times are we supposed to ask forgiveness of someone we've offended before we're off the hook? a. Once, b. Twice, c. Three times?" Answer: c. Or: "On Yom Kippur, some Jews wave *which animal* over their heads and then kill it and sell it, giving the proceeds to charity?" Answer: A chicken.

One year I put our family's names in a basket and each of us apologized to the person whose name we randomly picked, for anything we felt we could have done better in that relationship. There was something tender about having to summon a mea culpa on the spot.

I'm sorry I didn't make time with you alone last year.

I'm sorry I said you should cut your hair.

I'm sorry I snapped at you when I was carving the turkey.

I feel more and more sure that if kids have something to do, they're more likely to remember. Frontal lessons don't stick. I know how I felt in my teens—bored and deficient—when Mom explained the holiday basics at the Kol Nidre table. This year, in light of my holiday plunge, I'm more resolute than ever to try to connect the liturgy to real life so that, when the kids are in synagogue, at least one prayer makes sense and feels familiar.

As my family heaps hummus and baba ghanoush in our annual speed-eating ritual, I circulate a bowl filled with slips of paper and ask each person to take one. On every paper is typed one sin from the list of forty-four failings that will be read several times during services. Each line begins with *"Al cheit"*—"for the sin . . ."—followed by a specific offense. It was easy to find the "al cheits" online:

> For the mistakes we committed before You through wronging a
> friend.
> For the mistakes we committed before You by degrading parents and
> teachers.
> For the mistakes we committed before You by being arrogant. . . .

I ask each person to share an example of when he/she committed the "al cheit" in their hands. The personal confessions are unvarnished:

> *I wished that my friend at school would get a poorer grade on a test
> we both took.*
>
> *I lost my temper too quickly with Mom.*
>
> *I treated that waiter dismissively.*

When anyone at our table is stumped about whether an "al cheit" was committed, the rest of the group is eager to produce an example for him or her. It's an exercise that makes us laugh, but also makes us confess real things. It's hard to capture the moment when intimacy ratchets up in a room, but this is one of those times. We're a little closer afterwards.

After cupcakes and brownies, as I start rushing everyone away from the table to get to synagogue on time, my seventeen-year-old nephew, Ethan, suddenly shouts, "Where are our commitments from last year?"

He's remembered something I've forgotten: the previous year, I'd given everyone an index card to write down something they vowed to do better. We'd sealed the cards in envelopes with our names and the date to be opened: 10-3-14. Tonight was the moment of truth. I run to the cabinet where I keep things I don't want to misplace, and when

I open it, there they are: a pile of thirteen brisket-stained envelopes. We rip them open to see what we promised ourselves.

I read mine aloud, because my seventeen-year-old son, Ben, gives me permission: I'd vowed to nag Ben less and just appreciate him more. Boy, had I failed. I treasure my son beyond language; what Jewish mother doesn't? He's magical to me in a million ways. But I had not for a moment stopped pestering him. And on this particular Yom Kippur, when he's applying to college, I am hit with the stunning fact that he won't be living with us this time next year, that my on-site parenting will be finished and our face-to-face interactions will no longer be daily. How could I have spent these past precious months noodging Ben so predictably? Why do I feel compelled to ask if he's finished the essay yet, signed up for Driver's Ed yet, or remembered to write that thank-you note?

I show my index card to Ben, who—true to form—just gives me a knowing smile and says I'm forgiven. "I know you nag me because you love me," he says matter-of-factly. He gives me an easy pass, and I take it. But I look at that index card, want to tape it to that stupid goat and send it off to Azazel, that vague place in the Bible to which the animal is exiled, a word that, according to some, means "for the complete removal." I would love "the complete removal" of my screw-ups.

I've decided to attend the start of services at my mother and father's synagogue instead of going with my husband and kids to mine, because I want to make sure I see how other shuls do it, at least for an hour or two. Being with Mom and Dad takes me back to the time I used to go to High Holy Day services with them in my teens, how I always felt somehow like a tag-along, aware that Mom's synagogue wasn't really mine, that she was heading into familiar territory, which was, to me, largely foreign.

B'nai Jeshurun (known as BJ) is a popular Conservative synagogue on the Upper West Side known for exuberant dancing in the aisles on erev Shabbat and for its erudite Argentinian-born senior rabbis, whose accents have their own mystical effect and whose sermons are often impassioned and dense. BJ rents out a hall at Lincoln Center on Yom Kippur because they've also outgrown their space.

This service marks the kickoff to twenty-five hours of food-free hard-core penitence. The central Kol Nidre prayer is technically not a prayer but rather a legal declaration—an appeal to a court of three judges, asking to have vows annulled so that atonement may commence. The three judges are symbolized by the cantor flanked by two Torah-carriers (or three Torahs displayed) on the bimah, and the haunting melody is sung three times, louder each time, repeated thrice so latecomers don't miss it. Its text has been both controversial and confusing for generations.

> All vows we are likely to make, all oaths and pledges we are likely to take between this Yom Kippur and the next Yom Kippur, we publicly renounce. Let them all be relinquished and abandoned, null and void, neither firm nor established. Let our vows, pledges, and oaths be considered neither vows nor pledges nor oaths.

It reads as if we're being absolved of promises we'll definitely break. What? What's the point of making vows we're sure to violate and be forgiven for? There is a common theory that the Kol Nidre "prayer" was added when Jews were in a time of extreme persecution and forced conversions. Jews needed to know that God would forgive any promises they were forced to make renouncing Judaism.

Historically, Kol Nidre has been invoked as proof that Jews can't be trusted because it basically asserts that we promise to renege on our promises. In the mid-nineteenth century, congregations in Europe wrestled with whether to rewrite or jettison Kol Nidre. The Reform Movement took it out of its prayer book in 1844, then put it back in 1961. Some congregations today recite the Hebrew without translating it in English on the page.

So Kol Nidre is obviously a thorny non-prayer, but I look forward to hearing it this year, now that I understand its complexity. For Jews who have grown up with its melody (and despite my childhood syna-gogue deficit, I'm one of them), Yom Kippur *is* the sound of Kol Ni-dre. The tune is melancholy and reliable to me, and it's beautiful to hear in BJ's temporary sanctuary tonight—the Frederick P. Rose Hall of Jazz at Lincoln Center. Because of the amphitheater's design, it feels like we're embarking upon penance-in-the-round, which seems apt: we should have to look at each other when we're thinking about hurting fellow human beings. The rabbis explain that we're only par-doned for vows we made to God—not to another person. For those sins against each other, we have to face the people we've wronged and hope they absolve us.

Mom and Dad find seats in the orchestra, but—since I know I have to cut out early—I find a chair in the "bleachers," high up behind the bimah, a perch that ends up being dramatic theater in itself. Whenever Rabbi Marcelo Bronstein (who could be cast as a tall Tevye) and Felicia Sol (a steady, focused Golde) turn to face the ark (the Torah cabinet), they are turned toward me, and I can observe their more private de-meanor—eyes clenched, bodies rocking. I envy their catharsis. They look fervent and present. I imagine what it must feel like to be carried along by prayer, and wish I knew the liturgy by heart. Mom is visible across the auditorium, her eyes also closed. Dad looks indifferent, but I know he's content to be where he is every Kol Nidre: next to Mom.

It's disorienting to be away from my congregational home. I am not known here, and I feel like a tourist; the faces—and most of the mel-odies—are not familiar. However universal the prayers, every syna-gogue puts them to their own particular tunes, their own cadences and keys.

And yet one song, "*Ya-aleh*" (rise), is recognizable and, surprisingly, opens me up. I remember it from when my parents took me to BJ decades ago, and I notice now the ache of the music and the words, taken from a medieval poem, translated here:

> May our voices rise up at evening,
>   our righteous acts arrive with the dawn,
>   our redemption transforms the dusk.

I love this prayer's idea of multiple voices rising up together. Tonight amounts to a collective sorry. I like the notion that there's always the chance to behave better when the sun comes up.

After about an hour, I feel the need to be back in the company of my husband and children. I exit one Lincoln Center auditorium and walk into another, Avery Fisher Hall a few blocks north, where my own synagogue holds overflow services. I take my place next to Dave and Ben and we begin the work of Yom Kippur, side by side. I mentally run through my missteps—moments of insensitivity, inaction, impatience. Contrary to previous years, I'm not casting about for sins. They're all at my fingertips, thanks to weeks of advance introspection. My Elul training kicks in tonight.

I have no idea what my children or husband are thinking or regretting. But I also don't feel entitled to ask. Though Jews atone communally, the truest confessions are private. And I know that prying can ruin the experience. So instead of glancing sideways to gauge my family's expressions, I keep my attention on the rabbis and cantors, who gracefully move around the stage in white robes, bowing and swaying, singing and then sitting silently, hands in their laps or on their prayer books. The choreography feels as fluid and sacred as it did at BJ, but I am more connected here.

By the end of the service, the hunger rumblings have begun. As we cross Broadway to get a taxi, I calculate how many hours have passed since we finished dinner (four) and how many more remain. I'm already sinning anew, focusing on food rather than contrition.

The next day, Yom Kippur itself, is chilly and wet. I head downtown to the sprawling Javits Convention Center, the only space big enough to accommodate the massive numbers that attend High Holy Day services at what's known in New York as "The Gay Temple"—Congregation

Beit Simchat Torah (CBST), founded in 1973 as a home for LGBT Jews. The presiding rabbi, Sharon Kleinbaum, is somewhat of a celebrity because of her press-covered advocacy over the years, becoming this temple's rabbi in 1992—in the middle of the AIDS crisis—and, more recently, protesting "Don't Ask, Don't Tell" and the ban on women praying at the Western Wall. In 2011 Kleinbaum was filmed while heatedly debating same-sex marriage with an Orthodox man who called the rabbi and her allies "not Jewish" while Kleinbaum just kept repeating, "I will pray for you."

I am heartened by the hordes at CBST not only because it affirms the vitality of Jewish practice in general but of gay Jewish life in particular. It might surprise the skeptics to discover how traditional this service actually is. They cover more of the prayer book than many Reform synagogues. It reaffirms my remaining barriers: hearing prayers without elucidation still seems mechanical to me.

But I am moved by watching Kleinbaum make her way through the makeshift pews greeting people, knowing their names and those of their children. I overhear her asking after a sick relative, inquiring about someone's new job or commiserating over the latest affront to gay people in the news. I've met Kleinbaum at various Jewish events, and she stops to greet me, tallis around her shoulders, yarmulke capping her hair. She looks no worse for wear after her latest imbroglio. One month ago, during a regular September service, Kleinbaum read aloud the names not only of Israeli casualties during the 2014 war in Gaza, but also of Palestinian children killed in the fighting. Several of her members resigned in anger, including a member of her board. She was vilified on social media. But she remained clear about why she chose to offer a human nod to innocent children.

I leave the cavernous Javits Center before her sermon begins; once again, I'm eager to return to my family on a holiday I associate with family. I'm also feeling a little of what teenagers call FOMO—Fear of Missing Out.

Once back at Avery Fisher Hall during the "al cheit" litany, I glance at my children to see if the prayer rings a bell from the night before. Molly gives me a side-nod of affirmation. *"That's it,"* I think to myself.

That's what matters to me: my kids starting to connect the dots in a way I never did. A repetitive prayer comes to life because you recognize it. Because you unpacked it hours earlier, you now understand its purpose. Something opens up, lets you in. I glimpse that in Molly's face in that instant—*I know what to do with this prayer*—and it's priceless.

Rabbi Buchdahl's sermon on Israel is a sensitive one, as are all Israel sermons this particular autumn because of the Gaza war. It was a summer of vitriolic Facebook postings and strained family conversations, with many Jews showing little patience for contrary opinions. A *New York Times* article described the land mines clergy members were navigating as they wrote their High Holy Day sermons, wanting to say something forceful without alienating swaths of their congregations. Rabbi Buchdahl's sermon walks the line carefully and candidly. "I knew I had no choice but to speak about Israel tonight. I needed to say how high the stakes are," she says. "I don't know that any one sermon can persuade you that Israel should matter to you, if it doesn't already. But I had to try." She ends her twenty-minute speech by singing a fervent rendition of *"Al Kol Eleh"* (For All These Things) and as I feel myself choking up, the congregation around me is suddenly standing in a spontaneous ovation.

The worship continues with chest-pounding (we thump our hearts with our fists during the recitation of sins) and, after a small interlude, moves into the afternoon service with Central's quietly profound custom: "Torah meditation." It's a chance for anyone who wishes to go up to the bimah and stand for a few moments before one of three Torah scrolls. Two lines form quietly on either side of the sanctuary.

When my family takes a turn, I am again unexpectedly tearful. We stand wordlessly on the bimah with our arms around each other, facing the swaddled Hebrew Bible—a tangible symbol of endurance. I'm flooded with my blessings. The encounter, however brief, changes my Yom Kippur afternoon, a time I used to associate with endurance.

Later, Dave and I take a walk in Central Park and grab a quick nap before the afternoon Yizkor (remembrance) service to honor the dead. As always during these High Holy Days, congregants amble in and out of the sanctuary all day long, taking occasional breaks from the proceedings. I know my husband too well to ask his thoughts on atonement this year; he doesn't relish that kind of emotional question on any day, let alone when he's fasting.

The final service, known as "Neilah" (locking), begins around 5 P.M. back in Central's main sanctuary. Neilah denotes the moment when the proverbial gates close, symbolizing that we've run out of repentance time. It's an unnerving idea to think that the ten focused days of deliberation are ending and we won't know the verdict. Have we all been given another year? Can I tolerate the possibility that we haven't?

In the dimly lit synagogue, when the final imploring prayers build to a climax, I'm simply too distracted by the fact that there are fresh bagels and fried chicken, waiting uptown, to feel duly shaken. Even though I warm to the idea of a big finale, it's as if I'm already halfway out the door.

Breaking the fast with old friends is a tradition that Robin and I started in our twenties, when we were each newly married (both of us wed in 1993, just eleven months apart) and each tentatively starting Jewish homes. We wanted to create our own annual custom, apart from Mom's, which would gather all our Jewish friends and acknowledge that we're connected. So thirty-five to forty friends descend every year on Robin and Ed's house, where the table is laden with platters and the guests contribute dessert.

Ever since our children were little—and we needed to get the kids fed and to bed—we've cheated the starting gun of the first bite. But this year, I want to do it by the book, waiting till the Neilah service is entirely done, even if my friends start eating ahead of me. It would feel like breaking my own rules to flee before the final word, especially because I've never seen the ark actually close—the symbolic shutting of God's book.

As the ark doors slowly close, I feel that cinematic flash of panic: the drawbridge is going up before I'm surely, safely back in the castle.

But then I remind myself that it's a metaphor; I'm already either in or out of the Book of Life. Yes, the doors symbolize the closing of the gates, but my verdict is in. Standing in a pew with my husband by my side, it's a private, profound moment of defenselessness. Our fate is not up to us.

After one last taxi ride, I'm finally among my oldest friends who are already standing around Robin and Ed's dining table, buffet plates in hand, chewing happily, or sitting squished against each other on sofas and chairs, plates in laps, comparing lox to nova; recounting the day's sermons and hunger trials. Kids are running around loudly with cookies in hand, crumbs sprinkling the floor. It's chaotic and happy.

I heap my plate, though I always deliberate whether the first taste should be challah, a bagel, or fried chicken. Every cliché hits me when I eat again after twenty-five hours: *food is amazing.* Yom Kippur is an obvious, but weighty, reminder of want and need compared to plenty. We are so fortunate to get to eat so easily, whatever, whenever we choose.

Brushing my teeth later, it suddenly dawns on me that Elul is over. All the August-to-October introspection ends not with fireworks but with a bagel and a shmear. For forty days, I've done *cheshbon hanefesh* ("accounting of the soul") and heard the shofar blast each morning. That trumpet now falls silent until next fall.

So why, despite forceful moments, was I largely unresponsive through the final day? Because I didn't feel changed. There was no revelation. The words on the page didn't reach out and grab me the way Alan Lew said this holiday should. I can hear the rabbis scolding already: "That failure is on you, Abigail."

I should have heeded Rabbi Avi Weiss of the Hebrew Institute of Riverdale, who'd urged me to try the Yom Kippur ritual of dropping to the floor. This ancient tradition calls for prostrating oneself face-down to embody falling on God's mercy during *"Va'anachnu korim,"* which means "and we bend at the knees." Weiss tells me, "I think synagogues should be a place of baring the soul, taking off a lot of layers. Then you come to grips with who you really are, and a lot of people are uncomfortable with what they find."

I would have been "uncomfortable" making a spectacle of myself, and my fellow congregants would have been alarmed if they'd seen me buckle to the ground. Prostration takes a spiritual moxie I'm still lacking.

Rabbi Paley had warned me that High Holy Day transcendence is hard for a rookie. "You can't fully get it, Abby, because you simply haven't read the book as many times as we have. For rabbis, the text is never repetitive because each of the words hooks into something else and we're always seeing something new."

I did see new things. But not enough of them. Something got in the way of complete candor or apology, except when I stood in front of the Torah for two minutes with my family.

Maybe because real repentance is too raw to do in a public place. Maybe because I'm too afraid to really consider that I, or someone close to me, might have transgressed enough to be punished.

"My life is being weighed," writes Rabbi Yitz Greenberg; "I am on trial for my life. . . . If life ended now, would it have been worthwhile?"

I couldn't bring myself to answer that. And no prayer forced me to.

V'al kulam eloha selichot—s'lach lanu, m'chal lanu, kaper lanu: For all these sins, O God of mercy, forgive us, pardon us, grant us atonement.

Rabbi Sharon Brous
ON SUKKOT

It's hard to observe Sukkot. You have to be really invested. There are a lot of rules, specifications. You need two and a half walls minimally, preferably three walls. The Schach (roof) has to be something that grew from the earth but is no longer attached to the earth. More shade than sun. There are a lot of very specific regulations. It's hard to take on Sukkot in a small bite. At the same time, you can bring really secular and disconnected Jews into a sukkah, and they will have a profoundly moving experience.

Rabbi David Wolpe
ON SUKKOT

One reason why we go from the High Holidays to Sukkot is that, having had the world given to us on Rosh Hashanah—the world has been created, we now have to build something. We have to create something out of the world, and the sukkah is the first gesture. With the first nail that we drive in right after Yom Kippur, we say, "Having been redeemed and having the world be created, now I want to make it better."

Rabbi Naomi Levy
ON SUKKOT

On Yom Kippur, God is our judge. On Sukkot, God is our shelter. On Yom Kippur, we sit cooped up for endless hours inside. Sukkot is about space and breath. On Yom Kippur, it's all about "What have I done?" But on Sukkot, it's "What can

continued

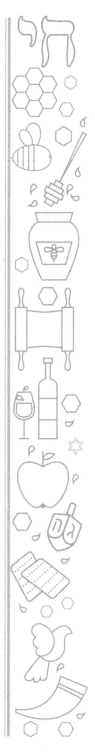

I do in the world?" On Yom Kippur, we deprive ourselves—
we starve! But on Sukkot, it's gratitude and about bounty,
sensuality, eating, and company. On Yom Kippur, we're in God's
house. On Sukkot, God comes to our house.

Rabbi Ed Feinstein
ON SUKKOT

I have a very radical idea—I've actually preached this in the
synagogue: Jews, as you know, show up three times a year—
two days of Rosh Hashanah and a day of Yom Kippur. I say,
"Those are the wrong three days to show up." First of all, they're
morbid holidays. And if there's anything our generation has
learned from the Holocaust, it's that God owes us a smile. So
don't come to shul on Yom Kippur, don't come to the synagogue
on Rosh Hashanah; come on Sukkot. Come on Pesach. And
then choose Purim or Simchas Torah—better both. And dance.
And sing. This is joy!! Why can't you Jews enjoy joy? Why can't
you embrace joy? These are High Holidays. Why can't Jews get
it? Because we love misery. And guilt.

6

SUKKOT IN LA

Serious Sukkah Envy

10.14.14

DIDN'T SCHEDULE FIVE Sukkot interviews just to stockpile rabbis. For me, the secret kick of this expedition has been the excuse to query some of the thinkers I admire most: "Tell me, Rabbi, why Sukkot matters in this day and age. Since it starts just five days after Yom Kippur, the holiday has always seemed to me like an excuse for a Jewish arts-and-crafts project that arrives too soon on the heels of synagogue saturation."

My first stop is the Manhattan office of Rabbi Michael Paley, the bearded, peppery Scholar in Residence at UJA Federation of New York. He's one of my favorite teachers, not just because of his obvious breadth of knowledge, but because, with Paley, no topic is taboo.

"Sukkot is about shtupping," he pronounces from behind the desk. I'm captivated already.

"Shtupping" (Yiddish for sex) is not what most associate with the harvest holiday. Your average Jew knows Sukkot to be the fall celebration that is tied to two main events: the annual end of the agricultural year in Israel, and the Exodus from Egypt, when the Israelites wandered in the desert, building *sukkot* (makeshift booths) for shelter.

I personally had thought the holiday meant decorating a four-poster wooden tent with garlands of fruit, topped by a leaky roof made of plant life. The holiday didn't figure prominently in Mom's Queens upbringing; she never took us to construct one or dine in one—as tradition instructs. And the prospect of now helping to build a hut was intimidating; wood shop was never my strong suit.

So during this year's holiday immersion, I'll be making up for lost time. And the more I read in preparation, the more Sukkot comes to life. I begin to feel not only intrigued but saddened: that I'd never celebrated this holiday before, that I didn't know its origins or how to wave the *lulav* (looks like a branch) and *etrog* (looks like a lemon)—two objects that are waved three times in six directions on the holiday, with particular choreography that involves thrusts in the air.

Which brings us back to the sex. Rabbi Paley says it's a given that erotic imagery has been found in the erectness of the lulav (comprised of a palm frond, two willow branches, and three myrtle branches) and the rotund juiciness of the etrog (a citron fruit). Call me naïve, but it had never occurred to me that the ritual dance of these symbols was racy.

"Sukkot is about shtupping," repeats Paley.

"Are you just being provocative right now?" I ask him.

Paley waves me off. "No! I'm in the text. *I'm in the text.*" Which is rabbi-speak for "The Torah and Talmud back me up."

"First of all," he continues, "you take a particularly suggestive fruit. Right? And you take a very long and tightly bound spear—the longer the better, to tell you the truth, with leaves at the base, just in case you *miss the point*—and you thrust in all different directions," he demonstrates the gesture, "thrusting, thrusting, and more thrusting. And then you march around like you're getting married with it, and then you do a little more thrusting. The sukkah is supposed to be like a huppah, the wedding canopy."

Paley has been teaching me every six weeks or so as part of a breakfast study group, which he leads over breakfast in my friend Gary's office. Moving easily between Rashi and Mohammed or Maimonides and Netanyahu with his trademark rapid-fire delivery, Paley will start one provocative thought and then go off on fifteen equally compelling tangents.

"Sukkot and Yom Kippur are connected," he insists—reminding me that we're supposed to build the sukkah as soon as Yom Kippur ends. We marry—or commit to—God on Sukkot after we beg God's forgiveness on Yom Kippur. Yom Kippur is a rehearsal for our death and then Sukkot is a wedding—with the sukkah as the symbolic canopy. "Wedding and shroud are connected," Paley continues. "We wear the same coat for each." He means the white coat—the *kittel*—worn by both a groom and a corpse. "You wear your love/death coat for Yom Kippur and your marriage."

It's already become a recurring epiphany: no holiday stands alone; all are intertwined. This harvest holiday used to appear like a non sequitur, veering jarringly from atonement to agriculture. Now I see it's the logical next chapter of a single story line, and Jews need to view several holidays at once to understand the one we're in.

I consult my informal kitchen cabinet, one of whom is Rabbi Naomi Levy, whose LA spiritual community is especially tuned in to outdoor worship, since her synagogue has no permanent building. I sit at my bedroom desk and call Levy to ask about Paley's marriage metaphor. "At Pesach [Passover], we and God got betrothed," she explains. "We started dating. On Shavuot—receiving The Ten Commandments, that was our *ketubah* [marriage contract]. What is Sukkot? It's our huppah. Sukkot is the wedding. And the huppah and a sukkah are really parallels."

Levy invites me to come visit her sukkah in Venice, California, and I jump at the chance to see how Jews do it in the sunshine. I plan to be an efficient sukkah-sampler, hitting four huts in two days.

I start by driving my rental car to Rabbi David Wolpe's mega-shul sukkah in Beverly Hills. The quick-witted veteran leader of Sinai Temple, known for his sermonic agility, Wolpe has become a friend over the years; we've ended up sitting at the same Jewish conferences, bemoaning the atrophy of Jewish conferences. He's an influential voice in Conservative Judaism because of his well-received books, literary sermons, large Persian congregation, and huge Facebook following

(61k+ at this writing). Sinai's sizable sukkah is pretty—braided with paper chains and flowers—and it's peaceful to sit in the open-air dwelling, which has been constructed according to ancient codes still followed today:

- The roof must be porous, made up of raw vegetable matter detached from its source of growth and whose branches leave space to see the sky and stars;
- The sukkah requires two walls and part of a third (ideally four), which do not need to touch the ground but should be able to resist the wind and be big enough to fit at least one whole person inside;
- The sukkah should be no larger than thirty feet tall, no less than three feet high.

"In some ways, the most beautiful part about the sukkah," Wolpe says, as we take chairs opposite each other, "is that you know it's fragile and temporary, and yet you have to be able to look through the roof and see the stars; because if you can't see the heavens, the sukkah isn't kosher. In other words, as you sit in the midst of fragility, you also have an eye on eternity." This is what I started this project to hear— ideas that change my perspective. When do I sit with fragility and contemplate eternity? "The impermanence of Sukkot," Wolpe continues, "is why there's this paradox that the holiday is called *Z'man Simchateinu*, the time of our joy. You wouldn't think that something that emphasizes the fragility of life would make you happy, but the truth is that everything in life depends on its one day ending."

The certainty of ending heightens what exists. Yom Kippur already hammered home our temporality: *you could die this year, and God is deciding that in real time.* Sukkot keeps up the pressure: *your home and belongings are fragile, not just you.*

I need this reminder because, like all of us, I get lazy about taking material things for granted. We run through days that feel sturdy, moving from house to gym, office, kids' school, shul, surrounding ourselves with "reliable" stuff, nice furniture, clothing, efficient home appliances. But they obscure life's precariousness. The bible's book of Ecclesiastes is read every Sukkot, with its clear-eyed message: belongings and buildings are pointless. *"I multiplied my possessions. I built myself houses and I planted vineyards. But all is nought"* (Ecc. 2:4).

So it would behoove me—at least annually—to sit under a roof that won't protect me, one that deliberately lets the rain in. Or to sleep under the stars. These holidays can heighten what I've already accumulated, whom I love, what lasts.

When Wolpe asks if I know how to properly shake the lulav and etrog, I'm embarrassed to confess that I don't. Standing near one of the tables in his sukkah, Wolpe guides me through the ritual, directing my hands with his. I'm self-conscious, not knowing in which direction we're headed next, the unwieldy stalk and fruit feeling like foreign objects whose choreography isn't intuitive. To defuse my clumsiness, I tell him about Paley's ribald lesson. Wolpe nods, chuckling. "You can't have Sukkot's agricultural imagery without sexual imagery," he affirms. "Plants flowering, bulbs bursting, trees growing, shooting up, dropping seeds, all of that is full of the imagery of sexuality, too."

Wolpe's agricultural list of symbols—bulbs, trees, and seeds—resonates in my next sukkah, situated near an actual farm. Okay, it's a miniature one: the backyard of Rabbi Naomi Levy's bucolic home. She happens to know Wolpe from when they were both students at JTS, both studying with Burt Visotzky, my Rosh Hashanah guide. Levy has a devoted following and could be considered The Sukkot Rabbi, because she founded a spiritual community in 2004 without a home. Nashuva ("Return") has no membership, no tickets, and a website slogan that says, "A soulful community of prayer in action." The small plot behind her house is an advertisement for mindful, earth-conscious living, with an impressive vegetable garden and a miniature animal farm that includes egg-laying chickens and two goats—one named "Goldie Horn," which I find hilarious. (For those under forty, Goldie Hawn is an actress, popular in the 1980s.)

Levy says her journalist husband is really the farmer of the family, and she offers me a stem of his fragrant verbena. "Smell this." I inhale the herb in my fingers and find myself violating the Tenth

Commandment (thou shalt not covet) as I covet California. I wish my family had this light, this yard, this verbena. Maybe it's the unique morning sun or more of that soft air, but Levy's modest acre seems utopian. Her sukkah, erected with metal poles and diaphanous curtains, appears less like a jerry-rigged prop than a sacred sanctuary. Though not yet decorated, the shelter is ethereal just as it is, with gourds on a white tablecloth and translucent "walls" that lift with the breeze.

When Levy and I sit down to talk at her sukkah table, she expands again on Paley's metaphors of the flesh, albeit with a little less porn: "The etrog is a breast. It actually has a nipple. The pitam [one of the etrog's stems] is a nipple. I mean, there are so many phallic symbols within every tradition. Let's look at it this way: Moses had a staff. Miriam had a well. The lulav is a phallus and the etrog is a breast. Is sukkot about sex? I would say sukkot is certainly about sensuality."

But she warms more to the symbolism of sukkah and huppah. "What do I always say to couples under the huppah? I say, 'This is the metaphor for your lives. That structure over there,'" she gestures to her home, "'that building that's my house—is offering me just the *illusion* of shelter. Because we all know that structures fall down and they offer only illusions of shelter.'"

The illusion of shelter. I'm beginning to think that Judaism is obsessed with brevity and instability. But rather than finding the message depressing, it's clarifying. The more temporary things are, the more precious they become.

The third sukkah I visit belongs to yet another JTS graduate: Rabbi Sharon Brous, who founded IKAR ("essence"), a spiritual group in West Los Angeles known for drawing young families and requiring community service as part of its membership. Over a platter of fruit in her backyard's flower-bedecked sukkah, Brous highlights the holiday's agrarian themes more than its symbols of marriage or impermanence.

"This is one of the holidays that reminds us of our connection to, and responsibility for, the earth," she says as I chomp on the grapes. "As contemporary Jews, I think many of us are so disconnected; we're urbanites."

Guilty as charged.

"We don't know different spices."

True; I'm stumped after oregano.

"We don't plant or harvest our own food." I once grew tomatoes. Slugs tunneled through them.

"And so this is one of those moments where the smells of the outdoors are with us throughout all of our meals."

It hits me like a ton of grapes: I've been sukkah-deprived. As a child, I didn't have Jewish rituals that took me outside—to a river on Tashlich, to a sukkah on Sukkot. I was never taught how to sit under a porous roof or wave a palm frond. This, I realize, may require some Jewish psychoanalysis, because I can't get those sukkahless autumns back.

Brous enthusiastically describes how her kids "grab basil" out of their garden, host big "Sukkot Sleepovers," and recall ancestors—real and biblical—an act which fulfills Sukkot's obligation to invite in *Ushpizin* ("guests" in Aramaic). I once again idealize California Judaism and kick myself for cheating my kids of fresh pesto.

"We spend all year building these structures, working on our homes, building additions for the homes, buying stuff for the homes," says Brous, a mother of three. "Then, we go outside into this very simple structure—which we tried to make look lovely, but it's not at all like our homes—and we say, 'Here's what matters: sitting at a table with someone you love and sharing a meal and knowing that at the end of the day, it's love that will persevere and persist.' What sustains us is not the fancy addition that we may or may not put on to our home, but the relationships we build."

I'm somewhat spellbound, sitting in Brous's sukkah, nodding my head at every word, hoping that Ben and Molly have absorbed this message but knowing I never physicalized it—by taking them out into a thatched home that we built in a day. It would feel forced and self-conscious to introduce a Sukkot habit at this point in my teenage kids' lives. But then again, the whole point of My Jewish Year is that it's never too late.

I have to visit one last JTS alum before I leave LA, Rabbi Ed Feinstein, because his jocularity and bluntness precede him, and because I admire any rabbi who has the chutzpah to critique his own religious institutions. In 2013, Feinstein said at a conference about institutional Judaism titled "The Conversation of the Century": "Our house is on fire. . . . In the next ten years you will see a rapid collapse of synagogues and the national organizations that support them. . . . What I'm missing at 'The Conversation' is a little bit of screaming. So I wanted to scream a little bit. At least someone here should."

You can see why I wanted to meet this guy. He greets me cheerily at the entrance to his synagogue, Encino's Valley Beth Shalom, and guides me to his shul's sukkah, which shows the wear and tear of kids having run through it—decorations askew, mashed pomegranates underfoot. Feinstein is as advertised—a Falstaff-like presence as brash as Rabbi Levy was serene. "Sukkot is a forgotten holiday because the Jewish tradition forgot that people have bodies. And this is a holiday that's *visceral*. This is a holiday about your body. You build something. One of the reasons for Sukkot is for Jewish men to prove to their wives, lovers, and daughters that they can actually build something with their hands."

I have to laugh: "You mean because Jewish men aren't handy?"

"Because Jews think that Black and Decker is a law firm," he replies. "This is a holiday about the body. This is a holiday about feasting. This is a holiday about dancing. This is a holiday about sitting outside and letting the sun shine down on you and feeling it on your face. Once a year on Sukkot we get kicked out of our house."

When Feinstein insists I drive to see the amazing array of creative sukkot in the Pico-Robertson neighborhood, an Orthodox enclave fifteen miles away, I thank him and head in that direction.

Behind Pico-Robertson's main drag of Jewish bakeries and businesses, shuttered for the holiday, I come upon rows of well-tended suburban homes, their front yards dotted with families in black hats and headscarves chatting between services. As I watch couples walking leisurely home from shul, calling *"Chag Sameach!"* ("Happy Holiday") across the street to each other—several pushing strollers with lulavs jutting out of the storage baskets—I can't help but envy not so much their orthodoxy, but their routine. Today there is zero reason to hurry; it's a simple itinerary of shul and sukkah. Prayer, family, food.

I get out of my car and walk a bit, venturing to ask a couple where I might view some inventive sukkot (the structures are largely hidden from view by hedges and fences). To my surprise, I'm instantly invited in to see theirs.

And then their son next door invites me to see his.

And his neighbor insists I visit hers.

For an hour, I am given proud "house tours" of sukkahs with chandeliers and velvet walls, with silky tablecloths and verdant roofing. I receive tutorials on how to build a solid-but-porous roof, how many guests a sukkah can accommodate. No one seems in a hurry for me to leave, except for a couple of barking dogs who sense I'm a trespasser.

I could have sukkah-surfed all afternoon, if I hadn't had a plane to catch. Part of me wanted to stay in these simple temporary dwellings a little while longer.

"Strip away all our privileges and luxuries; we'd still be full," Brous says. "We are all we need."

Rabbi Naomi Levy
ON SUKKOT

I find it fascinating that on Sukkot, you're commanded to have joy. It says *"v'samachtah b'chagecha v'hayita ach sameach—*You shall rejoice on your festival and you shall only be happy!"* You're *commanded* to rejoice. I've thought about that a lot; what does it mean to be *commanded* to rejoice? Well, it must mean that, on some level, joy is a choice.

Rabbi Avi Shafran
ON HOSHANA RABBAH

Every Jewish holiday has not only a theme and particular observances but its own mystical coloring as well. None, though, perhaps, as much as Hoshana Rabbah.

Technically just the last of the "intermediate days" of Sukkot, Hoshana Rabbah (literally 'many hoshanas"—"hoshana" being an entreaty to G-d for salvation) is marked with its own special liturgy and ritual. And a strange ritual it is: the beating of the aravot—one of the "four species" taken up on each of the holiday's non-Sabbath days—against the ground. The spectacle of Jews smashing stalks of willow leaves against the floor is, at least to an uninitiated observer, exceedingly strange.

Stranger still is the fact that the ritual's meaning is entirely obscure. In the times of the Holy Temple, the aravot were given a special prominence on Hoshana Rabbah. According to the Talmud, the aravot-focus is based either on a single word in the Torah or on an entirely oral "law given to Moses at Sinai." When the Temple is not standing, as today, the taking the aravot alone, without the other three species, on Hoshana Rabbah has the status of a prophet-declared "custom," which came to include beating the branches.

The aravot-banging comes after the congregation makes seven circuits around the bima, where the Torah is read. Each of the previous days of Sukkot (save Shabbat), a single circuit is made. Hoshana Rabbah's seven circuits recall Joshua's seven circuits around Jericho, before the city's walls fell. That Joshua's name, Yehoshua, has the same root as hoshanna is surely not meaningless. . . .

Perhaps, as we leave each year's "Days of Judgment" on Hoshana Rabbah, we act out our determination to become something more in the coming year than we were in the one left behind—to beat ourselves, so to speak, into Jewish shape.

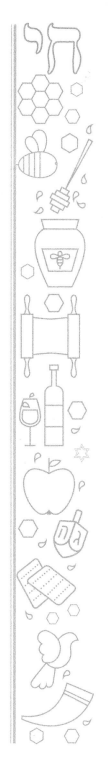

7

HOSHANA RABBAH & SHEMINI ATZERET

Left Out, Then Lingering

10.17.14

OSHANA RABBAH GETS short shrift because it's the caboose of Sukkot, not its own thing.

And yet I kept hearing from rabbis that this seventh day of Sukkot *is* very much its own thing—with its own special name and distinct synagogue service. And since I've vowed not to skip a holiday, no matter how little-known, I'm not skipping this one.

Hoshana Rabbah means literally "Great Supplication." But when this non-holiday-holiday arrives, I'm not sure where I should go to supplicate, because my research hasn't turned up the must-see, hardcore Hoshana Rabbah destination.

Then a pal, David Kalb, a Modern Orthodox rabbi who followed my series in the *Forward* and teaches some adult classes at my synagogue, tells me there's a jubilee over at the Carlebach Shul. So I head over to West 79th Street, where the small synagogue founded in the 1940s is tucked in between apartment buildings, with a burgundy awning, wooden doors, and a stained-glass window that says "Serve G-d with joy." This shul is best known for its charismatic spiritual leader, Shlomo Carlebach, who died in 1994 but whose spirited musical compositions have outlived him in many congregations.

On Hoshana Rabbah, God apparently decides how much rain will fall in the coming year, which was critical for crops in the ancient world and remains relevant today for parched areas. Tradition dictates that a hoshana (entreaty for abundance) should be recited seven times while circling the bimah seven times holding lulav and etrog. Then willow sprigs are beat against the ground so that the leaves fall off, representing raindrops. It's an exuberant seven laps to thank God in advance for a year of plenty.

I get to Carlebach late and unprepared—sans lulav, etrog, or willow branches—but there are some extra lulavs at the entrance for the taking. Instantly I see that men and women are separated, so I find a seat in the narrower female section on the right.

When I say "find a seat," it isn't difficult: the women's side is noticeably sparse. There is a smattering of women, sitting mostly apart from each other. The men, by contrast, are jammed shoulder to shoulder on the other side.

I was hoping to get through this holiday year without debating the *mechitza*—the divider (or, sometimes, balcony) that separates the genders in Orthodox synagogues, because I'm committed to sampling observance without judgment, including segregated worship. I have heard all the reasons why the mechitza was established, namely to preserve women's modesty and men's attentiveness to the prayers.

But the fact is, my Hoshana Rabbah induction is hindered by the physical barrier; it feels like I'm missing the holiday even while it's happening right in front of me. On the men's side, worshippers rock and chant under prayer shawls, so turbocharged in their singing that the room shakes, thrusting their lulavs to the sky or to the east, fervently kissing their yellow etrogs. This scene alone—a sea of tallises among upraised branches—is stirring. The smattering of women seems anesthetized by comparison: a little sway here, a limp lulav-wave there. The energy can't compare to the ecstasy next door. It's as if two entirely different rituals are occurring within spitting distance of each other.

Despite what some might assume about me, due to my mother's public role as an activist in the women's movement, I don't feel like an outraged feminist. I feel like a sidelined Jew. I want to be where the excitement is. Separate isn't equal here. I don't fault Carlebach. Its history is venerable, the music is beautiful, the congregants seem very content. But this is the first time I've come up against Judaism's barriers: *You see that happy group over there? You cannot join them, even if you want to. You cannot stand, move, or sing with them. Sukkot's credo, "z'man simchateinu" (the season of our joy), is just a little more joyful over there.*

I spot David Kalb, one familiar face, and we share an awkward glance that seems to acknowledge the oddness of the rules. I can't sit with the one person I know.

The hoshana plea for rain showers was interpreted more dramatically by the Zohar (the chief text of Jewish mysticism) to suggest that we're making one last petition to be included in the Book of Life. On Rosh Hashanah, our verdicts were written; on Yom Kippur, they are sealed; on Hoshana Rabbah, they're delivered. Which means (who knew?) we had an additional *eleven days to appeal*, to alter our decrees, a final shot at redemption.

God told Abraham (according to rabbinic commentary): "If atonement is not granted to your children on Rosh Hashanah, I will grant it on Yom Kippur; if they do not attain atonement on Yom Kippur, it will be given on Hoshana Rabbah." Ah, so *that's* why the traditional Yiddish greeting on the seventh day of Sukkot is *"a guten kvitel"* ("a good note"). It means "Your verdict should be positive"; the verdict is still out.

It's hard for me to think about how God will rule in The Case of Abigail Pogrebin. I *believe* I've been kind in the last year, but maybe not kind enough. I've tried to be less quick to impatience, but I'm still exasperated when I get stuck behind a slow walker. I've tried to avoid making close friends feel like I'm always rushing, but I'm still overscheduled. I promised myself I'd call my brother more, but I fell short. I donated money, but one can always give more. I volunteered at Central's soup kitchen every week, but gave up tutoring children in Harlem. I didn't consistently separate my garbage. And, of course, I'm not even mentioning more private lapses.

It occurs to me that I might be damaging my verdict right now at Carlebach by grumbling about the divider at Carlebach. I leave the service after about two hours and check my Google calendar for the next holiday's starting time as I walk across town, amazed anew that, in the fall, the holidays come fast and furious.

There was little daylight left in the afternoon to ruminate either on my Carlebach struggle or on my final day of judgment. The very next morning would bring everyone's hands-down favorite festival (drumroll, please). . . .

SHEMINI ATZERET!!

What's the easiest way to stump a Reform Jew? Ask him to explain Shemini Atzeret.

What's the easiest way to stump an Orthodox Jew? Ask him to explain Shemini Atzeret.

That's a bit of an exaggeration, but it gets at something true: everybody is a little fuzzy on Shemini Atzeret. The holiday is not tied to any commandment and has no historical narrative. In Reform shuls and in Israel, it's celebrated simultaneously with the *next* holiday, Simchat Torah, which marks the completion of one Torah cycle (reading the end of Deuteronomy) and the start of the next (the first lines of Genesis). Everywhere else, Shemini Atzeret is marked on the day *before* Simchat Torah. Stay with me.

On its face, Shemini Atzeret—literally, "the cessation of the eighth day"—is simply the eighth day of Sukkot ("Shemini" means "eighth").

Except that Sukkot is *seven days*, so the eighth day isn't technically Sukkot anymore.

Except that some Jews still sit in the sukkah on the eighth day.

Except that some of those sukkah-sitting Jews believe they should no longer *eat* in it on the eighth day.

And some ditch the sukkah entirely and go inside, because at the end of Sukkot, we're supposed to consciously return to our homes.

Leaving aside whether Shemini Atzeret is Sukkot's last gasp or its own separate holiday, there's no question that it's a dud. No wonder it gets no respect. But in my research, I do discover one intriguing kernel: after the unceasing intensity of Elul, Rosh Hashanah, Yom Kippur, and Sukkot, God is asking us to stay just a bit longer. "Atzeret" means stop, which the rabbis interpret as God's plea for us to tarry one more day after all the weeks we've spent together during these holidays of repentance and petition.

"Oh, won't you stay . . . just a little bit longer?"

The 1960s lyric by Maurice Williams and the Zodiacs was invoked by Rabbi Kalb, when he gave a lecture on Shemini Atzeret the year before at my synagogue. He moved quickly from his pop source to a medieval one: Rashi, the eleventh-century French commentator, whose interpretations visibly anchor every page of Talmud. Kalb said Rashi likens God's request on Shemini Atzeret to a king who asks his children to linger at his feast: "Please, stay with me just one more day, [for] it is difficult for me to part with you!"

I call Kalb before this vague holiday begins, to revisit that Rashi quote. "What Rashi is really saying," Kalb tells me, "is that God wants *us*; God needs *us*. It's funny to talk about God's wants and needs. . . . There's something very compelling about God having issues. Yes, we need God on these holidays, but God needs us, too."

It's a softening portrait, which suggests that God could be a friend. I've never heard the deity—commonly referred to in our prayer books as *Malkeinu* (our King)—described as needing us. It's a depiction that affirms a connection to God that I already felt but was embarrassed to admit. I haven't written about God easily (or ever), but the truth is, I'm a believer. Not in God as all-powerful, but in God as protector and healer, as an instigator to make us notice each other's suffering and be moved to relieve it. I do pray. I do feel somehow heard, watched over, guided. At the same time, going into this year of immersion, I wasn't sure God paid equal attention to the less devout, or whether I was entitled to a personal dialogue since I lack proficiency. Rabbi Kalb reassures me that my private relationship with God is not only affirmed by this holiday, but is, in fact, mutual.

Before even deciding which Shemini service to attend, I want to probe further the idea that God is accessible. So I phone Kalb's fellow congregant, Asher Lopatin, a Modern Orthodox rabbi who is the president of Yeshivat Chovevei Torah (YCT), a progressive Orthodox rabbinical school founded by Rabbi Avi Weiss in Riverdale, NY. Lopatin delivers every teaching with a kind of twinkle in his voice, as if he's constantly delighted by Judaism's many refractions. He, too, sees Shemini Atzeret as a tender, bonus moment with the Almighty, in contrast to God's severe evaluation during the Days of Awe.

"This is the intimate holiday," he tells me. "*Atzeret* means detaining. We're ending this period of holidays and pulling everything together." I could use a breath to pull everything together; I'm feeling buffeted by the marathon that started in August. "The term *atzeret* means stop and come in," Lopatin continues. "As busy as God is with the whole world, God is also interested in what I'm doing. There are no special customs. No special foods. No crying. No shofar. The message is, 'Just sit there and be there.'"

I need more "atzeret" in my life.

For the service itself, I drive on a sunny Thursday to the Bronx shul of Lopatin and Kalb, Hebrew Institute of Riverdale, which has, for years, forged a more progressive Orthodoxy under founder Rabbi Avi Weiss.

When I arrive at their light-filled, recently renovated sanctuary, the service is under way and feels at first like any impenetrable Jewish proceeding. The prayers keep coming in lightning Hebrew, everyone knows when to rise or sit; I'm at sea. But, unlike at Carlebach, here I feel welcome. I'm greeted warmly at the door by Lopatin, Kalb, and Weiss himself (whom I interviewed for a *New York* magazine profile years ago). When I take a seat, the woman next to me introduces herself and helps me find the right page number. The mechitza in this synagogue is less forbidding because the men's and women's sides have comparable amounts of space, the dividing wall is low, and the bimah is centered, suggesting more democracy. It's a glimpse of how separate *can* feel more equal.

It occurs to me that the Jewish door can swing wide open or remain just ajar. People won't walk through if they feel as if they have to knock or might be interrupting something. If God is asking us to "atzeret"—stop and come in—then every synagogue should, too. On my very first Shemini Atzeret, I feel invited to tarry, to continue the conversation, to "just sit there and be there."

Rabbi Avi Weiss
ON SHEMINI ATZERET

Shemini Atzeret is extraordinary because there's nothing between me and God. Every other holiday is full of ritual—on Sukkot, we wave lulav and etrog. On Rosh Hashanah, we blow the shofar. On Pesach, we eat matzah. Even Shavuot is centered on the Torah. Shemini Atzeret—it's just me and God. It's just the two of us.

Rabbi Dov Linzer
ON SHEMINI ATZERET

Shemini Atzeret is for me a day devoted to transition. It's the day we come in from the sukkah—from feeling our vulnerability and our need for God's protection—to live in our firm, sturdy house. Finally, no more holidays and we can get on with our lives. But then, what was the point of it all? Shemini Atzeret tells us—give yourself a day to transition back, to ask yourself: How am I going to integrate what I've learned and experienced this High Holiday season? It is a day that says: don't let this be like coming home from a conference all fired up with new ideas, only to forget them the minute you step off the plane. It is a day that says: make sure that something gets brought back home.

8

SIMCHAT TORAH
The Mosh Pit

10.20.14

I AM DETERMINED TO meet Simchat Torah head-on: dancing wildly with the scrolled law, holding it like a dance partner. But I'm nervous about boogieing alone. So I ask my family as the holiday hour approaches: "Anyone want to come dance with the Torah with me?"

Blank stares.

Daughter: "I have *so* much homework, Mom."

Husband: "You're seriously going to dance with strangers?"

Son: "I love you, but you're on your own."

Me: "Fine. Abandon me."

Simchat Torah (rejoicing of the Torah) marks the day we complete the Torah and start it all over again. The last verses of the last book (Deuteronomy) are read, followed by the first verses of the first book (Genesis). It's a clear snapshot of how we hold both the ending and the beginning in the same moment, not to mention that the ending never ends. After this celebration, the cycle restarts on the next Sabbath and then continues every Sabbath going forward, with sections read or chanted chronologically, weekly, in synagogues everywhere.

The *eve* of Simchat Torah is always the big kickoff. There are high spirits and literal spirits: people get amply inebriated ahead of time.

My kids would call it "pre-gaming." The rabbis tell me that single malt is the drink of choice on this holiday. So I stand in my living room and pour myself a shot of Macallan. The first sip doesn't go so well; I brave a second and stop there. Okay, call me a Simchat Torah lightweight. But I won't wimp out on the dancing.

The question is where. When I ask my rabbi "consultants" to point me to The Place To Be on this holiday, the near-unanimous response is B'nai Jeshurun—BJ—my parents' synagogue on West 88th Street.

The line extending down the block is my first confirmation: this is a happening. I'd been told it was popular, but the numbers astonish me. Jews, Jews, and more Jews—notably a critical mass in their twenties and thirties, a group considered to be the demographic sweet spot by Jewish professionals who fret about Jewish continuity.

These youngsters are queuing as they would outside a hot nightclub, waiting to get into the bash we can hear from the street. When I finally get inside BJ, a worn-but-beautiful building, it's like entering a raucous wedding reception, midstream. The sanctuary, cleared of chairs or pews, throbs with music, singing, and dancing.

By dancing, I mean stomping and clapping; bouncing and hopping; do-si-doing and tango-ing; human chains connected by hands on shoulders weaving in and out of other human chains, dodging smaller circles of carousers encircling someone bobbing with a Torah.

Torahs are passed around liberally, handed off with a tallis so that whoever dances with the scroll can be draped properly in a prayer shawl.

In the bedlam, I find two friends from my synagogue: Associate Rabbi Maurice (Mo) Salth and Interim Rabbi Andrew Straus, both of whom clearly got the same memo that BJ is the Studio 54 of Simchat Torah. I also spot rabbis from other shuls: Irwin Kula, who cofounded CLAL, a center for learning; and Elliot Cosgrove, who heads Park Avenue Synagogue where I spent Selichot; plus Amichai Lau-Lavie, spiritual leader of the experimental Lab/Shul who led my Tashlich tour of Hell's Kitchen. Knesset member Ruth Calderon is also in the house. This scene offers something I haven't yet experienced in my holiday escapades: a service that brings together leaders from disparate institutions, all dressed in weekend clothes, schmoozing and cavorting. It makes me feel happy, and also hip. I'm in the hub of the holiday.

Rabbi Mo has been to this hoedown before, so he explains the lay of the land: BJ's two senior rabbis, Rolando Matalon and Marcelo Bronstein, are taking turns at the microphone, leading rousing niggunim with the help of their beloved senior cantor, Ari Priven. Each niggun represents one of seven hakafot—the circuits taken with the Torah when it's removed from the ark, which calls to mind the seven circles under the wedding huppah. The Torah is the ketubah; we're wedded to The Book. I recall that I missed the seven circuits taken on Hoshana Rabbah and how wise Judaism is to think constantly in symbols and numbers. People remember numbers the way children remember rhymes. They stick in your head: forty days of introspection, Ten Days of Awe, forty years in the desert. Seven days of creation and Sukkot, eight days of Hanukkah and Passover. Memory itself is recurrence, going back over things. The repetition is starting to feel resonant to me. It creates a rhythm. Each repeated ritual is an affirmation that we're Jewish and therefore we do these specific things on these specific days. We believe there's meaning to be found every single time, and that the echo of our ancestors, heard in these rites, informs the moment we do them today.

Each hakafah lasts at least fifteen or twenty minutes and begins by inviting one age cohort to walk under a human-made bridge formed by the rest of us. I've arrived just after the 40 to 49's have ducked their way through. It reminds me of my childhood "London Bridge" or "Red Rover, Red Rover." Since the next hakafah group is just over my bracket—"everyone 40–49"—I leave Mo and Andy, find a spot on the bridge-line, and tent my arms across from a stranger. As the fifties group snakes its way through our gauntlet, it's impossible to miss how giddy people look—a marked difference from the solemn faces of Yom Kippur. We hold the bridge till everyone has walked under it, many holding Torahs, while the rabbis lead us in a recurring call-and-response prayer: *"Aneinu B'yom Korienu."*

I find Mo in the crowd again and ask him to translate that refrain. *"Answer us, on the day that we call."* I like that language. It's another example of how Judaism beseeches, cries out—in this case, for another beginning, another Genesis, a connection to Torah. "Answer us" cements the idea I keep hearing during these holidays: God answers us. Or might. It's reassuring and rousing, both.

A line-dance has started to conga through the sanctuary while many of us still stand clapping on the perimeter. I'm tempted to join, but too bashful to leap. Since Mo is holding his four-year-old son, he has no free hands to latch on, but Rabbi Andy and I exchange a glance that signals "Should we brave it?" and we break one of the chains to join it, jogging to keep up with the frenzied pace. The exhilaration is instantaneous. I ignore how clumsy I look, how badly I sing, how sweaty are someone's hands on my shoulders behind me. I just find myself laughing.

"If you jump in, you get caught up in it. It really opens you up," says Rabbi Asher Lopatin, whom I interviewed with the phone to my ear, laptop on my lap, before the holiday began. He says he always looks forward to the unfettered whirl. "You don't have to know any fancy dance steps. There are no complicated lyrics; just 'lai lai lai,' or 'dai dai dai.' The tunes go over and over again." He likens it to King David dancing before the ark in the Book of Samuel. "On Simchat Torah, we don't worry about the usual decorum in the synagogue—*Kavod hatzibur* [public dignity]," Lopatin says. "We get rid of those inhibitions and connect with the Torah and with each other."

His words prove true. I toss my inhibitions and "connect." It actually hits me that this is what I was missing: primal Judaism. Gut spirituality. A night like this, where it doesn't matter what age, aptitude, or denomination you are. Simchat Torah is a level playing field, no experience required.

David Kalb told me—also before the holiday began—that this night eliminates factions. "Sometimes I'll just stop in the midst of the dancing and say, 'This is the way things should be,'" he says. "When you dance with people in a circle, you don't worry about their politics or whether you agree with them. You put everything aside. The fact that we're ending this holiday with that experience kind of says to me, 'Why can't we be like this all the time?'"

I'm asking myself the same question as I careen around the sanctuary: "Why can't all Jews be like this?" I have that sudden, hopeful thought that if we all gathered to dance unrestrained once a year, we would not only have fewer internecine frictions, we'd be putting a firmer stake in the ground for Judaism overall. Men are dancing with women here. Reform Jews with Conservative Jews, Reconstructionist with Renewal, labeled Jews with unlabeled Jews.

"How powerful is it," Kalb says, "that the Torah is something so sacred—we're so careful with it all year round—but at the end of the day, we're dancing with it. Passing it. It's out there. It really makes a statement: the Torah should be out there in the world. It shouldn't be sequestered."

Communing with Torah. It's my second time in twelve days that I've been close to it: first the private moment on Yom Kippur afternoon at Central, now this revelry. "Where in the world is there a people that loves a book so much that they dance around with it?" Kalb asked me. "It's a celebration of the biggest book club in the world."

I remember how moved I was when my children had the heavy scroll unfurled in front of them when they became bar and bat mitzvah. Ben and Molly looked so small as they stood behind the large podium on a step stool, in order to be able to view the calligraphy on parchment. They touched the fringe of their tallis to the starting place in the Torah and then kissed the threads. I thought, as I watched them chant assuredly: "Our tradition essentially says 'Take hold of this luminous thing; it belongs to you, too.'"

The holiday of Simchat Torah is not found in the Bible; it's an invention of the ancient rabbis, who made a *separate* holiday out of the *second* day of Shemini Atzeret—which, just to confuse me, is the eighth day of Sukkot. So essentially Sukkot runs for eight days and then the following day is Simchat Torah.

"Scholars think this holiday emerged in the tenth or eleventh century," says Rabbi Michael Strassfeld, a learned presence whose fascination with the holidays' origins is contagious. (His book *The Jewish Holidays* has been one of my staples.) I interview him at his Reconstructionist synagogue, Society for the Advancement of Judaism (SAJ), New York's Reconstructionist SAJ, on West 86th Street. He says, "The creation of Simchat Torah probably has to do with the two Torah-reading cycles," referring to the two ways our tradition reads through the entire Torah: over the course of three years, or one. Once the method changed to the one-year cycle in the Middle Ages, the moment of concluding the Torah and restarting it again was considered cause for a party. And the crazy dancing came from the Hasidim, who tend to celebrate in that style of ecstatic rocking out (see the *Fiddler* wedding scene). "When the *annual* Torah cycle started to dominate," Strassfeld says, "then Simchat Torah emerged. Because there was this sense of 'Oooh, look, here's a great thing. We're finishing Deuteronomy and starting Genesis again. We're showing the cycle is an unending cycle.'"

That "unending cycle" can look redundant or rich, depending on your slant. An observant Jew has no choice in the matter; he or she is obligated to repeat, whether they find resonance or not. And I understand why the redundancy on its face can lose people—especially those who would rather read a new book than reread an ancient tome every single year. When I ask Strassfeld how he breathes life into the repetition, he harkens back to the metaphor offered by his pal Rabbi Burt Visotzky in my chapter on Rosh Hashanah preparation: "The repetition of the Torah and the holidays," says Strassfeld, "*is* like therapy in the sense that you come back to the same truth again and again, but you come back to it in a somewhat different way each year. You understand it more deeply, or you come back to it thinking more deeply about it. . . .

"So, yes, it's autumn again," he continues. "But I'm actually a year older and this thing happened in my life between last fall and this fall. I'm not the same person, even though I'm coming back to the same place. Both things are true: I'm the same, but I'm different. The Torah is the same, but it's different."

That could be our slogan, since we seem to need one these days: "Try Judaism: The Same Is Always New."

"How was it?" my husband asks when I limp in the door.

"Actually, pretty wonderful," I answer. "But I need a shower."

The next morning, I take an Advil for my disco-hangover and rush to get to a service for Simchat Torah itself. After the holiday's rockin' eve, the daytime observance is entirely teetotaling. I head to a venerable institution, Park East Synagogue, the 126-year-old Orthodox shul led by Rabbi Arthur Schneier. Women sit in the balcony, and I take my place among a smattering of hatted ladies in the upper pews while admiring the stately sanctuary, with its two circular stained-glass windows at the front and back. Schneier, a Holocaust survivor born in Vienna, stands mostly toward the rear of the bimah, draped in a tallis that shimmers with mirrored squares, calling up male congregants for the honor of an aliyah, the summons to read Torah.

As they come forward, he turns to publicly praise them for their devotion to Torah, and then they go to stand under the huppah to chant, bent over the open scroll, aided by the hazzan (cantor) who stands beside them.

I'm less attentive to the text because I'm glued to the ballet on the bimah, watching the seasoned senior rabbi hanging back, clearly intentionally not making himself the center of attention, the cantor and the more junior rabbi greeting readers—sometimes their sons—as they approach the scroll. No women are called up. There's a brio to it all.

Repetition is inclusion on Simchat Torah because every person who wants an aliyah gets one today, which means the aliyot go on as long as necessary until each person has had a turn. "It's not like needing tickets on the High Holy days," Rabbi Asher Lopatin says. "Everyone is welcome. The rabbis say that the Torah belongs to every single Jew. You're not coming as an outsider but as an insider: it's your Torah. Come as an owner."

I don't feel yet like an owner. Definitely a renter. But I'm feeling more and more at home.

As I leave the shul in the sunlight on the Upper East Side, it dawns on me: Simchat Torah is about access. It's a holiday that announces, *This Torah is yours. To dance with. To talk to. To encircle. To lift up. To chant. To hold.* That's what will stay with me: the Torah was brought close.

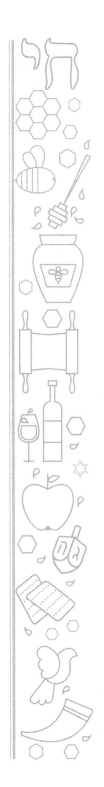

Rabbi Sharon Kleinbaum
ON HANUKKAH

I love the anti-militarist aspect of the story of Hanukkah, despite its being about a military episode. We are celebrating the miracle of the oil, instead. That's remarkable—that here is this great military event, but what we're actually remembering with the ritual of lighting the candles is that somebody had the chutzpah, the faith, the hope, to take a tiny little vial of oil and imagine that it would last. I think that's so profound for us today. You can imagine everybody around him or her, saying. "Nudnik, why are you even lighting that little oil? It's not enough, give up, don't even try. What's the point?" That speaks to all of us today who feel such despair about the conditions in the world, our ability to have impact in our lives. The hanukkiah, or menorah, says, "Start with whatever you have, use it well, and trust that there will be a future beyond that one day."

9

HANUKKAH RECONSIDERED

A Split in the Jewish Soul

12.11.14

H ANUKKAH WASN'T COMPLICATED for me until this year.
I grew up with the basics: lighting the menorah (the Hanukkah candelabra, technically the "Hanukkiah") for eight nights with a
candle added each night; spinning the *dreidel*, the four-sided top with
Hebrew letters, twirled expectantly by us three kids—(if it landed on
our letter, we got to open a gift); eating latkes (potato pancakes) made
expertly by Mom with crispy edges, sour cream on the side; and belt-
ing out a few songs, including the obvious standards, "Hanukkah, Oh
Hanukkah" and "Maoz Tzur" (Mighty Rock).

I knew the story of the brave Maccabees, the family that fought off
the Jew-hating Greeks, because Mom retold the tale when we were
little and we acted it out in costumes at the annual friends-and-family
Hanukkah party. The Cruel Greek King, Antiochus (usually played
by my twin, Robin, in a Tudor crown), decreed that all Jews must stop
practicing Judaism; he set up idols for the Jews to worship instead of
their God, and led his army to seize the Jews' holy Temple. But the
Jewish warrior, Judah the Maccabee (usually played by me), and his
Maccabee brothers (all played by my younger brother, David), fought
back valiantly, and reclaimed the Temple.

For costumes, we turned bedsheets into togas, which seemed like good, all-purpose ancient garb. Our relatives and parents' friends cheered as we stomped around with cardboard swords and shouted in British accents (when in doubt, use a British accent). I'm sure the audience enjoyed Mom's spiked eggnog more than our thespian exploits.

The Hanukkah story ends with the miracle, of course: when the Maccabees reclaim the Temple, they try to rekindle the menorah, which was lit daily at that time. But when they look for oil to reignite it, they find only one jar—enough for a single day. They burn the one cruse of oil optimistically, defiantly, and lo and behold, it lasts eight days. Amen.

I grew up loving this holiday, and not just because of the big party or the presents Mom wrapped in blue and silver Hanukkah colors. I loved the way the house glowed differently during Hanukkah week, how I looked forward to my siblings and me being called from our bedrooms to light the menorah, deciding whose turn it was to strike the match when we were old enough to hold a flame, counting how many candles were to be added.

It was a halcyon holiday. That is, until this year, when I learned the dark side and felt like a kid discovering that there's no Santa Claus. It turns out that Hanukkah is, in part, a tale of Jew vs. Jew.

Come again? Us against us? Whatever happened to Jew against Greek; Maccabee vs. Antiochus? The more complete story, asserted by rabbi after rabbi, is that the Maccabees (aka the Hasmoneans) took on not just Antiochus IV, who in 167 B.C.E. forbade Jewish practice. The Maccabees challenged their *fellow Jews for selling out*—embracing Greek culture, Hellenization, because they were either seduced by it or afraid to disobey authority.

"Hanukkah grows out of a split in the Jewish soul," writes Rabbi Irving Greenberg in his book *The Jewish Way*. "In most of the battles in that extended war, Jews fought among themselves as soldiers in the armies on both sides."

"A split in the Jewish soul." I see the potential for this in arguments over 2014's Israel-Gaza war. And I've seen it in the fault lines between the Orthodox and Modern-Orthodox. Between Conservative and Reform. Ashkenazi vs. Sephardic. Zionist vs. Anti-Zionist. I've been attuned, during my current expedition, to the Opted-In vs. the Opted-Out Jew. The former has an ease with Hebrew, ritual, kosher rules, holiday customs. The latter doesn't power down on Shabbat, reads the prayers in transliteration, and doesn't know it's a Jewish holiday on Shemini Atzeret. I get the difference, and it didn't used to bug me, but then it started to. Which is partly why I chose to do this project. But even a few months in, I'm straddling the two camps and alert to how each group judges the other, drawing conclusions about what brand of Judaism is "Jewish enough" or "too Jewish," exclusive or welcoming, cursory or rigorous.

Obviously Jews will always disagree (two Jews, three opinions), but there's something deeper dividing us: a sense of who's authentic and who's not. I have my own anxiety about where I fall or how I'm perceived. Which is why this new Hanukkah angle triggers something personal.

I know it's too simplistic to say the Maccabees stand in for the observant while the rest of us are Hellenized. But implicit in so many of the Hanukkah teachings I'm now reading is that Jews are in danger of losing our direction—our *distinctiveness*—and abandoning the traditions, language, and texts that make us Jews.

Am I Hellenized? Would the Maccabees have viewed me as a threat to Jewish life? Hanukkah makes me question this for the first time.

I order an Earl Gray at Alice's Tea Cup with Arthur Kurzweil, a writer and speaker with a copious gray beard who counts as his mentor the legendary Talmud scholar Rabbi Adin Steinsaltz. I've asked him to talk to me about Hanukkah because I've found his lectures refreshing: he never says the politically correct thing.

Sure enough, even before I've poured Splenda into my teacup, he says that the Hanukkah story "is about Jewish intolerance in the best sense of the word," when strict Jews were intolerant of lax ones. "I mean 'intolerance' in the sense of 'I don't want to just blend in with the majority unconsciously,'" Kurzweil tells me.

He believes too many of us have "blended in," or assimilated, by default, opting for an "anything-goes" Judaism that isn't Judaism. "I don't know who said it originally, but I think it's a great analogy: baseball has four bases. You can invent a game with five bases; maybe it's even a better game. But it's not baseball. So I think Hanukkah is trying to say, 'Judaism is not whatever you want it to be.'"

I can hear the counterarguments—that Judaism *is* individual and valid in every form. But the Maccabees didn't think so. Neither does Kurzweil. He disdains DIY Judaism, Torah groups that spend more time inviting personal takes than teaching the sages: "I'd rather go to a doctor for a medical opinion than the guy on the street."

Although Kurzweil doesn't point a finger at me, I'm clearly implicated as a member of his Hellenized camp. Before we part ways, he urges me to interview his mentor, Rabbi Steinsaltz, with whom he's studied and cowritten two books: *On the Road with Rabbi Steinsaltz* and *Pebbles of Wisdom from Rabbi Adin Steinsaltz.* The master rebbe is visiting New York from Israel this very week. I say yes instantly, because Steinsaltz is the Beyoncé of Talmud.

In the meantime, I prepare for my kids' Hanukkah, which means wrapping presents in Hanukkah paper—hard to come by at CVS, where rolls of Christmas paper dominate the aisles—and making sure I have Mom's recipes for latkes and eggnog. I know eggnog is a Christmas thing, but it's always been the taste of Hanukkah to me, thanks to Mom's creamy tradition, which involves folds of cream, swirls of dark rum, and sprinkled nutmeg (I was given the virgin edition before drinking age).

Steinsaltz, seventy-seven, a frail but fierce recipient of the prestigious Israel Prize, has an office on West 45th Street at the Aleph Society, which exists solely to fund his work: translating Talmud and making it accessible. He spent forty-five years translating the Talmud to Modern Hebrew, an enterprise he completed five years ago, to much acclaim. His colleague, Ruth, joins our meeting, in part, it becomes clear, to help me decipher the rabbi, whose wispy voice is hard to hear.

When I tell Steinsaltz about Kurzweil's view of Hanukkah, Steinsaltz agrees. "The Maccabean Revolt was a war that Jews fought to remain Jews." He underscores the idea that the enemy was internal—Jews who embraced Greek culture, adopted Greek names, rules, and ideals. "The idea of the Maccabean fight was, *Can you keep your identity?* . . . And that fight, in a certain way, exists today. The Jews disappeared as a people. They became a part of a general multitude."

It's an indictment I've never considered—that so many of us have faded away as a people. Not completely, but noticeably. Maybe this Jewish Year is my personal attempt not to fade.

When I ask Steinsaltz whether it's fair to assess the quality of someone's Jewishness, he doesn't mince words. "There is good art and bad art," he asserts. "You make judgments about good and evil, beautiful and not beautiful, right and wrong. When you read a piece of trash, you see that it's trash. Of course you are judgmental. Why shouldn't you be judgmental?"

I don't know many Jews—or frankly, human beings—without judgment. We're all wired to weigh in—often rashly—on other people's choices or conduct. Judgments are made about Jews with Christmas trees, Jewish women in wigs, Jews who eat cheeseburgers, and Jewish men who won't sit next to a woman on an airplane. So maybe Steinsaltz is just affirming what the rest of us gloss over: we decide daily whether a painting is masterful or mystifying, whether a novel is brilliant or boring, and whether one person's Judaism is thin or substantive, relatable or alien.

I have four different menorahs, none of them special, except one: the flat wooden board with eight stainless-steel nuts glued to its face, sloppily decorated with red paint and glitter. It's the menorah Ben made when he was four years old. I put it on the kitchen table, along with my travel menorah, and the one I bought at the Museum of Modern Art store. I like to have them all on display with a full box of slender tapers at the ready and a few colorful dreidels circling the tableau. It signals to my kids that the holiday is just a few days away, and hopefully gives them a sense of the anticipation I felt at their age.

This year, we haven't even lit the first candle before my head is spinning from all my preparatory conversations. To sort through the Kurzweil and Steinsaltz indictments, I call my college friend Rabbi Mychal Springer, who presided at Ben and Molly's baby naming ceremonies and is now the director of the Center for Pastoral Education at the Jewish Theological Seminary.

"I think Judaism has survived *because* of Hellenistic impulses," she says. "Over the generations, we've incorporated good things from the world around us. Judaism isn't ossified. And sometimes we get frightened and say we've gone outside the bounds, but that's part of the process of recognizing what's sustainable. I can't only be afraid of external impulses, of absorbing. I don't think they're only bad."

She offers a concrete example of where modern Hellenization has been important. "The Conservative movement has had a major revolution around sexuality and gender over the last thirty years. . . . The idea that nothing changes is *ahistorical*. Judaism has always evolved. Hanukkah isn't commanded anywhere in the Bible. And suddenly we invent Hanukkah and we say we're 'commanded' to say these prayers for this holiday we invented. So even Hanukkah itself is a radical act. You always have to be incorporating the story of your people in its own day. In fact, Hanukkah is the great symbol of our evolution. Where do you find Hanukkah in the Bible? You don't! The closest you get is Sukkot."

Sukkot? What does that have to do with Hanukkah? Glad you asked. The ancient Jews, oppressed by Antiochus, had to *skip* Sukkot because the king forbade all Jewish practice. So when the Jews retook the Temple, they made up for the missed Sukkot by celebrating it, belatedly. That Sukkot-redo became a new holiday, Hanukkah, which means "rededication." I get it now. Since Sukkot lasts eight days, so does Hanukkah. "Historically, Hanukkah is simply a late Sukkot," Springer clarifies. It demonstrates how Jews will not be denied their schedule—the one I'm trying to follow now; they'd rather celebrate a festival two months late than miss it entirely.

At home, I get sentimental when I see my children dive into Hanukkah, the candlelight in their eyes. I flash back to their toddlerhood, when their smaller faces showed the same concentration as they held the *shammes* (lighting candle), often with my steadying hand or Dave's. My recurring regret this year has been discovering all the traditions I never gave them. But *this* holiday is one that's ingrained, secure.

Ben and Molly know Hanukkah—how to set up the menorah, adding the new candles right to left (the way Hebrew is read), lighting them left to right (newest candle to oldest). They're familiar with the blessing, the songs, the dreidel game, my pyramid of gifts, how one night is reserved for giving, not receiving: as soon as they were old enough to have a conversation, we discussed what kind of organization or cause they'd select for our "Giving Night." It strikes me, on this holiday this year, that tradition can be easy or shaky—easy if you start early, shaky if you never began.

Still intent on adding facts to the rosy-colored Hanukkah story, I go the whole nine yards and call Seth Schwartz, the hard-hitting Professor of Classical Jewish Civilization at Columbia University. I want to make sure that Kurzweil's Jew vs. Jew paradigm—Hellenist versus Traditionalist—is rooted in scholarship.

Schwartz says it isn't. Or at least that it's an oversimplification. As we sit in his classic-academia office on Columbia's campus, Schwartz says the Maccabees (only one faction of the Traditionalists) weren't rebelling chiefly against assimilated Jews, but rather against Antiochus's royal edict to stop Judaism. "The Maccabee revolt was not a civil war between progressive Jews and reactionary Jews," he says, calling this an exaggerated subplot that "many liberal rabbis learned in rabbinical school." Schwartz contends that, in some American Orthodox circles, the Hanukkah story has become a rallying cry—"We have to fight against the Jewish Hellenizers of our own time."

I ask his reaction to those who say the Haredi (Ultra-Orthodox) of today are the Maccabees of yesterday. "Historians exist in order to make people not say things like that," he says, clearly irritated.

As to whether Jews like me can be called Hellenists, Schwartz instead suggests that we are materialists, pointing out that Hanukkah was never a major holiday until Christmas exploded. "Three generations ago, who cared about Hanukkah?" asks Schwartz. "Our ancestors in the Old Country, they lit candles on Hanukkah. That was it. There wasn't a fuss about it. We needed a big story to compete with the Christmas story. So I think it's specifically American."

I leave Schwartz's office feeling sheepish about my kids' present pile.

On top of all this Hanukkah-homework, I've been asked to orchestrate a Hanukkah event at the Jewish Theological Seminary, the main training academy for Conservative rabbis and scholars. Rabbi Burt Visotzky, who oversees some of JTS's special programming, has asked me to create, with Amichai Lau-Lavie of Lab/Shul, a captivating Hanukkah experience for four hundred people in early December.

That's a tall order, especially for a well-versed Jewish audience, and since Amichai and I are so busy, we do most of the planning by phone. We efficiently "cast" the panel—trying to achieve some balance in terms of denomination or Jewish perspective, looking for participants who will eschew stock answers about Hanukkah's meaning.

We get fast yesses from Rabbi David Ingber of Romemu; Bruce Feiler, author of *Walking the Bible*; Rabba Sara Hurwitz, the first woman to be ordained in Orthodoxy (though much of the Orthodox establishment refuses to recognize her as clergy); Rabbi Jill Hammer, Director of Spiritual Education at the Academy for Jewish Religion;

and Burt. We ask each person to prepare one aspect of the holiday: Ingber will focus on light, Feiler on Christmas envy, Hurwitz on *pirsum hanes*—publicizing the miracle (the command to put the menorah in the window), Visotzky on Hanukkah history, Hammer on the winter solstice.

But we're still missing an ultra-Orthodox rabbi, and no one will come aboard. It's hard for me not to see the echoes of Maccabee–Hellenist tensions when I invite the participation of representatives from Chabad and Agudath Israel (an Ultra-Orthodox communal organization). Chabad puts me off till it's too late anyway. Agudath says they can't—or won't—sit on the JTS stage with non-Orthodox rabbis. "Agudath Israel's policy with regard to involvement with non-Orthodox institutions prevents me from accepting," writes Rabbi Avi Shafran, Agudath's Director of Public Affairs, who invited me, as part of my exploration this year, to spend a Sabbath with his family.

His email goes on: "That policy is a sort of 'civil-disobedience statement,' intended as an alternative to shouting from the rooftops that we don't accept any model of 'multiple Judaisms.' So, instead, we opt to not do anything that might send a subtle or subliminal message to the contrary. Sorry. Really. But I do deeply appreciate your reaching out on this."

When I tell Shafran that I'd like to quote his email in my holiday dispatch, he asks me to "please make sure the readers know that I consider all Jews to be my brothers and sisters, regardless of affiliations or levels of observance."

I can't help but feel disillusioned. I'd been aware of these philosophical divisions, but I hadn't anticipated the impossibility of sharing a stage. Is it really so verboten for an Orthodox rabbi to have a public conversation with non-Orthodox clergy about Maccabees?

I call sociologist Steven M. Cohen, a non-Orthodox-but-well-versed Jew, to explain it to me. "To sit with you and me individually in a café is fine," he said. "Possibly to sit with you and me and speak at a JCC may be okay. But the second that you bring in a rabbi, then you bring in a religious functionary who represents a system of thought and culture that actively denies some of their deeply held principles. So from their point of view, they can't do that—they can't extend any honor to a rabbi of a non-Orthodox tradition."

I'm nervous about the JTS evening as it approaches, but it's packed and joyful, with a palpable holiday energy in the auditorium. We open the proceedings wearing props that set the tone—I'm in a menorah headband; Amichai in his "Ugly Hanukkah Sweater." The panel discussion is lively, and, after a musical pause for a Hanukkah rap, we invite twenty-five cantors onstage to sing "Light One Candle" by Peter, Paul, and Mary. The surprise of the evening is that Peter himself is here—Peter Yarrow, who has agreed to lead the assorted cantors in the song he wrote in the eighties, which has since become a Hanukkah anthem.

> Light one candle for the Maccabee children
> Give thanks that their light didn't die. . . .

Watching twenty-five cantors singing in unison proves more persuasive than any argument. I look out at my family in the audience, singing along, and think to myself: as complex as Hanukkah is, it can be very simple. And though the historical nuances offer food for thought, I'll always be that nine-year-old who rushed downstairs when Mom said it was time to light the menorah.

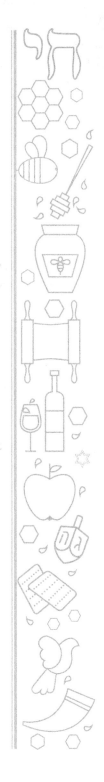

Rabbi Burton Visotzky
ON HANUKKAH

The rabbis really couldn't stand the Maccabees. In all 2,700 folios of Talmud, the Maccabees got just one page. If the rabbis could have, they would have suppressed the holiday entirely—because it's militaristic, and frankly, as far as the rabbis were concerned, the Maccabees were on the wrong side of the divide. The Battle of Hanukkah, which took place in the second century before the Common Era, was a battle within the Jewish community, not unlike the one we're fighting now, between zealotry—those who wanted very little to do with the outside world—and those Jews who were willing to live in accommodation with the outside world, who were willing to Hellenize to a greater extent. And that battle disturbed the rabbis, who were a people who liked to get along to go along. So seven hundred years—seven hundred years!—after the Maccabees fought their fight, the rabbis discovered a cruse of oil. What?, you say, *the rabbis* invented the oil? Yes, Virginia . . . It's kind of astonishing how the rabbis shifted from the battle to the light. For the rabbis, it was always about adding light. That's what they did. They wanted no part of either the military aspect of it, or the Hanukkah that was anti-assimilationist.

10

HANUKKAH AT THE BEDSIDE AND THE WHITE HOUSE

Unexpected Light

12.23.14

Sitting in the Chicago hospital room where my father-in-law, Milton, has often resided since November crystallizes the meaning of Hanukkah. So many rabbis have talked to me about light. And I see it there.

Milt's wife, Phyllis, and twin daughters—Sharon and Fern (both of whom also live in Chicago)—never leave. They just sit, read, or play word games on their iPhones (Phyllis is unbeatable at Scrabble). They worry and chat, knit and parse blood-pressure readings and dialysis cycles. They don't tire or grow restless; they just stay. When Dave and I fly in from New York with our children during Hanukkah, we all camp out at the hospital, too. As I watch Milton battle a failing kidney in his green patient gown, all the Hanukkah metaphors rush to mind—the miracle of the oil lasting one more day; the miracle of doctors who keep trying; the miracle of a family that never leaves your side.

Each person who shows up at the hospital—niece, brother-in-law, friend—seems like another candle, and the room grows palpably brighter with each arrival. My mother-in-law, Phyllis, leans over to me at dinner one night after we leave the hospital and says, "I can see the difference in Milt when everyone is there."

We add another candle to the menorah that night, when we get home to Phyllis's condo on a golf course.

I've read so many teachings about adding light on this *chag urim* (Festival of Lights), how we illuminate the darkest time of year and trust there will be a brighter day. "Jews light lights not to banish the darkness," writes Rabbi Barbara Penzner in *A Guide to Jewish Practice*, "but to be reminded of the miracles of everyday life."

The next morning, Milt regales us with his dramatic dream of the night before, about two planes—one loaded with nuclear weapons—and the conundrum of whether to shoot down one, both, or none. Then he goes on to deconstruct the American folk ballad "Oh My Darling, Clementine." I watch Ben and Molly draw him out, encourage his narrative, however disjointed. They make sure he feels taken seriously. My husband even asks some follow-up questions, which Milt is eager to answer. It's a long yarn and we have plenty of time.

We add another candle that night.

I call Rabbi Mychal Springer to ask her about Hanukkah light—specifically the dispute between ancient rabbis Hillel and Shammai over how to properly light a menorah. Hillel's approach, which virtually every Jew follows today, adds one candle each night to build up to eight. Shammai, by contrast, lights *all* eight candles the first night and decreases one each day to end up with one.

While I've only known the Hillel way—adding candles—Mychal prefers Shammai's, subtracting. "Shammai reminds me that we treasure that light for as long as it remains, without needing to pretend that it's going to last forever," Springer says. I summon her words during Milt's waning days, as I write my Hanukkah dispatch—*"We treasure that light for as long as it remains"*—having no idea that, two months later, he'll be gone.

The menorah itself offers another Milt metaphor. Jews usually light Hanukkah candles in a cluster of family or friends. A menorah gathers us. So does a sick parent.

"Every night of Hanukkah," says Mychal, "according to Shammai, we're witnessing that there's less light, but the people are still together, night after night, and the diminishment of light is possible, or tolerable, because of the people being together. There's a commitment to not walking away that brings light. As the light is dimmed, the people keep coming back." And so we do. We keep returning to Milt, even when he's moved from hospital to nursing home to hospice. We're there for "the diminishment of the light."

I'm invited to the White House Hanukkah party by Matt Nosanchuk, President Obama's director of Jewish community outreach, who the preceding September was a fellow attendee at a three-day conference run by *The Jewish Week*.

I invite my teenage daughter, Molly, to be my guest. My mother, Letty, has also been invited, and she brings my brother, David, as her plus-one. My reporter-twin, Robin—also invited—brings her husband, Ed. My family is excited to be together but a little embarrassed, feeling slightly overrepresented.

We're all freezing cold as we join the queue snaking down Washington's 15th Street. I see so many familiar faces—people I've been with at Jewish conferences; Jewish journalists; friends of Mom, etc.— that the line begins to feel like a cocktail party of its own. All of us note that Hanukkah at the White House would have been unimaginable to our ancestors.

Once we make it through security and enter the glowing White House, the public rooms look like set pieces from a twinkling Jimmy Stewart movie, with overflowing Christmas decorations, elaborate trees, wreaths, and garlands. I glimpse Hanukkah light not in the outnumbered menorahs but in the five hundred milling Jews—many in yarmulkes, some in *sheitels* (wigs)—eating latkes and lamb chops from a White House kitchen made kosher for the occasion.

Molly and I wander from the red room to the blue room to the ballroom, taking selfies and marveling at the oversized gingerbread house, which Gwyneth Paltrow (her dad was Jewish) is also admiring with her daughter, Apple.

My congregation's senior rabbi, Angela Buchdahl, is here with her husband and three kids, having been invited to lead the blessings over the candles. She's been on Nosanchuk's radar since she made a certain kind of Jewish history—the first woman to lead Central Synagogue in its hundred-plus years, the first Asian-American rabbi to be ordained, widely respected for her vibrant worship.

My family and the Buchdahls are enjoying latkes at one of three enormous buffet tables, when suddenly the Buchdahls are ushered away by White House staff for a brief private audience with the president and his wife before the ceremony. (As the rabbi bids a hasty good-bye, I remind her to remember the proletariat.)

The formal program begins, and the crowd jockeys for a view of the small stage, iPhones furiously clicking photographs of the Obamas. Buchdahl guides us all in the Hebrew blessing over the candles, and there's an undeniable magnificence in that unlikely tableau and in the sound of a Jewish prayer filling The People's House. "Our founding fathers," Buchdahl says in front of the attentive Obamas, "could not have predicted in 2014 that there would be a female Asian-American rabbi lighting the menorah at the White House for an African-American president." Huge cheer.

The menorah for this event has been created out of olive wood, clay, and iron by the children of Yemin Orde Youth Village in Israel, a residential program for at-risk children, which made a powerful impression on my kids when we visited three years ago. Damn the clichés: there's light in the White House on this Hanukkah.

Back in Chicago, I sense a different illumination.

When I hold my father-in-law's hand and he says, "What's shaking, baby?"

When I watch my mother-in-law monitor Milt's care more vigilantly than any physician.

When seventeen-year-old Ben climbs onto Milt's bed to chat.

When my husband rests a hand on his father's head.

"We are called to bring together the sparks to preserve single moments of radiance and keep them alive in our lives," wrote the philosopher Rabbi Abraham Joshua Heschel, a seminal thinker and social-justice activist of the twentieth century, "to defy absurdity and despair, and to wait for God to say again: Let there be light. And there will be light."

Maybe it's because I'm watching my children grow up, or seeing my father-in-law falter, but I want so much "to preserve single moments of radiance." So I'm sappy about these holiday symbols—the enduring menorah, the lifted darkness, the waxing and waning flames. This year's Hanukkah meets me right where I am.

Rabbi Adin Steinsaltz
ON HANUKKAH

We display Hanukkah candles in the window. And they are not for beauty. They are just to show we are fighting for the light. The point of the light is that it's a symbol of what we are. We were fighting for the light and we won. And so we light a candle and another candle and another candle.

Rabbi Chaim Steinmetz
ON THE TENTH OF TEVET

A siege is more than a military maneuver; it is a psychological attack. Armies in biblical times used various tactics, including destroying trees and shouting slogans, to encourage surrender. What makes the Tenth of Tevet relevant is that the psychological element of siege has remained a part of Jewish life. Throughout the years of exile, Jews were under an invisible siege, in ghettos with or without walls; and more than a few Jews surrendered, happy to get away from the adversity of being a Jew. Even today, this siege remains a part of Jewish discourse. When Conor Cruise O'Brien wrote his history of Israel in 1986, he entitled it *The Siege*, a reflection of Israel's isolation; whether this depiction is still true today is a matter of debate. Indeed, many argue that we must change our mind-set, and that a siege perspective is paranoid and self-destructive; yet at the same time, Jews in places like Paris, Tehran, and Sderot are still under siege. What is certain is this: Nebuchadnezzar's siege of Jerusalem in 587 B.C.E. has been a part of the Jewish experience ever since.

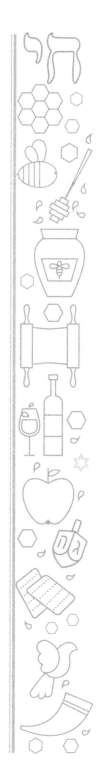

11

THE TENTH OF TEVET
Starting the Secular Year Hungry

1.5.15

DON'T RECOMMEND FASTING on New Year's Day. Starvation is not the best cure for a hangover.

But the Jewish calendar isn't known for convenience, and this year, the Fast of the *Tenth of Tevet—Tzom Asara B'Tevet* (shorthand, 10 Tevet)—happens to land on January 1.

What a rollicking way to ring in 2015: revisiting the destruction of the First Temple. Hanukkah was the most recent holiday. Tu B'Shvat (the new year of the trees) is next. So, naturally, there should be a fast between celebrations. We Jews purge between parties. And Temple destruction is about as sober as it gets.

It may be difficult for most of us to fathom how important the Temple was. This impressive structure in Jerusalem was not just the symbolic hub of faith; it was where most observance took place. Animals were brought there for sacrifice, its hallowed inner sanctum was soaked with blood from slaughtered offerings. The Temple embodied Judaism. When it was destroyed the first time (586 B.C.E.), the Jews were exiled to Babylon for seventy years. When it was re-constructed and then destroyed a second time (70 C.E.), the Jews had to build a faith without a building, to codify a tradition that would no longer rely on four walls, high priests, or dead goats. Judaism became more portable; pray where you are. Rabbis became the transmitters of the law and the ambassadors of worship, wherever they happened to be.

So the destruction of each Temple was seminal. Which is why we honor its loss with four separate fasts—Tzom Gedaliah, named for the last Jewish governor, Gedaliah, who was assassinated after the First Temple fell; 10 Tevet, which marks the Babylonian siege of the First Temple; 17 Tammuz, which recalls the day the Romans breached the Second Temple's walls in 70 c.e. and begins three weeks of mourning; and Tisha B'Av, the final and sixth mega-fast, which peaks the mourning and commemorates both Temples' destructions—each of which happened to occur on the same day (the Ninth of Av) about 655 years apart.

It's like a slow-motion action sequence, stretched out over the entire year: the Temple dies and dies again. No other event gets this much holiday-play. (The two other fasts are not Temple-related: Yom Kippur, for atonement; and pre-Purim, for Esther. No Temple hook.)

For this 10 Tevet, my "fasting chum," Jeremy, will join me remotely from across the pond in London (he's visiting his dad), which I tell him is kind of unfair because British daylight is even shorter than ours this time of year, so he'll be suffering for less time.

Even with the fast's brevity in New York, I am agitated; not eating is not my forte. (And I've been cheating a bit on the not-drinking rule. A few sips of water to keep the splitting headache at bay.) My friends are staying with us at our Connecticut lake house, and, after a somewhat raucous New Year's Eve dinner, they're enjoying pancakes and maple syrup in the morning while I'm reading up on King Nebuchadnezzar of Babylonia.

"What's this fast for?" my friend Catherine inquires mouth full.

"Our Temple was destroyed by Babylonians," I say, crankily.

"Ahhhhh." Catherine turns back to her pancake stack, albeit sheepishly: it's hard to eat in front of a fasting friend. But it would be hard for me to make the case that she should be fasting with me. This rite feels like an intellectual exercise more than a visceral return to expulsion from Jerusalem. And it's no wonder. The Tenth of Tevet gets no star billing. "Except for fully observant Jews," said Rabbi Yosef Blau of Yeshiva University, "no one knows anything about it."

That may be an exaggeration, but not by much. Attempts to raise the holiday's profile have met with varying degrees of success, but its original importance is plain:

> "And in the ninth year of his reign, on the tenth day of the tenth month, Nebuchadnezzar moved against Jerusalem"—2 Kings 25:1–4.

Blau believes there is a powerful lesson in marking the start of this devastation. We should notice the clouds; they could warn of an approaching tornado. "There's a sense on the Tenth of Tevet that we should always be concerned about what things may lead to, instead of waiting for some tragedy to happen," Blau says. "We should be alert to the early stages of the process. The fact that we fast even for the *beginning* of the destruction, not just for the destruction itself, is probably a reminder that we should be sensitive to dangers even early in the game."

I like that: Heed the signs. Care about the start of something bad, don't wait for it to grow worse. Of course I harken back to Europe in the 1930s. Ten Tevet is perhaps one more reminder that evil seeds propagate faster than we can fathom.

Blau stresses that he's not a catastrophic thinker, nor suggesting we face similar peril today, despite the facts that French Jews are buying homes in Israel (just in case) and anti-Semitism is a growing cancer on college campuses. "I'm not an alarmist saying 'Anti-Semitism is rising and if we don't move to Israel next week, it's all over,'" he says. "It's not because I think Judaism is doomed."

But the disquieting signs are being catalogued by the press—heightened religious bigotry all over the world. Ten Tevet tugs at my conscience: Should I spend this fast day getting involved in something that calls out hatred before it can harm? I scold myself for needing a holiday to goad me. But I'm floundering a bit with 10 Tevet, which doesn't offer a clear to-do list. I get back to my reading.

While my houseguests take midday naps, I learn that this holiday was picked to honor the Holocaust, but the concept fell short. On January 11, 1949, four years after the concentration camps were liberated, the Chief Rabbinate of Israel declared that 10 Tevet would become a day of remembrance for those who had died in the Holocaust without anyone to say the mourner's prayer—Kaddish—for them. This new holiday was dubbed Yom HaKaddish HaKlali, translated as "The General Kaddish Day."

"There was a feeling of 'What are we going to do with these yahrzeits [the anniversary of someone's death] for all these people we don't know?'" explains Rabbi Ethan Tucker from his office at Mechon Hadar, an independent seminary he cofounded in Manhattan. "I don't know why they picked this fast day as opposed to the others, but I think this particular fast—*Asara B'Tevet* [The Tenth of Tevet]—was a little less burdened with other memory and ritual."

I'm fascinated by the image of rabbis casting about for underutilized holidays on which to pin a new one. They decided which holidays could afford to shoulder more meaning, and this was one of them. But the newly declared memorial didn't catch on for what Blau describes as two reasons, firstly the invention of Yom HaShoah—"Day of the Holocaust"—created two years later, in 1951, to devote one day to remembrance. That new dedication eclipsed 10 Tevet as the day to honor the six million dead. Yom HaShoah was chosen to coincide with the Warsaw ghetto uprising, which began on the eve of Passover, April 19, 1943. "We didn't want to just mourn those who died; we wanted to talk about the Jews who fought back," Blau said. "So Yom HaShoah won out."

Ten Tevet also lost its Holocaust remembrance to Tisha B'Av, which was already well established from biblical times. Tisha B'Av— the last fast of the Jewish year, known as "the saddest day" in the calendar—takes place in late summer, and has evolved to encompass most Jewish tragedies, including the Temples' destruction *and* the Holocaust. So what was 10 Tevet left with? A fast of foreboding, yes, but also a fast for current suffering. And if people *aren't* suffering, we can actually eat.

Excuse me? You mean this fast is optional?

Tucker tells me, 10 Tevet is "actually only obligatory during *a time of persecution.*"

And who decides whether or when we're in a time of persecution?

"There's a lot of disagreement," Tucker acknowledges. "The rabbis ask, 'Does that mean each person decides? Each community decides? A Jewish court decides?'"

This suggests I could have eaten on New Year's Day, if I'd found a pro-nosh decider who would declare we're not currently oppressed.

Tucker sums up the Talmud's take: if we're in a time of persecution or suffering (*shemad*), then fasting is obligatory; if it's a time of peace (*shalom*), fasting is forbidden and these fast days turn into celebrations; it means the Messianic time has arrived.

I think about who is in a time of shemad right now. People living under despots. Trafficked young girls. Hostages. Refugees. The wrongly convicted. And then there is the more personal shemad: a violent marriage, child abuse, illness, addiction, loneliness. But when it comes to Jewish persecution, I would not characterize this time as a time of shemad.

The Talmudic rabbis were divided on whether fasting was required back when there was no Temple and no persecution. More recently, rabbis pegged the arrival of shalom to 1948 with the creation of the State of Israel, arguing that the fasting could then stop. Today, many say that the ongoing strife in Israel can't be considered shalom, so the fasting should continue.

Tucker is less concerned with parsing whether we're in a time of peace or persecution. He says *we're in a time of need*, and therefore this holiday should focus on helping, not about prayer, or whether we can eat.

"If you go back to where these fasts are first talked about, in the book of Zechariah," Tucker says, "there are two things which are really important: one is that the point of these fast days is not to do some religious act of piety which God needs, but to actually motivate people by turning their attention to be politically and socially active— to make sure the oppressed and the weak in society are not oppressed and are not weak."

I remember the surprising words of the prophet Isaiah, who condemns an empty fast that is more about self-importance than saving others.

> Is this the fast that I desire? A day for people to afflict their bodies
> ... lying in sackcloth and ashes? Do you call that a fast? ... No,
> this is the fast I desire. ... To untie the cords of the yoke. To let the
> oppressed go free ... to share your bread with the hungry, to take the
> poor into your home (Isaiah 58:5–7).

Tucker underscores this: turn the spotlight away from yourself. If Yom Kippur is about a fixation on our souls, 10 Tevet should move it to those of others. "These fast days are not about 'How do I become a better person?'" he says. "They're about the question, 'Why are you eating? There is so much work to be done in the world. How could you possibly just take the time to take care of yourself?'"

That might smack of a guilt trip; but his point seems crucial, and I'm challenged by it. Our tradition doesn't care about whether you're sated, but about what you *do*. So what am I doing? That question distracts me from my self-deprivation on January 1. I'm focused less on the pancakes I can't have and more on the good deed I'm compelled to complete before sundown. Since Judaism says that the noblest gestures are made without recognition, I will keep mine to myself (it ultimately involves a donation and signing up to make sandwiches for the homeless).

I spend the bulk of the day reading in the living room with my family, trying not to smell their grilled cheeses at lunchtime, and then finally going to a movie with the houseguests, which is probably sacrilegious, but I need something to pass the time.

Almost forty minutes into *Wild* with Reese Witherspoon—which is slightly relevant, since she has to survive on few rations—I break the fast mid-movie, with a Polly-O String Cheese. I brought it with me, since I knew sundown would happen at 4:39 p.m., while we're still in the theater. It feels both odd and meaningful to eat it in the dark, imagining the Jews in my time zone who are also taking their first bite after so many hours. Fasts connect me to strangers.

I can't say I'll be fasting on future 10 Tevets. But I will commit to doing something concrete for someone else, whether or not I'm nursing a New Year's Eve hangover. And Tucker's words will stay in my head:

"What the fast day is really focused on is, how do you get someone to not focus on their own needs but to focus on the needs of the other, the condition of the Jewish people, and to focus on increasing God's presence in the world?" he says. "If you're really focused on that, there's not a lot of time for lunch."

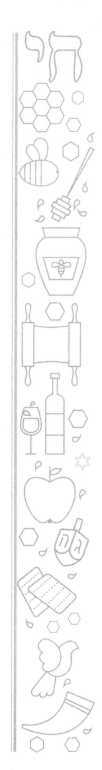

Judith Shulevitz
ON SHABBAT

When you put the devices down on Shabbat, you actually have to look at each other. We have no devices at the family dinner table on a regular weekday night, but after dinner, everyone sits around the living room looking at their screens—you know that scene. But if one day a week, you can't look at your screens, then you actually have to look each other in the face and talk to each other. Especially now, when work and entertainment and social connection are all merged into one device, it's a real slippery slope from texting your best friend or child to playing a video game, to answering a work email. It's all happening on the same device now. So you put that away, and you have to look at each other. I do think it's hard. Social mores have an incredible force; we cannot buck them. It's a real battle. If you want to have the perfect Shabbat, you have to really fight for it.

12

SLOUCHING TOWARD SHABBAT

The Most Important Holiday of All

1.26.15

'M FAILING AT Shabbat, which most rabbis say is the most important holiday of them all. On the seventh day of the week—just as
God rested on the seventh day of Creation—we're supposed to stop
working, which includes: creating anything, shopping, driving, writing (or erasing), doing laundry, using fire, or electronics. The fourth
of the Ten Commandments instructs, "Remember the Sabbath day,
to keep it holy."

It's not that I'm skipping Shabbat entirely. For the past eight years,
I've gone to synagogue services most Friday nights and several Saturday mornings, which are the weekly worship slots for this holiday.

I buy a challah every Friday. My family, when we're all together,
duplicates my mother's Shabbat, lighting and blessing the two candles, holding up the cup of wine, and reciting Kiddush, tearing pieces
of the braided challah bread.

So I do feel *some* Shabbat differentiation, or separation—the rabbinic interpretation of the word *kadosh*, also meaning holy—which
divides the six weekdays from Shabbat.

But this year, because of my holiday expedition, I have to ratchet
up my kadosh—my separation—to create a firewall from the rest of

the week. So I decide to add one challenging embargo: no looking at email on Saturdays.

For the first six Friday afternoons of my Jewish Year, I go to the "vacation responder" under my Gmail settings and input a message that says I won't be reading email from Friday sundown to Saturday sundown.

Friends who receive my automatic message are taken aback. "Wow. You're really doing this," one writes. My mother calls and leaves a message: "I had no idea you'd be Shomer Shabbos!" That's the term for one who observes the Sabbath commandments, and it doesn't apply to me. I'm not adhering to the directives. Jews are supposed to refrain from any of the thirty-nine kinds of work that were required to build the Tabernacle (the portable temple that carried the Ten Commandments in the desert), including sowing, plowing, baking, flaying, kindling, you get the idea.

But I am trying to disconnect. And it's harder than I thought. Moreover, it doesn't by itself make me feel the supposed tranquility and blissful cessation of Shabbat, what Rabbi Abraham Joshua Heschel called "a palace in time." I've heard rabbi after rabbi tell me just to keep at it—opt out of work, efficiency, travel, technology, and commerce; see where it leads. "The solution of mankind's most vexing problem will not be found in renouncing technical civilization," Heschel writes in his prescient 1951 book *The Sabbath*, "but in attaining some degree of independence of it."

But I can't pull it off. At least so far. I still find myself violating the Fourth Commandment to "Remember the Sabbath, to keep it holy . . . you shall not do any manner of work." I still read the *New York Times* on my phone. I catch up on *Homeland* on the exercise bike. I call my sister. I carry a purse. I buy milk.

To be clear, this is not a plea for Shabbat Rehab. As much as I appreciate those who have offered to guide me through an immersive Shabbat, I already know the rule book. I'm just not following it.

I decide to talk through my Shabbat crisis with the writer and scholar Judith Shulevitz, author of the captivating 2010 book *The Sabbath World*, which explores the day of rest from every angle—historical, theological, and sociological. I made sure to underline the book before my Jewish Year began because so many rabbis stress that Sabbath is the fundamental holiday. But reading about Shulevitz's personal observance-ambivalence doesn't clarify my own. When we meet in person, the author generously acts as my Shabbat therapist.

"For me, I keep the Sabbath in the spirit of knowing what I'm *not* doing, how far I am from the ideal Shabbat," she says over a cup of tea at a café near her home. "Nobody can get there. It's an unachievable utopia. It's this dream of community, oneness, wholeness, rising outside of yourself into this perfect world. In some weird way, Shabbat is about coming to terms with imperfection."

That's a hard thing for a neurotic perfectionist (and realist) to hear. Meaning: at the same time that I wish I had more Shabbat in my life, I know it's hard to put more Shabbat in my life. But I haven't given up entirely.

Shulevitz's book helps, not only because she unpacks the Sabbath's evolution, but also because her initial resistance to the Sabbath's system affirms mine. "I still like the idea of the fully observed Sabbath more than I like observing it," she writes. "I feel guilty about not building better fences around the day, but apparently not guilty enough. Partly, it's because each step up in observance paralyzes me with indecision. Why follow this rule and not that one? . . . My religious commitments remain too abstract to overcome the inconvenience of making them."

"Inconvenience" is one of my hurdles. It's inconvenient to live by rules that feel antiquated: not cooking, not calling, not riding, not carrying, not "working"—to the point of tearing toilet paper squares in advance to avoid any such effort on Saturdays.

I once attended a Jewish conference where making hot tea was prohibited, even if the water was on a burner that had been turned on before Shabbat, because the tea bag leaves would be "transformed" by the hot water in a way that constituted cooking.

The various bans have evolved over the centuries. With each chapter of modernity and technological advance, rabbinic decisors (fancy word for deciders of law) have adjudicated what is permissible or barred. Yet, Rabbi Yitz Greenberg maintains that the holiday is not about injunctions. "The Sabbath is actively to achieve *menuchah* (rest) through self-expression, transformation, and renewal," he writes in his book *The Jewish Way.* "On this day, humans are freed and commanded to explore themselves and their relationships until they attain the fullness of being."

Ah: it's that "fullness of being" thing I'm missing.

And yet I'm not missing it; I don't feel empty.

Does one need to feel the *lack* of Shabbat to *seek* it? I'm not missing spirituality; I'm missing tranquility. There's a difference.

"There is no better point of entry to the religious experience than the Sabbath," Shulevitz writes, "for all its apparent ordinariness. *Because* of its ordinariness. The extraordinariness of the Sabbath lies in its being commonplace."

I love that notion—that the mundanity of Shabbat is its magic. But if my Shabbat is not yet "commonplace," as Shulevitz puts it, getting to its "ordinariness" seems to require extraordinary effort. I'm daunted by the upheaval it demands.

What *does* enthrall me is the notion of quietude. Reading hardbound books. Being unreachable. Closing every screen.

My family doesn't lack for interaction; we're close and chatty, despite our technology dependence. But I wish that, years ago, when our kids were small, my husband and I had delineated a formal period of undistracted togetherness.

And friends often remind me that I could use a weekly dose of stillness. I'm not the most stressed person I know, but no one would call me Zen; my mind races with a buzzing list. It's difficult to power down.

"If you're in the habit, it becomes natural," Shulevitz counters. "Sometimes out of that, you have the subjective, transformative experience and sometimes you go through the moves. I don't think the feeling comes first. I think the doing comes first."

Do it and you will feel it. That's another theme of this year. Fast and you will feel others' pain. Dunk in the mikveh and you will feel cleansed. Sit in a sukkah and you will feel fragility. Dance with the

Torah and you will feel close to it. Light the menorah and you will feel community.

That approach is underscored by Rabbi Lauren Berkun, the director of Rabbinic and Synagogue Programs at the Shalom Hartman Institute North America. "When Moses is presenting the Torah to the people on Mount Sinai, the Israelites say *'Na'aseh V'nishmah'*—'We will do and we will listen,'" she reminds me on the phone. "The commentators remark on the strange order: We will first *do* and *then* listen? In Judaism there's a certain amount of a leap of action. First, you do." In other words, add Shabbat boundaries and the rest will follow.

"Immerse yourself in this way of walking in the world," Berkun suggests. "Then you'll understand the meaning. It's often the reverse of how liberal, Western Jews operate when they essentially say, 'First convince me this is meaningful, and then I'll do it.'"

She's right. So many of us take a skeptical posture: "Tell me why I should care about this today." Okay, I should just speak for myself: *I'm* skeptical. But this project represents a continuous effort to get past misgiving. I have to plow through the doubts or I won't do anything.

Berkun's own Shabbat conversion confirms that it's never too late. After a secular childhood, she did not become observant until college, and then found it revelatory. "I remember that feeling of total liberation, of walking out of my dorm room without even a key in my pocket and just feeling free," she says (I forgot to ask her how she got back into her dorm). "Even though I was keeping all these picayune laws, the experience of doing that was this feeling of emancipation."

The concept of limitations being freeing sounds right to me. If you can't do certain things, you do less. If you can't be efficient, you slow down. If I couldn't text or telephone a friend, I might see her in person. If I couldn't get in a cab, I'd walk. If I couldn't write, I'd read.

It's certainly easy for me to embrace Shabbat's mitzvah of hospitality; I love hosting Friday night dinners, hearing my friends bless, in unison, the challah that I bought at Fairway Market (so-so) or Silver Moon bakery (better). Somehow this small act, by itself, affirms that we're in a separate vessel together, following the Sabbath Strait. And I'm glad there is a map to follow.

But I'm not comfortable at other people's Shabbat tables, where the Hebrew is recited at breakneck speed and the songs are new. My unsophistication is embarrassing. When I started this expedition, several observant Jews generously invited my family over to share their Friday dinners. But for now, I'm more at ease in my modestly literate Sabbath habit, which—on closer look—already does include sacred moments at my synagogue:

The 6 P.M. service shimmers like a beacon at the end of each week—a welcome respite. I am stirred by the sight of multiple generations crowding around two flames on the bimah after lighting the Sabbath candles. I review the week in depth during silent prayer. I listen to the ballad "Hashkiveinu" with the lyric "Guard us from all harmful things," and feel protected. I close my eyes during the *Shema*—the most sacred avowal of commitment to God. I finally know Kaddish, the mourner's prayer, by heart. I pray for the sick, and focus, as I never used to, on the weekly tally of struggle and loss: my friend Julie's unending cancer treatments, Milt's weakening liver. I take a "gratitude inventory" when we sing the *shehecheyanu* blessing, which thanks God—communally—for bringing us to this moment. I want this mindfulness in my life. I'd go so far as to say I've come to need it. As Shulevitz writes, "We all look for a Sabbath, whether or not that's what we call it."

Berkun encourages me to just begin keeping the Sabbath, even if the rest of my family doesn't come along with me. "It is possible to be a lone soldier," she says. "Whether the people around you are doing it as well is secondary." But it isn't secondary to me; I need allies to change my life so dramatically. As each week goes by, I find it hard to go offline solo. I feel compelled to accomplish things. Maria Popova wrote on her popular *Brain Pickings* blog: "Most of us spend our days in what Kierkegaard believed to be our greatest source of unhappiness—a refusal to recognize that *busy is a decision* and that presence is infinitely more rewarding than productivity." Presence over productivity. Decide not to be busy. I should, but I'm squirming.

Shulevitz told me she still wrestles with her Shabbat practice, invoking theologian Franz Rosenzweig's reply when asked whether he put on tefillin—the prayer phylacteries: "Not yet."

"I'm still in the 'not yet,'" she says.

Me, too.

Dr. Yehuda Kurtzer
ON SHABBAT

I had an epiphany about Shabbat recently. Theologians and Jewish law scholars love Shabbat for its mystique (think "a cathedral in time") and for its arcane rules. I've observed Shabbat strictly all my life, and I, too, have been seduced by these framings. But a recent Shabbat spent on the beach on Tel Aviv (in walking distance, natch) changed things for me. The image that sticks in my mind is of a secular-ish Mizrachi family, feasting in bathing suits on a traditional buffet—served from a cooler—of shnitzel, jachnun, borekas, and other delicacies sourced from the history of the Jewish dispersion and now serving as the Israeli Shabbat food canon. Beach Shabbat is the unique contribution of Israeli Jewry to the Jewish liturgical year, and it is transformative: it reminds us that Shabbat is, first and foremost, the weekly vacation day for a frenzied people so often weighed down by the burdens of history, a respite from creation for the processes of individual and collective recreation. Beach Shabbat is a success story for secular Zionism—its capacity to claim sacred ritual in unexpected places. And, if the proliferation of kippot on the beach is any indication, Beach Shabbat offers something of value to traditionally observant Jews as well. We are a people that did not merely cross the Sea to become who we are; we also recline beside it to fulfill who we need to be.

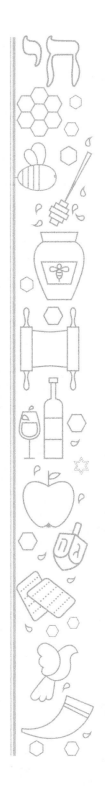

Rabbi Micah Greenstein
ON TU B'SHVAT

Tu B'Shvat is a holiday for skeptics and mystics alike. You don't have to be a mystic to be enthralled with trees. Just ask a New Englander in October, or a visitor to Northern California's Muir Woods any time of year. In the presence of nature's greatest wonders, even a skeptic would concur that behind all the brokenness we witness in the world and in our lives, there is an awesome beauty and unity.

As a giant metaphor for the interconnectedness of all things—people, nature, and time itself—Tu B'Shvat speaks to the world. And for the wondering Jew, the message is even more direct. However one chooses to plant this precious seed of Judaism—with love and care—will reap a lifetime of meaning and blessing, beyond one's lifetime, too. "Because my parents planted trees for me," the Talmud teaches (Ta'anit 28a), "likewise I am planting trees for them." For the sake of our children and our world, keep planting.

13

TU B'SHVAT

Sometimes You Feel Like a Nut

2.2.15

IKE WALLACE, THE legendary *60 Minutes* correspondent, kept to a Tu B'Shvat diet.

When I was one of his broadcast producers years ago, Wallace prided himself on his intake of nuts and raisins, insisting they were the secret to his longevity and jet-black hair.

Mike, rest his soul, would never have called his regimen the Tu B'Shvat Diet, because he couldn't have told you what Tu B'Shvat was (he was a proud Jew without ritual), but it occurs to me that he was on to something. Because he lived to ninety-three and never went gray.

Tu B'Shvat was dubbed by the Talmud rabbis as a Rosh Hashanah (a new year) for the trees, because it began the tithing cycle, in which a farmer had to tithe his crops either to the poor or to Jerusalem, depending on the year. It was reimagined by the medieval Kabbalists as a celebration of creation and the bounty of the earth, with a "seder" consisting of nuts and fruit eaten in a certain order.

These days, we're supposed to plant trees on Tu B'Shvat. Or plant plants. Or give money to enable others to plant plants.

This holiday, I've now learned, was the ancient precursor to Earth Day. It should make us alert to the preciousness of air, water, animals, and foliage, as well as all that we're doing to destroy them.

I dial up Rabbi Michael Cohen of Israel's Arava Institute for Environmental Studies. "We are partners with God," he says. "We've been given this earth on loan, and we need to take better care of it."

It's a very Jewish idea: we've been given life that can't be taken for granted. It's why observant Jews thank God every morning—simply for another morning. Life isn't a given. Neither is land, water, sun, or trees.

The Arava Institute educates students from Israel and abroad to be environmental leaders, while also conducting research on projects such as solar power fields and sustainable water management. Cohen says Tu B'Shvat has become an important conservationist holiday in the last three decades, thanks to an increasing Jewish awareness of natural resources in peril. "The overwhelming scientific world says, 'The crisis is here, it's now and it's happening,'" Cohen says. "The religious response to that reality is that we need to do something about it."

Rabbi Arthur Waskow, founder of the Shalom Center in Philadelphia, who, at eighty-one years old, fits the part of the quintessential bearded sage rabbi, says: "Tu B'Shvat should affirm the importance of physical creation and healing the physical damage." He calls out those people who say either, "It doesn't apply to me," or "I'm too overwhelmed to act." I fall in the latter camp. Waskow says I should feel galvanized, not helpless. "The same scientists reporting the danger are saying we do have a window of time when we can make a difference," he says. "If we don't do anything, it's unimaginable."

He says our gluttony today echoes the gluttony of Adam and Eve. The Tu B'Shvat seder was created to repair original sin. "The big mistake of the Garden of Eden," he explains, "is that God said, 'There's incredible abundance here. Eat from it, enjoy. Just exercise a little self-restraint. You see this particular tree here? Don't eat from it. Reserve it. Show some self-restraint in the way that you deal with the abundance of the earth.'"

We all know how Adam and Eve responded. Waskow says we've repeated their mistake. "If you gobble up everything, you produce disaster and abundance stops."

Waskow suggests I take a small first step by planting parsley to use in my Passover seder—which is two months away. Not only does spring feel distant, but it's odd to learn that there's a seder before the seder, just as there was a fast before The Fast back in the fall. As I'm discovering again and again, Jews repeat tropes. Or have multiple iterations of the same ritual. But he's right: the parsley could be a nice link between both seders. I can get in touch with the earth for one supper by planting herbs for the next.

I buy a packet of seeds, a flowerpot, and some soil. I spread newspaper on my kitchen table, cut open the peat, and scoop the earth into the clay pot with a soup ladle. Then I embed the seeds in the soil, according to the packet instructions. Inconsequential as this project is, I'm enjoying the warmth of the loamy dirt and the idea that these kernels could actually morph into edible herbs. When I pour a little water on my planting, it feels holy.

Setting aside whether I'll be able to till parsley successfully (not a safe assumption), I return to the nuts. I need to understand the nuts because they are prescribed at any Tu B'Shvat seder, along with the seven species associated, in the book of Deuteronomy, with the land of Israel: wheat, barley, grapes, figs, pomegranates, olives, and dates.

"The Tu B'Shvat seder is extraordinary because the eating of fruits and nuts does not require the death of any animal whatsoever," Waskow says. "It's the most deliciously life-filled meal because it doesn't require any death." I'd never thought of that: how many species died for my meal.

Tomorrow night, I'll attend my first Tu B'Shvat seder, a ceremony invented by seventeenth-century Kabbalists in the Israeli village of Safed, to honor nature, the Tree of Life, and the four worlds—or four levels of creation, as the Kabbalists defined them.

I had no idea there were four worlds, but they tug at my environmental consciousness and make this holiday more complex. As I read about each one, I try to personalize it. That's the only way I can connect to this mystical stuff at all.

The world of action (*Assiyah*). This makes me think about what I actually *do, or don't do*—for my family, community, and strangers—and for the future. When do I act, when am I inert? I realize few of my friends devote any time to rescuing the environment, but nor are they indifferent to the importance of clean air and oceans. So what rouses our "assiyah"?

The world of formation, reinterpreted as emotion (*Yetzirah*). Okay, I can get emotional. But I'm also impatient with those who exhibit *too much* emotion. At the same time, I'm wary of people who seem detached. Who gets worked up about the danger to nature these days? And when people are vociferous about the ecological emergency, do we write them off as grating or overzealous? If we were forced to grasp the severity of the threat, maybe we'd all be more outraged. Maybe, on some subjects, we've muffled our "yetzirah."

The world of creation, reinterpreted as intellect (*Beriyah*). I respect intellectual mastery and covet it, too. I'm grateful to the people who spend most of their time thinking about the planet we're going to leave to our children and grandchildren; they're doing the heavy lifting for the rest of us. While I'm anxious about the environment, I'm not radicalized. Which makes me more anxious, which makes me think my Yetzirah is at least functioning.

The world of emanation, reinterpreted as the spirit (*Atzilut*). The spirit—like the spiritual—has always been a mushy area for me. But when I do feel transcendence, it's admittedly often in nature. The poetry and power of a glassy lake or a snowy mountaintop is hackneyed for a reason: so many of us have felt the same enchantment when we look at those vistas. I can easily name the moments when I've felt God, and they often involve streams, peaks, deserts, glaciers, forests, oceans, or cliffs. It's harder to list the steps I've taken to safeguard those scenes. The *Atzilut* hasn't yet been translated to *Assiyah*.

It's challenging to memorize the four worlds (I've already forgotten them), and their accompanying four fruit-types (which I'm about to share), but the metaphors are provocative and also kind of childlike in their literalism:

For the world of action, the mystics tell us to eat fruits with hard shells and soft insides, such as walnuts and coconuts.

For the world of emotion, we eat fruits with soft shells and hard insides, such as dates and plums.

For the world of intellect, we eat fruits that are wholly edible such as grapes or blueberries.

The world of the spirit is not represented by any fruit.

Is it too much of a stretch to liken ourselves to seder produce?

"It's not going too far at all," Waskow replies. "The fruits and the nuts of the Tu B'Shvat seder clearly represent different kinds of human beings. Human beings with tough outsides, but soft insides; those who are open, soft, you might say, to each other with *chesed*—loving-kindness—outside and inside. So when we go through the Tu B'Shvat seder, we should be asking ourselves: 'When do I need a tough outside? When do I want to make sure my outside is soft and my inside is clearly strong? And when do I want to be open—outside and in?' They're all legitimate parts of us. The question is how to judge which part of us is the *life-giving* one for the moment that we're living in."

I'll be asking myself that at my first Tu B'Shvat seder tomorrow.

And in the meantime, I'll remember to water my parsley plant. Because I've failed at every vegetable I've ever tried to grow before, but this time I'm on a mission to produce greens for the seder plate, a small stab at ecology.

My Tu B'Shvat baptism happens at Romemu, a spiritual community that I choose for its amalgam of orthodoxy and mysticism. It strikes me as exactly the right place to experience this environmentally responsible holiday.

Romemu was founded in 2006 by Rabbi David Ingber, who is considered one of the leading lights of reinvigorated worship. In 2011, when I complimented him at a Jewish learning-binge conference called Limmud NY, he informed me—with a smile—that my brother accidentally broke his nose years ago when they were playing ice hockey together in a pickup game.

Since Rabbi Ingber is away in Israel on the night of the Tu B'Shvat seder, we are guided instead by his frequent partner in prayer, Romemu's sprite-like music director, Basya Schechter, who fronts a musical group, Pharaoh's Daughter.

There are no assigned seats in the church basement on the corner of Amsterdam Avenue and 105th Street. Volunteers have decorated the plain hall with strings of orange lights and a few small potted trees.

Thirteen tables of ten are set with yellow paper tablecloths (crayons scattered, if we're inclined to draw), and a platter is piled high with the prescribed fruits and nuts: figs, walnuts, pomegranates, clementines, blueberries, and almonds.

I never thought I'd pine for Manischewitz. But the odd wine fusions prescribed by the Tu B'Shvat seder will make me yearn for the sugary Passover wine.

The Kabbalists who created the Tu B'Shvat seder in the Middle Ages chose to include four cups to mirror Passover. But at some point, their wine directives took an odd turn.

The first cup we drink is just red wine. (Other Tu B'Shvat seders start with just white; the choice is optional.)

The second cup is red wine *with white wine added* (I'll be honest: can't recommend it).

The third cup is white wine *with red wine added* (even stranger). Other seders suggest a *full mixture* of half-red, half-white. Either way, it suddenly feels like I'm a kid in chemistry class.

The fourth cup is just white, where apparently other Tu B'Shvat seders do just red for the last cup. It feels backwards to go from red to white, but I roll with it.

Some add a fifth cup. For Romemu, it's vodka. No objections there.

Each cup represents one of the worlds, which were linked to one of the fruits; talk about symbolism-saturation.

Sitting next to me is a twenty-nine-year-old woman who says she majored in biological anthropology and has bought a one-way ticket to Israel to work on organic farms, leaving tomorrow. She admits that her parents wish she would stay home and find a husband, but she's disregarding their advice. She seems to unwittingly affirm the invitation printed in Romemu's Haggadah, "to set a kavanah/intention for your own personal unfolding."

I'm pretty folded-up myself, at least at this seder so far, especially when we're directed by another leader—"spiritual storyteller" Carole Foreman—to get up and circle our tables while singing *"Zeh ha-schulchan asher lifnei Adonai,"* "This is the table that is before God." Maybe if vodka had been the first cup instead of the last, I'd be more game for circling.

But Basya's beautiful singing does make me exhale a bit, and sets the tone for openness and a lack of inhibition. She is casually dressed in a skirt, tights, and a floppy winter hat, and her huge smile is infectious as she introduces the first world, *Assiya*, which their Haggadah defines as "Actualization = the physical world, earth winter."

"Find a fruit on your table that is hard outside and edible inside," Basya instructs. "What are the challenges we have in our lives that are almost impenetrable?"

My tablemates pass the platter of banana halves, clementines, and walnuts.

"Some things are difficult at the start," Basya continues; "but once we go further, they soften."

Fruit therapy, I think to myself.

Basya's questions bounce in my head and I try to answer them inwardly, honestly. When did I meet a barrier that then softened? My Hebrew skill. A chilly friend. The Jewish holidays.

Yitzhak Buxbaum takes the microphone. A self-described "teacher and storyteller" with a gray ponytail, who has written ten books on Jewish spirituality and Hasidism—and happens to be married to Romemu's storyteller, Carole Buxbaum—he reminds us that the "sap is starting to move in the trees," despite the fact that we're in extreme winter. "At least it is in Israel," he clarifies, winking. In the depths of winter, it is reassuring to be reminded that spring has started somewhere.

He continues: "The Tu B'Shvat seder is a *tikkun*—a mystical repair of the sin of Adam and Eve. . . . The sin is that we ate wrongly. So we repair the sin by eating in a holy way." Eating in a holy way on Tu B'Shvat seems the antithesis of Passover's excess. Tu B'Shvat's nuts and oranges are the antidote to Pesach's gefilte fish and brisket. A cleaner meal. (I may need pizza later.)

Basya says we've now come to the second world, *Yetzirah*; "Formation = growth, creativity, water, emotions, spring."

"Find a fruit on your table with a pit inside and an edible outside," she directs us.

My tablemates take dates, which turn out to be faulty because someone brought pitted ones in error. We're missing the rigid centers, which means we're missing the metaphor.

"These fruits are representative of all the things that we start that seem easy at first, and then get hard: our spiritual practices, our exercise regimens, our relationships," Basya says. She adds a personal insight—"I'm good at many things really quickly and then I hit a wall"—and encourages us to think about the times we've hit walls and broken through them.

My walls come easily to mind:

1. Slowing my thoughts.
2. Slowing my coffees with friends.
3. Slowing my device-dependence.
4. Slowing. Period.
5. Golf.

This holiday trek is another personal example of wall-defiance. In the past, I hit barrier after barrier whenever I tried to gain more grounding in Jewish tradition. I kept being reminded of how much I didn't know, how unyielding prayers can be. This project has been an attempt to push through.

Basya recounts out loud a conversation she had that morning with Larry Schwartz, who teaches meditation at Romemu and is in attendance at this seder. "This is one of four Jewish new years," he told her, "Elul, Rosh Hashanah, Tu B'Shvat, and Passover. Look at how many chances we have to start again."

So many chances to start again.

I can't think of one person in my life who hasn't wished they could start over in some area of their lives. I love that teaching. Judaism gives us another go. Four times.

The third world is "Briah," "Creation," which the Haggadah says equals "thought, air, summer season." We now eat fruits that are wholly edible, through and through: blueberries, strawberries, grapes.

For this category, Basya quotes an eighteenth-century Hasidic sage, Rabbi Nachman of Bretslov: "There is no such thing as obstacles." Would that this were true. But maybe it is. Maybe the obstacles we perceive are largely self-constructed and not impassable. Maybe we see hard pits when the fruit is permeable.

Larry Schwartz takes the microphone to guide us through a meditative eating practice:

"Look at your piece of fruit and think about where it came from, what it required to get here: sun, soil, planting, pruning, picking, packing, driving, unloading, packaging. . . . Farmers, pickers, drivers, grocers. . . ."

I pick up a strawberry slice and a snapshot flashes: my teenage daughter picking fruit last summer with two friends, running from bush to bush, clearly excited at the surfeit and the sweetness. Strawberries in February seem defiantly optimistic.

"Roll it around in your fingers," Schwartz says. "Notice the different colors. Smell it."

He instructs us to put it in our mouths without biting or chewing it. "The temptation to bite is strong, but resist it. This is really difficult."

I'll say. Delayed gratification is ungratifying. I lack the discipline of delay. I've seen glimpses of suspension or deferral in several holidays so far—the Days of Awe (we await forgiveness), the three fasts (we delay food), Sukkot (we suspend routine), Shemini Atzeret (we stay back with God), Shabbat (we suspend work)—forced intervals that require waiting, postponing, patience. Taste the strawberry without chewing it.

Finally we're permitted to bite it. One bite only. Then a second. At last we can masticate to completion.

"Notice how you swallow it. We feel gratitude. For the sensations. For our ability to taste. And for being together."

I've lately been keenly aware—as I watch people like Milton age or decline—of what a loss it is to no longer be able to taste or swallow. The thought spurs panic. How often I gloss over the microscopic joys of a good meal. I won't take them for granted again. Tu B'Shvat brings home not just the riches of the earth but the laziness of our pleasure in it.

The seder breaks for the buffet dinner, and we fill our paper plates with chickpea patties, rice, a fattoush-like salad, and lentils.

After eating and talking, it's time for the fourth cup, for the spirit—*Atzilut*. The Haggadah describes this world as "Emanation—World of the Aleph, world without words. . . ." Indeed, I have no words for this world because I don't understand it. I also lack the fruit for *Atzilut* because none is assigned to this world. The Romemu Haggadah says, "We are beyond eating, beyond speech. . . ." (I'm never beyond either, though I could certainly do with less of both.)

The vodka marks the fifth and last cup—a Romemu invention, with a world described as *Yechidah*—literally "single one," which tonight's Haggadah describes as, "Outside of time, presence = the highest of the highest are humor and music. . . ." I'm not sure I'd say "the highest" world is humor, but I'm game for the next seder stop: comedy. A Romemu congregant does some standup, and a few volunteers play "Name that Fruit" with Yitzhak Buxbaum. I'm the only one at my table who finishes my vodka.

Basya sings a final song, and as she does, I take my pen and underline one part of a verse they've included in their Haggadah. It's by Reb Nachman: "*Do you know that every blade / of grass has its own poem?*"

As I bid good-bye to my tablemates and return to the snow detritus outside, my answer is yes. Every blade of grass has its own poem, indeed. I will taste things a little differently now. I will do more to guard the earth. I will aim to repair (or at least not repeat) the original sin of excess. I will think about the worlds of action, emotion, intellect, and spirit, and the fruits that correspond—where I'm hardened or porous, when I've given up or pushed through. *"Every blade / of grass has its own poem."* Every Tu B'Shvat is a second chance.

Rabbi Joshua Davidson
ON PURIM

The truth is, most of us live with a sense of foreboding about the future, and we could very easily succumb to our anxiety. But Purim admonishes us not to. On the contrary, it says, even in the face of danger and fear we should celebrate the miracle of deliverance that allows us to survive another day. It commands us to lift the glass, or even a few. We are permitted to forget from time to time just how challenging our lives can be. Still, on a communal level, the holiday does sound an alarm we can't ignore. Haman's xenophobia (his rationale for destroying the Jews—that they were different) is alive and well in the twenty-first century. The more frightened we become about the world's instability, the more intolerance rears its ugly head. Ours is the task to stamp it out wherever it remains.

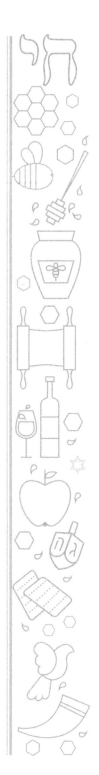

14

TZOM ESTHER & PURIM

Preparing to Fast and Spiel

3.3.15

IT WAS HARD to get in a party mood for Purim because Milton died fifteen days ago. At the moment he drifted off (that's how it appeared—nothing violent nor discernible), Dave, Ben, and I were in Milt's room at the nursing home, with Dave's mom, sisters, and nieces. Molly was in London with her synagogue confirmation class. The private details of the scene are calcified in my memory, as they are, I'm sure, for all of us who were present for Milton's last moments. Dave and I weighed whether to call Molly, but knew how upset she'd be across the ocean. We decided to wait for her to return two days later, to tell her in person.

"Who will live and who will die?" The words of the High Holy Day prayer come back to me, unsparing, irreversible. When we recited that chilling liturgy five months ago, I didn't think it would touch us. But built into Jewish poetry is reality: inevitable losses and some immutable, unknowable plan about who will be taken and when.

Dave invites me to say a few words at Milt's funeral, which I consider a privilege as an in-law, a chance to say out loud what I learned watching Phyllis and her children attend to Milt so lovingly in his last months. "They never announced their devotion," I write. "It was just

159

there—in every large and tiny moment, in every errand, every meal, every phone call, text, touch, and gesture—so small you could sometimes miss it. . . . Just today there's an essay in the *New York Times* by Dr. Oliver Sacks, the neurologist and author, in which he writes about being told his cancer is terminal. 'I cannot pretend that I am without fear,' he writes. 'But my predominant feeling is one of gratitude. I have loved and been loved.' Milt, you have loved and been loved. There is no greater legacy." (Sacks died six months later.)

The shiva at Sharon's house is intimate and brief. Phyllis doesn't want more than one day of communal mourning, and that makes sense. She and Milt were not observant, and the traditional seven days of visitors and condolences would be excruciating for Phyllis, who weeps whenever Milt's name is spoken. "Jewish law protects mourners in two ways," writes Princeton professor Esther Schor, "by ensuring that they are never alone and by limiting the duration of the mourning period." I remember one rabbi comparing the end of shiva to Sukkot, which kicks us outdoors after days of atonement in synagogue. We are nudged back into life after a death. Routines resume; we have to breathe the air again.

The reception at Dave's sister's home is more cheerful than any of us expected. So many people show up from different stages of their lives—the old Irish neighbors, Milt's nephew, Dave's childhood friend's dad. As we stand around the living room and kitchen, Phyllis's rabbi leads us all in brief prayers and announces that the mourners should be able to fill their plates first. Phyllis overrules the rabbi, and insists everyone dig into the deli spread laid out on the kitchen island. Fran Drescher once told me in an interview that, "Jews eat to celebrate and they eat to mourn." A truer word . . .

Two weeks later, I have to gear back up for a holiday that requires raucous revelry. Purim is a dark story marked by a crazy party. (I'm still unsure why a close brush with extermination became, in the Middle Ages, an opportunity for costumes and farce, but there you have it.) Milt's death doesn't have to be set aside, however. I've learned by now that Jewish tradition holds sorrow and joy in both hands.

So I dutifully dive into Purim, and first make sure I know the plot. (Leap ahead two paragraphs if you're fluent in Purim.)

It's the fifth century B.C.E., about a hundred years after the First Temple's destruction. The Jews who were exiled to Babylon are now ruled by Persian king Ahaseurus, who thinks highly of himself. In the city of Shushan, the king's adviser, Haman, is a cruel Jew-hater. He hatches a plan to kill all the Jews and draws lots ("purim") to pick the day it will happen, persuading Ahaseurus to go along. A proclamation is made throughout the kingdom: on that day, all Jews shall be killed. A Jew named Mordechai entreats his cousin, the gorgeous Queen Esther, to prevent it by pleading for mercy with her husband the king.

Esther was married to Ahaseurus essentially against her will. He chose her out of a bevy of prospective wives at a banquet after banishing his then-wife, Vashti, who refused to display her beauty for his guests. (Some say she refused to dance naked.) Esther's Jewish roots were kept secret when she married the king, so for her to now entreat her husband would mean exposing her Judaism. Not to mention that in those days it was life-threatening to approach the king without having been summoned. Nevertheless, she screws up the courage, successfully appeals to her husband, and foils the massacre. The king kills Haman and his sons, and then, because the proclamation could not officially be cancelled according to Persian law, the Jews can only defend themselves with a preemptive strike. Some say they took self-defense too far, slaughtering 75,000.

Purim's modern observance, at least in Reform synagogues I've visited, doesn't focus on that brutal coda, highlighting instead the reenactment of cruel Haman and courageous Esther. The ritual is to read aloud the story from a scroll of parchment known as the *megillah*, which has the biblical book of Esther inscribed on it. The narrative is then often theatricalized with wacky costumes, in a play called a *spiel*—pronounced "shpeel." Whenever Haman is mentioned during the satire, people "boo" vigorously or spin noisemakers, called groggers, to drown out his name.

Purim is, hands down, the biggest party of the Jewish year. Simchat Torah pales by comparison, with its sips of single malt. *This* is the Big Megillah (wordplay intended), and we're supposed to get so trashed that we can't tell the difference between Mordechai (good guy) and Haman (really bad).

I decide to sample some of the elaborate spiel-prep under way in New York City, so I spend an evening watching rehearsals at Stephen Wise Synagogue on the Upper West Side, where congregant Norman Roth, seventy-six, a retired accountant, has been writing and directing the shul's spiel for the last three decades. Some of his past triumphs line the stairway in colorful, theatrical show posters with titles like "Michael Jackson's The Thriller Megiller," "Les Mis—Les Megillah," and "Oh What a Spiel—The Jersey Boys Megillah." This year's theme is Elvis. One of Roth's lyrics riffs on "Blue Suede Shoes," when the king tells Haman, "Don't you step on my Shushan Jews," a reference to Persia's city.

Roth takes great pride in his spiel scripts—he tells me no one else works on theirs as long or sells them for $250 a pop. And he points out that, in his librettos, Haman never dies. "We have very few men in the show, so we need Haman for the closing number. We never kill him off. We always have a line—something like, 'You're going to hang on your gallows, but before you do, you've got to be in the final song!'"

I ask Norman if it gives him pause to know he's leaving out the real, bloody end of the story—the 75,000 slain. "I don't think God really let that happen," he says. "That's human beings writing that story; not God."

But it's in the megillah, I point out.

"It's not in *my* megillah," Roth counters.

It's a kick for me to watch amateur actors—committed congregants—moving through the choreography in sweatpants and jeans, trying to remember their lines, teasing each other, swaying those Elvis hips. I note how earnestly this is taken; these actors have a job to do and they're untiring. I'm laughing in the empty seats, wishing my synagogue had Roth's scripts so I could rehearse zany songs with fellow congregants and revisit my childhood theater obsession.

But my amusement is tempered when I remember I have to fast before this holiday.

It must be embroidered on a sampler somewhere: "Before Jews party, they should suffer." Wednesday, March 4, the day before Purim, is Ta'anit Esther (the Fast of Esther). This will be my fourth fast of the year, with two more to go.

Ta'anit Esther is not in the Bible, but was created by the rabbis in the eighth century. (Jewish tradition is, as I'm learning, an amalgam of rites and prayers, authored by ancient rabbis who invoked the Hebrew Bible to institute new rituals.) This fast springs from the book of Esther—in the Bible's "Writings" section—when Esther decides to prepare herself to confront her husband by fasting for a day.

One Esther-expert is Dr. Erica Brown, a D.C.-based author and educator who has been publicly applauded by her famous students, *New York Times* columnist David Brooks and former NBC anchor David Gregory. I've never met her, but I'm a fan from afar; she sends a weekly email blast with Torah ruminations that I find absorbing. She wrote her doctorate on Esther.

"The thing that I most admire about the Esther story," she tells me over the phone from Washington, "is its notion of the tests that are thrown at an individual and the way in which they transform themselves as a result." Esther was transformed by her newfound bravery. She took on a task that she first refused.

Brown continues, "Esther's cousin, Mordechai, says to her, essentially, 'How do you know you weren't put in this position of royalty for exactly this moment?' I would throw in the Sheryl Sandberg, *Lean In* way of looking at this: of initially having the insecurity to say, 'I'm not the right person. I can't do this for any number of reasons'; you opt out of your own future. And then you have someone like Mordechai who says, 'No, this is your time. Take advantage. Leap into that.'"

I think about the challenges I've avoided, the moments I've chickened out. A few come to mind, both large and quotidian: causes I didn't fight for (see gun control), people I haven't aided (see domestic-abuse victims and Rwandan refugees), articles I didn't pitch (a long list), physical feats I avoided (see parasailing).

But this holiday forces me to reflect on leadership, what it means to be thrust forward when that wasn't your plan. Seven months earlier, I was asked by the current president of Central Synagogue if I would be interested in succeeding him. The very request left me choked up. The job is not only a tremendous honor, but also daunting and important. I love Central in a way I never expected to love an institution. I've seen how clergy can deepen daily life, how a synagogue community can anchor a family. But if you'd asked me back in college, when I was focused on being an actor or writer, if I thought I'd end up as a shul president, I'd have said, "In what universe?" Now this invitation feels like a blessing and a test: Can you do your part to guide a place that has challenged and changed you? Obviously, being a board president isn't comparable to Esther's assignment. But Judaism is always asking us to apply epic stories to everyday decisions.

I say yes to Central's president and yes to Esther's fast, even though it's another holiday that few around me observe. This particular fast appears to be a gauge of loyalty: Can you do a hard thing to support the person doing the harder thing? Esther asked her people to fast with her before she risked her life. I will skip food and drink from dawn to dusk in solidarity.

"The joy of victory in her story is so much more colorful, rich, and deep when you participate in the suffering," Brown says. "The joy that I experience every Purim is heightened by the fact that I've fasted and I've tried to put myself in that moment of risk—leadership risk—that Esther took all those years ago, because so much pivoted on that one individual. So being with her in that moment of anxiety and suffering and worrying about the future helps me celebrate her."

I love Brown's term "leadership risk" because, as I get older, I've come to see how those words are conjoined. Trying to lead is risky, but, then, so is not trying. Despite my mother's feminist inculcation, I often worry that people will see audacity in my saying "I'm up to the task." Esther reminds me to stop apologizing for myself and get on with it. Then again, she was saving lives, which is a little more pressing.

Just when I think my Esther learning is complete, I stumble on another interpretation of the fast day. Esther is apparently not just a paradigm of fortitude; she has, in modern times, become a symbol of enslavement. She was "picked" by the king for betrothal and sexual satisfaction without much say in the matter, and therefore represents subjugated women everywhere.

Yaffa Epstein, a sparkplug who teaches Talmud at the Pardes Institute of Jewish Studies (based in Jerusalem) and at Yeshivat Maharat in New York (the first Orthodox Yeshiva to ordain women), tells me that the Fast of Esther was chosen in 1990 to be Yom Ha'Agunah— The Day of the Chained Woman. The *agunah* (chained woman) is the wife who cannot extricate herself from her marriage because, according to Jewish law, only men can dissolve a wedding vow. This forces women to remain in a loveless union or to carry the stigma of remarrying illegally, without a *gett* (divorce certificate).

During this particular year of my Jewish immersion, there have been headlines about Gital Dodelson, twenty-five, who waited three years for a gett, and Rivky Stein, also twenty-five, who testified in January about being unable to break free.

Three decades ago, the Day of Agunah was assigned to Ta'anit Esther very consciously by the International Coalition for Agunot Rights (ICAR). It shows me that ancient rabbis were not the only arbiters of holidays and symbolism; assigning meaning is still happening in my lifetime. "ICAR wanted to tie it to Esther," Epstein explains, "because Esther is this powerful woman who brought salvation, but also because she's trapped in this terrible marriage and is a victim of the king's power."

Blu Greenberg, who founded the Jewish Orthodox Feminist Alliance (JOFA) in 1997 and who is married to Yitz is an old friend of my mother's, was part of the early ICAR discussions about whether Ta'anit Esther was a match for Agunah Day. "Some women argued that it would muddy the focus on Purim and their rabbinic authorities would object," Blu recalls, adding that two coalition members pulled out in protest.

But the Agunah-Esther link won out, even though Blu cautions that symbolism and fasting are insufficient. "Hopefully the prayer and awareness on Ta'anit Esther will inspire us to activism. God is not going to solve this problem."

When I ask her for a suggestion as to what I might *do* that's meaningful during the Esther fast this coming week, she urges me to educate myself about agunot. A good place to start, she offers, would be to view the Golden Globe–nominated Israeli film (in theaters when we speak), called *Gett: Trial of Viviane Amselem*, which depicts a woman who is desperate to divorce. I look up a critic's review: "It's not Viviane who's on trial in 'Gett'," says the *Washington Post*. "Rather, it's the system that's perverse, in the way that it treats wives not like people, but property."

As I make my movie reservations on Fandango, I can hear some traditionalist readers insisting that it's a bastardization to make the Fast of Esther about Jewish women stuck in unhappy marriages. But Yaffa Epstein says the tie is appropriate. "It's an attempt to ground my reality in my ancient narrative. If the Fast of Esther was just about some woman who was the Queen of Persia, why should I care today? So we need to answer that question as a Jewish community: Where is the relevance? What can it teach me today?"

I have no personal connection to the agunah, but the notion that women can't get free of soured marriages does test my commitment to refraining from judgment this year. It's hard to square the message of kindness in Judaism with the severity of Orthodox divorce law. My answer is just to keep moving toward Purim itself, noting the discordance between Elvis's hips and chained women, between fasting and inebriation, between pride in Esther's valor and qualms about the 75,000 we killed after she saved us.

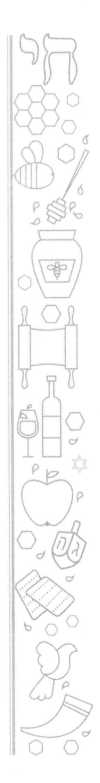

Rabba Yaffa Epstein

ON PURIM

Today we think about Purim as a day of partying and excessive drinking and masquerading and customs, but it's actually so much deeper than that. If we look at what's happened to the character of Haman, he has been imbued with every enemy of the Jewish people. Haman has taken on the face of whatever threat we Jews were, and are now, confronting. At different times in Jewish history, we've called Haman the different names of our oppressors. We've dressed him up in different garb and allowed him to represent each peril. There's always a Haman.

15

THE PURIM REPORT

Mirth and Melancholy

3.9.15

SET MY ALARM for 5 A.M. so that I can have a quick breakfast before the Esther fast begins at daybreak (6:26 A.M.) on Wednesday, March 4, 2015. I honor Elvis by eating his favorite sandwich—peanut butter and banana—because The King is the theme of the Purim Spiel at Stephen Wise Free Synagogue, where, a week earlier, I had sat in on intensive rehearsal.

I take a quiet pause in the dawn darkness to mark the reason for Ta'anit Esther: our heroine fasted and asked the Jews to join her before she petitioned for their survival.

I deliver to neighbors the holiday hamantaschen, which my daughter Molly and I baked together—our first flour-drenched foray into the cookies shaped like Haman's hat, folding circles of dough into three corners and filling them with jam. Amidst all of my holiday studying, this activity reminds me that the sweetest traditions often come down to tactile projects and the taste of a misshapen dessert.

Packaging three cookies in each cellophane gift bag—tying the openings with ribbons and a "Happy Purim" note—I drop the parcels on doormats in our apartment building.

I then attend an early-afternoon showing of the film *Gett: The Trial of Vivianne Amselem*—my small nod to The Day of Agunah, or "the Day of the Chained Woman," which some have assigned to the Fast of Esther.

I walk alone through Central Park, weary of the biting cold and the absence of anything green, aware of bareness in the city despite so many colorful Purim parties about to commence.

I enter Congregation Emanu-El on Fifth Avenue, the massive, cathedral-like synagogue whose members include Joan Rivers and Michael R. Bloomberg.

I'm here to attend my first "Purim Scotch Tasting," which I hear is de rigueur for Purim eve: the Esther fast ends with a cocktail. It's a preamble to the partying that Purim demands. We're supposed to get so inebriated that we can't tell the difference between Mordechai and Haman, the hero and the villain.

Presiding behind the makeshift bar is the convivial Senior Rabbi, Joshua Davidson, who has, in his brief two years at Emanu-El, already generated a buzz for combining intellect and wit.

"Macallan or Dewars?" he offers to those lined up for a sample. "Rocks or neat?"

I'm hesitant to drink before eating, but Davidson, whom I know because we both attended a Jewish conference the previous fall, waves me into the queue.

Jackie Mason had it wrong when he said gentiles are focused on the next cocktail and Jews on the next meal. I'm learning that Jews do their share of drinking on the holidays. There's wine every Shabbat, single malt on Simchat Torah, eggnog on Hanukkah (okay, maybe just in my family), four cups of wine on Tu B'Shvat, four cups on Passover—and now we're supposed to get blotto on Purim.

Since I have been fasting since sunup, I'm already a little woozy from hunger. But as they say, "When in Rome," or, in this case, in temple. So as soon as the fast ends after dusk—5:50 p.m. (believe me, I checked in advance)—I belly up to the rabbi's bar.

Suffice it to say that whiskey is not the best way to break a fast. To soften the blow, I reach for some of Emanu-El's hamantaschen. The cookies are nestled temptingly on a paper plate (their triangles neater than mine), and I try not to appear voracious as I take two pastries. There is barely a moment to revive before it's time for the megillah— the annual recitation of the Esther story. Scripts are distributed and one of the associate rabbis insists that I accept a role. As I demur (unsuccessfully), I watch Rabbi Davidson, standing now between pews, suddenly transform himself from jovial barkeeper to menacing Haman, as he dons a black cape, pirate hat, and black leather gloves. "I had to combine store-bought costumes for Darth Vader, Dracula, and Captain Hook," he says to me in a dry aside. "You don't come by a Haman costume easily in this town."

The assigned readers are encouraged to make use of the hats and props lined up onstage—a cane, boa, baseball mitt. All of us conscripted "actors" are responsible for recounting one segment of the Esther/Haman story, standing in front of a microphone at the front. I've been assigned the first section; no chance to learn from others' mistakes.

"Choose a prop!" someone commands. I reach for the crown.

"That was going to be MY prop!" shouts a girl (who looks six years old).

"Way to go, Abby, spoiling the kid's megillah," I internally scold myself. I surrender the tiara and grab the nose glasses.

Someone tells me to pick one of the slips of paper with the "directions"—each a prompt for *how* to perform your section while you read it aloud.

My instruction: "Act as if your leg is being bitten by a dog."

I gamely attempt to pantomime this as I recite the text about the town of Shushan and the king's banquet, but the applause isn't exactly deafening. Davidson's colleague Rabbi Amy Ehrlich is kind enough to capture the moment with an iPhone, and I find myself hoping that my dog mauling doesn't end up on social media.

The next reader has to enact "being swarmed by bees." She is better at the bees than I was at the dog. Her bee attack is totally believable.

The education director, Saul Kaiserman, rises estimably to his challenge: "Sing every line like an opera score." He kills it with a baritone.

Rabbi Davidson is Stanislavski-worthy. He has to read his part as if giving birth in the back of a taxi. If you'll excuse the pun, he delivers.

This ritual proves that the so-called "People of the Book" can also be the People of the Party—if only once a year and despite the somber source material. (Haman's plot to annihilate the Jews isn't exactly a laugh riot. Nor is the Jews' revenge—cast as self-defense—when they slaughter those 75,000 Persians.)

But the tradition also speaks to the importance of letting go a little, even as it stresses solemnity. We should revisit the past's calamities, yes, but also seize the chance to exhale. There's something undeniably spiriting—and arguably important—about watching our authoritative clergy leaders loosen up.

Just six months earlier, I had seen Rabbi Davidson in a very different context, as one of a few rabbis invited—along with Jewish journalists, educators, artists, foundation professionals, and social-justice activists—to a three-day conversation about all things Jewish, convened by the *Jewish Week* newspaper. In small breakout groups, we discussed loaded subjects ranging from the coarsening of Jewish disagreement to whether Chabad is the gold standard for Jewish engagement. I saw Rabbi Davidson thoughtfully grapple with hard questions. Now I am watching him simulate Lamaze breathing while reciting the words of Mordechai.

I leave this gathering wishing I'd grown up with spiels, performing them with my kids. Just like I didn't build a sukkah with Ben or Molly every fall, I didn't put them in costume for Purim every spring. My kids are too old now to be able to say, "I grew up playing Haman, Mordechai, or Esther. . . ." They didn't. They don't know the story by heart.

The next day is Purim itself (March 5), and I do a mental inventory to ensure I've observed all four *mitzvot* (commandments) of the holiday:

1. Read and hear the megillah: Check. (In nose glasses.)

2. Have a festive meal: Check. (At lunchtime, I enjoy a nice chicken paillard with my former Senior Rabbi, Peter Rubinstein, and hear all about his recent public dialogue with Cardinal Timothy Dolan.)

3. Bestow two edible gifts: Check. (The neighbors seemed to enjoy our deformed hamantaschen, though maybe they were just being polite.)

4. Give gifts to the poor: Check. (I donated to "charity: water," which builds wells in developing countries, and I made a date to go to a local eyeglass store with Betty, who sells newspapers on the street corner near my shul and has broken lenses.)

Purim reinforces the generosity that almost every Jewish holiday requires. On the High Holy Days we're reminded that *tzedakah* (charity) will "lessen the severity of the decree"; on Sukkot, we're supposed to feed guests in our sukkah; on Hanukkah, we're to reserve one of the eight nights to give instead of receive; on the Tenth of Tevet, the fast should focus us on the needy; and on Passover, we welcome the stranger. So it is not surprising that Purim also demands that we step up. Perhaps no other holiday so closely aligns self-indulgence and self-lessness in one twenty-four-hour period.

"The Jewish tradition asks us to stay in between these two extremes," says Yaffa Epstein, who teaches Talmud at the Pardes Institute for Jewish Learning in Jerusalem. "What's beautiful about that is, they're both necessary."

I keenly experienced these two extremes when I stood (pre-scotch, pre-spiel) in the pew next to Rabbi Davidson—who kindly invited me to join him—saying Kaddish for Milt.

The mourner's prayer—recited at nearly every service—reminds me how Judaism brings us back to those we've lost, no matter how merry the festival. We are repeatedly taught to hold two thoughts at once: after Rosh Hashanah (joyful), we enter Yom Kippur (ominous); on Passover, we eat *maror* (bitter herb) and *haroset* (sweet apples and nuts); in my shul on Friday nights, we say the *misheberach* prayer for the sick immediately followed by the shehecheyanu (gratitude) for our blessings. On Purim eve, we recite both a solemn Kaddish and a madcap megillah within the same hour.

In his 2013 Rosh Hashanah sermon, his first at Emanu-El, Rabbi Davidson said, "While our congregation celebrates countless joys, there exists enough suffering here to break the heart." He's right: Jews revel and weep in the same moment. That was evident at Milt's shiva and even ninety minutes after his passing. After the shock at his bedside, our tight embraces and the required phone call to alert the funeral home, my sister-in-law, Sharon, interrupted our weeping: "Should we still keep our dinner reservation at P.F. Chang's?" The laughter was instantaneous and restorative. We could smile despite the pain, hold our heaviness and our hearty Jewish appetites at the same time. Milt, too, would have laughed and insisted we go eat fried dumplings.

Yes, Jackie Mason, you're right: Jews are always planning the next meal.

Rabbi Rick Jacobs
ON PASSOVER

Who's the most problematic of The Four Children? It's not the wicked child and it's not the innocent (simple) child. It's the child that doesn't know how to ask a question. The wicked child you'll engage; that one is going to be alive, asking, "What's the point of all this nonsense? Why do we do it every year? I hate the food," etc. But the one who can't ask a question—whoa. That's the most critical challenge, because that child is not going to be able to engage in the world. The Four Questions are asked to put the children in the spotlight and remind all the adults, too, that our tradition is a religion that requires deep probing and asking of penetrating questions. And to make our Judaism alive to those questions.

And then at the end of the seder, we open the door for Elijah. All of a sudden you say to the children, "Go! You need to open the door!" But that's not just to keep them engaged. The young child who opens that door actually thinks that the Elijah or the Messiah might be there. The sense of possibility that that young person has can be seen in their eyes as they run to the door. They aren't jaded. They aren't convinced that it's just a ritual. We ask the young people to go welcome Elijah because we need to see in their eyes that sense of hope and possibility. It's not just to keep them absorbed and awake, it's actually to keep *us* engaged and awake.

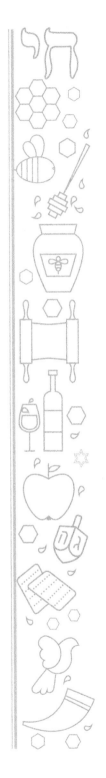

16

PASSOVER

Scallions and Rare Silences

3.25.15

M Y LOCAL JUDAICA shop sells the "feather set" we're supposed to use to scour the house for *chametz* (leaven). No leavened dough or anything made from leavened dough is allowed in the house during the eight days of Passover, and therefore it all must be expunged. The chametz ban honors the Exodus story, when the ancient Israelites fled their Egyptian captors in such a hurry, they had no time to let their bread rise. To remember that escape, we swear off bread (or any dough that ferments), which means cutting down on carbs. (There's an ongoing question as to the status of rice, but that's for another book.) I toss all the half-eaten cereal and Ronzoni boxes in the garbage, feeling guilty about the waste. I could "sell" the extra chametz to a non-Jew and then buy it back after Passover (that's the protocol for observant Jews), but instead I give it away to our apartment doormen, who seem slightly confused by all the Cheerios and Oreos, but appreciative.

Despite my intention to meet all holiday requirements, I am sheepishly skipping the full-kitchen purification that is routine for kosher homes. Since I haven't been keeping kosher all year, it would feel like paying lip-service to *kasher* (make kosher) my kitchen now. But I feel ashamed at the toil I'm avoiding, knowing that observant Jews are, at this moment, scouring, sweeping, and scorching their kitchens into Passover-readiness. The oven should be scrubbed and heated for one to two hours, with the top burners turned up till they're red-hot. The microwave should be cleaned and steamed. The sink should be sanitized, unused for twenty-four hours, doused with boiling water several times, then lined with foil. The fridge, freezer, closets, and table should be purified of chametz, vigorously cleaned. A separate Passover set of utensils, plates, and pans must be pulled out of storage and substituted—or the usual ones kashered, which is too elaborate to go into here. No wonder many observant families choose to go to a kosher resort for Passover week; the cleaning has been done for them.

My nod to kashering for Passover is to do *bedikat chametz* (search for chametz), the search-and-destroy mission, on the eve of the first seder, to find crumbs in the cupboards and shelves, using a candle to illuminate the farthest corners, and a feather to brush any stray bits into a spoon (made of wood so it can be burned later).

The shop's feather ensemble comes complete with white feather (bird undetermined), wooden spoon, candle, and printed blessing. I ask Molly to dust with me, and she's curious (and kind) enough to say yes. Having only done this once, when I was twelve, I've forgotten the technique. This year I want to get it right, so I read the enclosed instructions aloud with Molly. It's yet one more time that ritual brings my family together, and I'm actually moved by watching my daughter follow the directions on how to sweep and where. I light the candle and the two of us muddle through the task, half-giggling, half-somber. It's not easy to spot Oreo crumbs by candlelight, let alone scrape them onto the wooden spoon, but we put all the stray chametz we can find in a little bag and seal it. I don't burn the spoon as I'm supposed to, because I fear setting off the smoke alarm. Then we recite the enclosed prayer out loud (I do the Hebrew, Molly the English): *Blessed are You, Lord our God, King of the universe, who has sanctified us by His commandments, and has commanded us concerning the removal of chametz.*

Of course my friend Rabbi Dov Linzer, Dean of the Modern Orthodox seminary, Yeshivat Chovevei Torah, informs me after the fact that we were supposed to recite the blessing *before* the search. Oh, well; chalk it up to learning on the job. Dov also sends me an additional passage we could recite in the future—what he calls the "belt and suspenders" of the chametz purge: *"Any chametz that I did not see and do not know about, let it be nullified and ownerless as the dust of the earth."* This reminds me of the Kol Nidre declaration, how we nullified our vows before making them on Yom Kippur.

Parents are supposed to purposefully plant some crumbs ahead of time, so that the kids can root out the chametz like crack detectives. This holiday of Passover is indisputably oriented toward the younger generation. The Torah repeats and repeats: *Tell it to the children.* They'll grow up to be the tellers. When the children disengage, we've failed the mitzvah. I seek to meet the mitzvah when I lead the family seder. I spend hours in advance of the holiday's arrival, trying to come up with ways to keep the kids riveted. Even Chabad.org's online Haggadah acknowledges the hurdles of boredom: "Jews have prayed for thousands of years. With time, however, despite those helpful preparatory rungs, fresh and focused praying sometimes grew stale and could even lapse into rapid reading by rote. Our people's spiritual leaders labored to counter such an approach. . . ."

I pore through books about the Haggadah and peruse various modern Haggadahs along with online build-your-own-Haggadah sites featuring readings and blessings you can customize. I've learned that a Haggadah is not fixed like the siddur—the daily prayer book—whose name, similar to "seder," comes from the word "order." Though the Passover seder does indeed have a specific order of rituals or tasks, "Haggadah" means "to tell," and a telling is more open for creativity: what happens around the seder-signposts is fluid. I call Rabbi Arthur Green, an esteemed professor at Hebrew College in Boston, irreverent lecturer, and prolific writer. "The old-fashioned seder, where people's grandparents mumbled through the whole book," he tells me, "was in fact—even from the point of view of *halachah* (Jewish law)—a very bad way to do it. Because it wasn't really 'telling' your child; it wasn't really passing it on."

Passing it on feels doable to me. The Exodus is an epic story of oppression, resolve, and deliverance. The problem has always been, at least to my mind, that somehow the storyline gets lost in the Haggadah; the seder duties (dipping parsley, asking four questions) do not follow the Exodus narrative. I therefore grew up without really grasping the full tale; so, just in case you missed it, too, here are my Spark Notes. (Skip the next four paragraphs if you know the story cold.)

The Hebrews were slaves under the cruel Pharaoh in Egypt. He decreed that every Hebrew baby boy that was born should be cast into the Nile. One particular boy (guess who?) was born soon after this decree and, to save his life, his mother put him in a basket among the reeds by the bank of the Nile. He was found by Pharaoh's daughter, who named him Moses (meaning either "drawn from" or "born from" the water). Moses's sister, Miriam, had been hovering nearby, and offered to find a nursemaid for the baby. Pharaoh's daughter gave her permission to do so but did not know that the nursemaid turned out to be Moses's mother.

Moses grew up privileged in Pharaoh's house, but he could not remain complacent about the mistreatment of the Hebrew slaves, whom the Torah suggests he knew to be his brothers. One day, when he saw an Egyptian beating a Hebrew slave, Moses killed the master. Realizing that he was now in deep trouble, Moses ran away to escape punishment, becoming a shepherd and marrying a non-Hebrew named Zipporah. One day, God appeared to Moses in the form of a burning bush and charged him to return to Egypt to save his people. Moses demurred, but God pressed, assuring Moses that his brother, Aaron, would assist.

Moses returned to Egypt and appeared before Pharaoh, demanding in the name of God to "let my people go!" Pharaoh flatly refused. So God sent the first plague: blood. The rivers ran red with blood, frightening the Egyptians. Moses repeated God's charge: "Let my people go!" Pharaoh hardened his heart and refused again. Another plague was sent, ten plagues in all, each one harsher than the previous. Pharaoh flip-flopped—relenting and reneging—until God finally sent the worst and last punishment: killing the Egyptians' sons, a fitting cruel echo of Pharaoh's own decree, which had almost killed Moses at birth. To make sure the Hebrews didn't suffer this final plague by mistake, Moses instructed his people to smear lamb's blood on their doorframes so that God knew to pass over (get it—*Pass*over?) their homes when the tenth plague struck.

The Israelites escaped en masse the next day, racing into the desert with few belongings and no time to bake bread, eating flat pita instead, which had no time to rise (today's matzah stands in for the Torah's unrisen pita). Pharaoh sent his army to chase the escapees. The Israelites kept running until they hit a major obstacle: the Red Sea. Just when they felt doomed, Moses lifted his staff, the roiling waters parted, and Moses guided his people through to safety. His sister, Miriam, led the women in a celebratory dance on the other side, as the Egyptian army, in hot pursuit, were swallowed up in the waves. The end. (Or at least the end before they get to Mount Sinai, but Sinai's not in the Haggadah.)

When Mom handed off Seder Duty to me after my adult bat mitzvah in 2005 (she was a weary host and had earned a break), I was determined to accomplish one simple goal for my kids and their cousins, then ages four to eight: connect the story to the seder. I hoped the thirty-two relatives, from tots to tantes (Yiddish for aunties), would put the pieces together in a way I had not. To see, for instance, that Pesach means "pass over, to spare," and that the roasted lamb shank on the seder plate evokes the lamb sacrificed to smear its blood on our doorposts, signaling "Jews live here."

My childhood seders at my aunts' and uncles' were warm but uninspiring. We sat at the table and dutifully read through the Haggadah. There was little spontaneity. The only suspense was who would be asked to read aloud.

So I've tried, in the ten years since my mother passed the baton to me (after taking it from my uncle Bernie), to introduce at least one activity that captures the children's attention so they become *integral* players in the entire evening—not just to perk up during the four questions and "Dayenu," the centerpiece song that means "It would have been enough." One year, I invited the kids to each prepare a section of the seder (the four children, the ten plagues) so they could explain it in a format of their choosing: poem, song, rap, PowerPoint, iMovie, art. Another year, I put each of the seder's fifteen steps (composed by Talmudic scholars in the eleventh century) on individual index cards with two-sided velcro, shuffled them, and asked the kids to work together to put them in the right order on a poster board I had bought (and decorated) from Kinko's. As the kids matured, I made these exercises more challenging—putting debate topics under their plates and giving them each one minute to argue their side. They loved the gamesmanship, and I loved seeing them own the story enough to dispute it. Example:

Resolution for Ethan (nephew) to argue: *"Resolved: Pharaoh can't be blamed entirely for sending each plague, because according to the Torah, God kept 'hardening' Pharaoh's heart."*

Resolution for Ben (son) to counterargue: *"Resolved: Pharaoh should be blamed entirely for sending each plague because he could have done the right thing when Moses first asked."*

This year, I'm substituting the debate questions with more general, accessible queries for the entire table. So, instead of writing on index cards, I'm placing blank 3 × 5 cards under each plate, along with a pen tucked near each fork.

I always take pride in setting the seder table, which I liken to a theatrical event that requires multiple stage props. That includes not just plates, silverware, napkins, and glasses, but the seder plate with each of its categories filled—*karpas* (parsley) represents the spring; a *beitzah* (charred egg) reminds us of the burnt offering brought in Temple days and symbolizes the cycle of the year; the *z'roa* (lamb shank) stands in for the ancient lamb sacrifice on Passover and evokes the tenth plague, which Jews were spared by smearing their lintels with lamb's blood; haroset (the mix of fruit, wine, and nuts) stands in for the mortar used by Israelite slaves to build Egyptian cities; the maror (bitter herb) conjures the bitterness of slavery; one more bitter vegetable (*hazeret*) underscores servitude and is usually represented by a romaine lettuce leaf, which isn't actually bitter and which a lot of

Jews leave out because it feels redundant to the maror; and finally the feminist addition of an orange, to symbolize the inclusion of women and gay people.

Each guest has a small bowl of salt water (the salt of our tears) in which we will dip the parsley and, later, hard-boiled eggs. There are stacks of matzah on the tables and, near the seder leader, a silk case for the *Afikomen* (special matzah). The last three years, I've also placed one scallion next to each knife because Rabbi David Wolpe mentioned—and I was delighted by—the Sephardic tradition of inviting everyone to (gently) thrash his or her neighbor during the chorus of "Dayenu" to recall the whips of the Egyptians.

This year, Molly has decided to take on the matzah ball soup assignment, and she chooses a recipe from Joan Nathan's *Jewish Cooking in America*. My teenage daughter has always been far more at ease in the kitchen than I, and after she shops for all her ingredients, it's strangely comforting to watch her mash the matzah meal, egg, and dill as I sit nearby at the kitchen table, preparing the seder ceremony on my laptop. We're often a team, she and I, whether we're choosing her brother's Hanukkah gifts and wrapping them, or setting a birthday table with confetti and silly hats. She's a celebrator and an organizer who cares about marking things in a big way. Observing her efficiency and energy, I am reassured that she will carry on the holidays when I'm gone.

As Molly chops, mixes, and boils, I put three index cards under each plate, knowing I plan to pose three hopefully provocative questions at four different junctures in the seder, all of which the guests will answer anonymously and place in a bowl. The plan is to read them aloud without knowing whose answers are whose. I figure it will be a safe way to be honest, not to mention a chance to get to know some of the seder-themed truths in the room.

The Haggadah I've used for the last three years is homemade—a collection of questions rather than readings, again with the intention of keeping kids engaged. When kids simply recite, they zone out. I know I did. So I've assembled a Haggadah that meets all the seder requirements, while inviting constant participation.

Why do you think the Haggadah invites both "all who are hungry" and "all who are in need"? What's the difference?

Moses balked when God first asked him to lead; is it possible that a sign of great leadership is self-doubt?

The youngest guests are asked questions such as:

It's hard to eat the bitter herb without making a sour face because it tastes harsh—on purpose. If you had to pick a food to take the place of maror and get the same reaction, what would you choose?

Guests don't know who will be called on next, which keeps everyone alert. No mastery of Judaism is required; the point is not to highlight ignorance but to involve every participant. Each opinion is additive.

The evening arrives and we begin with our usual hugging and milling around, catching up loudly over wine and slivovitz, which is a tradition I stole from my sister Robin's in-laws (it's a liqueur that contains no grain, perfect for Pesach). After about thirty minutes, my family needs to be corralled forcefully into our dining room to start the seder, and they appear in good humor despite being packed so closely at three rented round tables. Each table has a designated candle-lighter, and we all say the blessing for lighting, a simple consecration that never fails to move me. There's something about the quiet around the flames as they're lit and seeing my family's faces illuminated, knowing how many families are lighting candles within minutes of each other. I ask for a moment of quiet to remember those whom we wish were still at the table: My father-in-law, Milton. My mother's sister, Aunt Betty, who used to host the seder. Her husband, my Uncle Bernie, who used to officiate in his kittel (white coat). Their son, Jeffrey, a social worker who died of AIDS. My dad's mother, Grandma Esther, who used to dependably complain that the seder was too long.

I remind everyone that the rabbis say each of us is a Haggadah, a storyteller. That seder means "order" and we'll keep to it, but the rest is ours to shape. I ask them to speculate why some say the Haggadah itself represents survival. Why the children are the most important audience. Why we choose to re-live slavery. Why we retell the Exodus story publicly. Lord Rabbi Jonathan Sacks wrote this about Passover: *"To be a Jew is to know that the task of memory is more important than history."* Is memory more important than history? The answers come fast and furious. Opinions are not hard to come by in this family.

Soon, I ask the first of my index-card questions. "Take out your pens and one index card from under your plate. Please write down an answer to this question—preferably legibly—and do not sign your name. *The Haggadah reminds us to remember the stranger because we were once strangers; name one time in the last year that you helped the stranger."* It's not meant to be a guilt trip but to trigger awareness. Each guest unearths a card and pen, writes an answer. I pass a bowl and it fills up with the anonymous cards. I mix them up and pass the bowl around, then each guest reads one answer aloud.

I gave a dollar to any homeless person who asked.

I tutored a third-grader in math.

I sent a donation to a cancer research.

People are listening to each other, unsure what will be shared next. I can't explain why the engagement matters so much to me. Something makes me feel strongly that this holiday, probably more than any other, should capture what Judaism can be. A seder should amount to more than the joyful chaos of a family reunion; that can happen without Judaism. It should make Jewish kids want to be Jews. Because our heritage is spirited, intimate, binding.

Before we do the first hand-washing, I pose the question about water in the Exodus story—where does it figure in? One nephew answers that Moses was sent down the Nile River as a baby; one niece notes that the first plague—blood—turns the water red; another nephew volunteers that God parted the Red Sea to allow the Israelites to escape; and Molly chimes in that Miriam led the people in dancing on the sea banks after they crossed to safety and then hydrated the Jews in the desert with her well as they fled to the Promised Land. The point is not to test knowledge, but to connect the dots. When we see the threads, the fabric feels stronger.

I ask for silence between the first hand-washing and the dipping and eating of karpas, which requires no blessing because we're about to eat a vegetable instead of bread, which does require a blessing. I never knew, till I researched it this year, that this silence was built-in. I'm aware of how rare silence is in the din of my exuberant family, and I make sure to honor two more silences later on: one between the second hand-washing and the blessing for the matzah, and another when we break the middle matzah to create the Afikomen, a word meaning "that which comes after" (i.e., "dessert"). The Afikomen is the half-piece of matzah broken off and set aside to eat at the end of the seder. I ask the table to think privately about when they've personally felt broken and also about who helped put them back together. I'm slightly amazed that no one balks and everyone seems to be actually thinking about someone who healed them. We talk about the Hebrew word for Egypt, *mitzrayim*, translated as "narrow place."

"Whatever it is that constricts you or enslaves you," says Rabbi Green, "you have to ask, 'What is holding me back, what is my inner slavery? What keeps me from being in touch with the deepest parts of myself, with the presence of God in myself, and how do I liberate myself from it?'"

One's personal "narrow place" may not be comparable to the narrow places of global suffering. But at the seder table, it's a small step to notice the pain close to home and then begin to fathom the struggles of populations far away.

I confess that I'm seldom galvanized by attempts to imbue the seder with contemporary issues. It's not that I don't feel compassion for the plight of sex slaves in Bangkok, or the poverty of Bengal. But I think there's something awkwardly heavy-handed about the way these modern plagues are often brought to the seder table. I do ask my seder guests—as I know others have—to think about today's Pharaohs, today's blights. To speak their names. But I have yet to find the exercise that connects the headlines to the holiday in a way that feels organically powerful, not artificially political.

Green agrees. "To make it about the political stuff is too easy. It has to be about *us*," he tells me. "I'm much more interested in spiritual liberation than in political issues. For me, it's about inner freedom, the mitzrayim of the mind, and the Egypt of the soul. . . . You have to talk about the places where we are enslaved; that's the real challenge."

I love his words but can't ask my family to name "the places where they are enslaved." Our rowdy Passovers, for all their poignant moments, don't offer the intimacy to share personal mitzrayim. And if I'm honest, I don't relish being confessional myself. My "narrow places" were exhumed back in Elul.

We move now to the Maggid—the telling of the Exodus story itself, and instead of reading it aloud from the Haggadah (typically a choppy, confusing account), we either recount it without text (taking turns telling the story, passing it along when we get stuck), or we play the kids' favorite game: "Speed Maggid." I divide the room into two teams, and one brave volunteer from each team comes to sit in the front of the room with a low side table between them, holding two hotel desk bells (ordered on Amazon). I ask a factual question about the story and they compete to hit the bell and answer correctly. If the bell-ringer gets it wrong, the opponent has a chance to get it right. You get the idea. After five questions, we move to the next pair of opponents and the next five questions.

I worried in advance that my cousins would judge this game: "There they go again, that competitive family." But on the contrary, everyone is maniacally absorbed—screaming, cheering, jeering. It's hard to control, to be sure, but the game achieves exactly what I'd hoped: the room is energized.

- Who finds Moses and pulls him out of the basket—
  Pharaoh's wife or daughter? (Daughter!)

- What does Moses say when God calls his name from the burning bush? ("Hineni"—"Here I am!")
- Name the second plague. (Frogs!)

When it comes to Jewish knowledge, I'm pro-competition. It should be cool to know the name of the guy who, according to Talmudic legend, entered the Red Sea first (Nachshon).

The kids recite the four questions ("Why is this night different from all other nights?") and read about the four children—the wise, the wicked, the simple, and the one who does not know enough to ask. This is honestly my least favorite part of the service, because the four questions have a tuneless tune and the four children are so befuddling. No amount of research or explanation satisfies me. The four children don't relate naturally or obviously to the four questions or to the Exodus story as a whole.

The plagues are much more fertile ground. Before we recite them in a singsong alternation of Hebrew and English, I ask a new question: Why do the rabbis say that the wine droplets we daub with one finger on our plates, one for each plague, symbolize the tears we shed for our enemy—drowned in the Red Sea after we crossed it? It's an important idea that I missed growing up: that it took others dying for us to be freed. And however necessary those casualties might have been, they should give us pause, not cause for celebration. Another rabbinic reading: we take the wine drops from our cups to diminish our bounty a little bit, to honor the Egyptians' suffering from the tenth plague. Even God, according to the Talmud, admonished his angels not to sing merrily when the Israelites made it to the other shore. "How dare you sing for joy when My creatures are dying?" (Talmud, Megillah 10b, and Sanhedrin 39b).

The Egyptians, our oppressors, were God's creatures, too. I watch everyone at the table take that in. One relative counters that it's perfectly understandable to feel relief and even joy at the death of those who have killed or mistreated your family. Another says it's not just understandable but appropriate. But someone else points out that our escape required the death of innocents—the Egyptians' firstborn. And that it's beneath us to exult at the miracle of the parting Red Sea and then cheer when the same sea closes, swallowing up the army that pursued us. The idea of moral ambivalence feels Jewish to me: we don't celebrate revenge, even when we need to exact it.

Before we sing "Let My People Go," I remind the children that Dr. Martin Luther King invoked the Exodus when he accepted the Nobel Peace Prize in 1964. His words: "The Bible tells the thrilling story of how Moses stood in Pharaoh's court centuries ago and cried 'Let my people go.' This is a kind of opening chapter in a continuing story."

"A continuing story." We talk for a bit about how the story has continued. Then we sing the seder spiritual, which was actually written by African-Americans during the Civil War and adopted at seders in the early 1940s. It has always been my father's strong suit. He sings it in a booming, dramatic voice that brings me back to childhood.

We then hold up Miriam's cup—a modern addition to Elijah's chalice—because Miriam helped save our savior, Moses, when he was an infant.

For the second hand-washing before the blessing for the bread—or in this case, matzah—I leave the room to ostensibly and theatrically "wash my hands," so the kids have time to hide the Afikomen, which is my family's tradition and kind of lame, because what's the point of hiding something the leader doesn't have to look for? In our annual charade, the leader ends up pleading with the kids to produce the Afikomen and the kids demand a ransom. Other families make the leader do the hiding and the kids do the finding, though that can result in a ransacked home. In any case, it feels too late to change our Afikomen custom now, so I guess we're stuck with it.

Together we recite the blessings for the matzah and eat our first piece. In addition to the Manischewitz-brand matzah boards on the table, I've piled a plate of *shmura* (watched) matzah—the darker, grainier, homemade matzah—because it feels more Old World. It's baked from wheat that has been guarded from the moment of harvest,

to make sure it doesn't come into contact with water or other mois-
ture, which would cause it to ferment and become chametz. I'm convinced this kind is more flavorful; but with matzah, it's all relative.

We eat the maror, the bitter herb, which has always been, if you'll
excuse the sexist bromide, a moment that separates the men from the
boys. Either you can take a hefty dose of the nose-clearing horserad-
ish or you can't. I encourage my kids to eat enough maror that they
feel it; if your eyes don't water, you've missed the point.

"Dayenu" ("it would have been enough for us") is the spirited high
point of any seder, but we never discussed its lyrics when I was growing up. "It would have been enough." If God had *only* given us the
Torah, had *only* given us Shabbat, had *only* delivered us from slavery,
any one of those gifts would have sufficed. But there was always more.
And then more. I ask the table, and especially myself: How many
times have we focused on what we have instead of what we want? It
may be a well-trodden idea these days, that noticing blessings makes
you realize you are blessed. But so many times this year I have been
reminded to focus on what's in my hands rather than what's out of
reach.

The scallions are a hit. Everyone is free to flog their neighbors
during the "Dayenu" chorus (only the chorus, or it's pandemonium),
and it becomes a rambunctious battle royal. It's hard to describe the
hilarity of watching my husband whip my second cousin or my son
lash his aunt. The added ritual has now become a boisterous
free-for-all.

We complete the first part of the seder in about seventy-five minutes, and then it's time for the meal. As I pass the hard-boiled eggs
around and the kids start ladling and distributing Molly's matzah ball
soup (delicious), it's gratifying to hear guests tell me that they'd lost
track of the time. Not because a seder should feel short for brevity's
sake, but because the reality of ritual, I've come to believe, is that
duration is not a value in itself and can be a deterrent. Boredom is
often considered a bad word in Jewish life—rarely confronted. But I
think it's worth noticing and countering, especially for kids. Because
when they're intrigued (and kept busy), they stay.

The meal is the easiest part. My family is like so many others: loquacious and loving. We're glad to be together this way, and it shows. We pick up where we last left off, no matter how many months have elapsed. And despite my stress (hosting is stressful: the spills on the floor, the chair scrapes on the walls, getting the coffee urn out and realizing I forgot to buy half-and-half for Mom), I try to tell myself not to worry about whether the macaroon crumbs are being ground into the rug, and instead notice that the seder is alive and bubbling the way it should be, that Dave is catching up with my second cousin, and Robin is grilling Ben on his girlfriend, and Dad is answering Molly's questions about her history reading. I also overhear some ribbing about the Speed Maggid winners. The buzz is satisfying.

Of course it's challenging, as always, to round up everyone to resume the seder after dessert. I can't continue the proceedings without the Afikomen, which the children will only produce in exchange for cash. After the typically heated negotiations, I proffer some single dollar bills and hand one to any guest under eighteen. I'd prefer to link the bartering to some kind of tzedakah in which one dollar goes to the child and the second dollar to a charity of the kid's (or the whole family's) choosing. But I know my family would roll their eyes if I tried. Too self-conscious. The Afikomen is soon back in my hands and we can get to the third cup of wine.

The Afikomen is supposed to be the last thing we eat, which is not realistic in a family that keeps picking at the desserts until they walk out the door. Mom's matzah-brickle (a variation on butter crunch made with matzah, caramel, and chocolate) is addictive and gets devoured even after we've downed the last cup of wine.

This year, despite waning attention spans, I hope to make Elijah— the prophet for whom we open the door toward the end of the seder— much clearer to the kids than he was in my childhood. Most Jews I know would be hard pressed to explain who Elijah is or why he comes to the seder at all. So we talk about how Elijah was considered a macho prophet who challenged the worship of a pagan god; how he is supposed to be the harbinger of the Messiah, who will arrive only when the world is healed and when we've done our part to heal it. We talk about how he's the only major character in the Hebrew Bible who never actually dies; instead, he ascends to the heavens in a chariot. We discuss how there are two Jewish rituals at which Elijah always shows up: every seder and every bris. But most importantly, I want us to focus on the rabbinic idea that Elijah *needs us*. He needs us to open the door for him so he can symbolically enter, just as he needs us to help fix the world so the Messiah can arrive.

There will be no Messianic time—no perfect world, nor even an *improved* world—without our participation. That's why some have introduced the ritual tradition of each guest pouring a drop of wine from our cups into Elijah's: to symbolize the cooperation it will take to heal what's hurt. It's mushy, maybe, but what else is Passover about? If we don't use the seder to think about what's left to repair and who is still enslaved, aren't we just revisiting a folk tale every year? The story has to make us care, and even act. "Next Year in Jerusalem," which we will exclaim as the last words of the seder, has to mean, in addition to the literal aspiration, "Next year in a better place." A kinder place.

But the seder doesn't just end with a message of repair; there's a message of revenge, too. My childhood seders left it out, even though it was there—in the Haggadah we used at Uncle Bernie's table. It's the prayer known as "Pour out your wrath," a plea to God to punish our enemies. I could skip it, because it's not the warm Passover message I want people to take away. But I also don't think the Haggadah should let us off the hook. People don't retain what's oversimplified; they retain what's challenging. If I've learned anything this year, it's that the thorns in the Jewish story—the intolerant Maccabees in the Hanukkah battle, the wholesale slaughter of non-Jews in the Purim story, and now this aggressive prayer—all make the tradition so much harder and so much richer.

So, as we open the door for Elijah and prepare to drink the final fourth cup, we read the prayer, *Shfoch Chamatcha*, added to the Haggadah in the eleventh century, words that many Jews excise or ignore, words based on Psalm 79:

Pour out Your wrath upon those who do not know You and upon the kingdoms which do not call upon Your Name. For they have devoured Jacob [meaning Israel, or the Jewish people] and laid waste his dwelling place (Psalms 79:6–7). Pour out Your fury upon them; let the fierceness of Your anger overtake them (Psalms 69:25). Pursue them in indignation and destroy them from under Your heavens (Lamentations 3:66).

Though I'm not an eye-for-an-eye type, I respect that this prayer was added in the Middle Ages, a time when Jews were horrifically persecuted. I'm cognizant that Jews, in generation after generation, had reason to invoke this appeal for payback, when anti-Semitic cruelties were unceasing. Today, the language feels antiquated and coarse—not the Jews we want to be. Yet this past year, many argued for exactly this kind of retribution during the summer's 2014 Gaza war, when Israel struck back hard in response to Hamas's rocket fire. Was Israel's response the equivalent of pouring out God's wrath? Does bloody retaliation have a place in the Passover message? Rabbi Green chooses to include the controversial section in his Haggadah every year, "though some of my guests are scandalized when I do," he admits. "It's a piece of Jewish history; I think we have room to be angry at what was done to us."

But he stresses that we have to turn the same mirror on ourselves. "It's not just 'Pour out your wrath upon the gentiles'—it doesn't say that. It says 'Pour out your wrath upon *those nations who have not known you.*' Sometimes we Americans or we Jews or we Israelis act as if we don't know the will of God. Then *we, too,* deserve that wrath."

At our seder, the family reflections are robust, with even some of the avowed pacifists in attendance defending the prayer, others disgusted by it. Once again, I sit back contentedly and let the seder be just as messy and lively as it should be.

I restore some order so we can drink the last cup and end on a cheerier, less militaristic note. We lift our glasses and recite the wine blessing in unison—one of the few prayers the entire room knows by heart. We then sing all the seder standards: *"Chad Gadya"* (One Kid), *"Echad Mi Yodea"* (Who Knows One?), *"Eliyahu Hanavi"* (Elijah, the Prophet). The tablecloth is stained, the rug sprinkled with matzah crumbs, everyone looks sluggish. But we've made a Passover and fulfilled the mitzvah: "On that day, tell your children. . . ."

Rabbi Arthur Green
ON PASSOVER

I've come to the conclusion there's only one mitzvah Jews are really committed to, and that is the mitzvah of "You shall teach them to your children." We have a sense that we have this legacy that we have to pass on. We got it from our grandparents; we've got to pass it on to our grandchildren. And if we don't do it, we have a terrible sense of failure. Even when the thick soup of tradition has been watered down to nothing, when people have no idea what they're supposed to be passing on in terms of content, there still is this sense that I've got to tell the story.

The whole seder for me is the tension between "We were slaves to Pharaoh in Egypt and now we're free . . ." and "This year we are slaves, next year may we be free." The seder lives in the tension between those two things. On the one hand, we're the most fortunate, liberated Jews in history; for God's sake, look at our tremendous privilege and freedom. But on the other hand, there are lots of things that enslave us. We have to liberate ourselves from so many things to be really spiritually free. And so we live in that tension between "Yes, we are free" and "No, we still have to become free."

Rabbi David Ellenson
ON PASSOVER

Every year of my childhood, Passover would always begin with my father, my brother, and me, along with my uncle and my cousin, walking to the home of a neighbor of ours, Mr. Brenner, for a private minyan. All the boys and men in this community would come together and daven Minchah (afternoon prayer)

continued

and Maariv (evening prayer). As a boy growing up, it never seemed odd to me that it was only the men who went to this, and then, when we'd come home, all the women would be waiting, particularly my mother, and they would have prepared the whole seder. I bring it up because I think about our Passover today, and the fact that my wife, Jackie, leads our seder so fully and remarkably. My sister and my mother were very strong people, but in this one way they were sort of disempowered. The contrast of my childhood tradition to my family's today is significant.

17

THE FEMINIST PASSOVER

A (Third) Seder of Her Own

4.8.15

ALL FIRSTBORN SONS are supposed to fast on the eve of Passover, to remember that God spared the eldest Jewish boys during the tenth plague.

Some Jews interpret the fasting mandate to apply to firstborn women as well.

This year, my mom, Letty Cottin Pogrebin, an un-shy feminist (and loving noodge), assumed that I'd be fasting as part of my holiday marathon.

"I'm not a firstborn son," I replied petulantly. (I frankly didn't relish starving all day before the first bite of matzah.)

She retorted, "But you're a firstborn!" (Come on, barely: I was born just one minute ahead of my identical twin sister.)

I didn't fold. "The tenth plague smote all Egyptian firstborn *sons*," I said, relying on Exodus. "I think the gender matters here. It doesn't apply to me."

The upshot: I did not abstain on April 3, the day that led up to the first seder at Robin's house, nor did I study a tractate of Talmud, which is the accepted alternative to fasting. But *after* our two family seders, when a place opens up at the Feminist Seder on Sunday night and Mom invites me along, I accept.

I go, not just to atone for my non-feminist non-fast, but also because I haven't been to the Feminist Seder since I was in college, and I remember how powerful it was in my youth, when I attended every year starting at age twelve.

I capitalize "the Feminist Seder" on purpose. Because although there are now hundreds of feminist seders around the world, this is the original—the revolutionary ritual started in 1976 by the late Esther Broner (an esteemed academic and spiritual presence) in collaboration with a group of women who came to be known as "the Seder Sisters," which includes my writer mom.

The Feminist Seder reimagined a ritual that had largely sidelined women in the Bible, Haggadah, and the seder ceremony itself, wherein men would traditionally do the praying, reciting, recounting, and discussing, while women did the cooking, serving, clearing, and cleaning.

This innovative women-only observance was a highlight of my youth in the seventies and eighties, when I was still wearing the Danskin pantsuits Mom insisted looked good on me.

Each year, after my childhood family seders at Uncle Danny's (first night), and Aunt Betty's (second), I looked forward to a whole new world the third night, in New York City's SoHo or Chelsea. There was the improvised "table"—patterned fabrics spread on the floor of someone's loft, the pile of pillows we all brought to sit on in a huge circle, and the myriad platters that each guest contributed for the potluck meal.

I remember being soothed by Esther Broner's ethereal voice, being riveted by her poetic asides, pushed by her incisive questions.

I felt privileged to be a "Seder Daughter," sitting among leaders of the women's movement—Gloria Steinem and former Congresswoman Bella Abzug, who always kept her famous hat on and was the only one who insisted on a chair.

I remember listening attentively to the incantatory teachings of writer Phyllis Chesler (usually in a caftan); artists Bea Kreloff and Edith Isaac-Rose (the first lesbians in my life); filmmaker Lilly

Rivlin—cousin of the current Israeli president, Reuven Rivlin, and the director of *Esther Broner: A Weave of Women*, a 2013 documentary that chronicles this seder's evolution.

But for reasons too complicated to enumerate here, one year the Seder Daughters were not included, and that sadly ended a precious tradition for me. I suppose I could have invented my own version as an adult, but life gets in the way.

When Esther Broner died in 2011, the eulogies at her memorial service resurrected her voice in my mind—her ability to make examination feel holy, her reflexive warmth.

This year's seder is a confirmation of her legacy, the fortieth celebration of the rite she conceived, led collaboratively by a smaller group of her devoted friends, including Rivlin; her sister, Dot; my mother; Canadian writer Michele Landsberg; Carol Jenkins, the former news anchor, now president of the Women's Media Center; Sue Leonard, editor of *Persimmon Tree*, which features the writing of women over sixty; Jewish Federation executive Anita Altman; classical pianist Gena Raps; and Esther's daughter, Nahama Broner, a professor of psychology who was always decidedly more hip than me and Robin (no Danskin pantsuits for Nahama).

Our host Sunday night is Barbara Kane, a psychoanalyst who, when she lost her husband to Lou Gehrig's disease—also known as ALS—in 1995, invited her close friend Esther Broner, and Robert Broner, Esther's artist husband, to move in with her. Bob's art is all over Barbara's walls. The framed work he created out of the Seder Sisters' list of "women's plagues" is an amalgam of words thrown out that particular year by participants: "exhaustion," "fear," "breast cancer," and "GW Bush."

After greetings and wine, Kane asks us to begin the seder out in her hallway. We crowd into the narrow space outside the front door and cease our kibitzing as Kane reads aloud some words she drafted on her iPhone:

Together we create this oasis, a space sacred in time. Let the magic begin. We who know the wound that never heals and the fire that never goes out come together this evening to help this strange seder story evolve, this odd story with its gaps and omissions. We will ask questions: important, even crucial ones. . . .

The twelve of us file into her apartment silently and take seats around Kane's large square coffee table, set elaborately with ceramic dishes, a copper seder plate, various individual candles, earth-colored cloth napkins encircled by delicate jungle-animal napkin rings, and bowls containing the requisite *haroset, maror,* matzah, and salt water.

As has been the custom for the past forty years, each woman introduces herself by her matrilineage, and it is unexpectedly powerful for me to invoke, for the first time, my teenage daughter: "I am Abigail, mother of Molly, daughter of Letty, daughter of Ceil, daughter of Jenny."

Rivlin asks us to "bring an invisible guest" to the table—a woman, living or dead, whom we wish could be present. Nahama Broner brings the unnamed women of the Exodus story—the female Hebrew slaves; the seven daughters of Midian (not sure who they are, but Midian is where Moses escaped after he killed an Egyptian slavemaster); the Israelite women who danced on the shores of the Red Sea. She also brings her own daughter, Alexandra, who is currently doing development work in Kenya and who dials in via Skype to greet everyone.

Landsberg brings Ernestine Rose, a little-known abolitionist and women's-rights pioneer of the nineteenth century, who felt alone as a Jewish atheist among Christian activists. Rose told her friend Susan B. Anthony in a letter, "I expect never to be understood while I live." That is a poignant quote to me, even taken out of context. It strikes me that this is something for which we all strive: to be understood.

My mother "brings" my late aunt Betty, who warmed to the women's movement after initially resisting it, and who eagerly participated in the Feminist Seder for years until she died in 2013. Anita Altman kindly adds her memory of meeting my aunt back in the nineties, just after Betty lost her son, my cousin Jeffrey, to AIDS, and had decided to become active in PFLAG—Parents, Families and Friends of Lesbians and Gays. Jeffrey was my introduction to male homosexuality, and, though I wasn't close to him, I will never forget Betty's agony and helplessness at losing him.

Kane's "invisible guest" is Sabina Spielrein, a patient of Carl Jung's who became his student and ultimately his colleague, one of the very first female psychoanalysts, though unsung to this day. She was killed by a Nazi death squad.

Jenkins brings her five-year-old granddaughter, who happens to love the opera, and who, during their recent excursion to *Aïda* (which includes slave characters), asked her African-American grandma, "What's slavery?" Jenkins said it was surreal to find herself explaining such a basic inhumanity to her progeny—"It's when someone owns another person and tells them what to do." That, by itself, was a profound evocation of the Exodus story.

After the blessing over the candles, we are asked to bless the woman to our right in some private way. My mother blesses me—a little overemotionally, but I can see it's sentimental for her to have one of her daughters back at this ceremony—and then I bless Kathleen Peratis, an attorney specializing in workplace discrimination and a writer who has taken many fact-finding trips to the West Bank and Gaza. I quietly thank her for the staunch friendship she's shown to Mom for decades, and also for her mettle; she asserts controversial opinions without any discernible fear—a courage I lack.

Peratis's charge Sunday night is to offer a modern interpretation of the seder plate. She says the scorched egg reminds us that "some of our dreams are toast," and the matzah symbolizes simplicity. She recently listened to a public radio interview with Bruce Kramer, an ALS patient who said his fatal disease "cured him of planning." Peratis pointed out that most of us are crazy planners and should remember, "All that really matters is simplicity." That kicks me in the head: all I seem to do is plan, and how would my days change if they had more space and spontaneity? It harkens back to my wrestling with Shabbat.

Sue Leonard uses the Ten Commandments to talk about the plight of public education.

Jenkins uses the fiftieth anniversary of the Selma march as a metaphor for coming out of the desert.

Mom asks us to take turns reading "The Ten Plagues According to Women," an essay she wrote back in 2010, wherein "beasts" are those who "attack women and children behind closed doors, some with mezuzot on their doorposts," and the ninth plague of darkness is the "dark hole in Jewish history" with too many women "unnamed, unseen, unrecognized."

I veer, as I often do, between feeling involved and like a spectator—admiring the fact that these women still call out injustices, but not galvanized to do more to correct those wrongs myself. I see the specters of sexism but don't experience most of them. The Four Questions are similarly more interesting than they are relatable:

Why is this Haggadah different from traditional Haggadot? Because this Haggadah deals with the exodus of women.

Why have our mothers on this night been bitter? Because they did the preparation but not the ritual. They did the serving but not the conducting. They read of their fathers but not of their mothers.

Three hours elapse as we discuss the seder symbols and pile our plates with Kane's delicious meal. It's nostalgic to be back in this group, but it doesn't feel like it used to. There's less anger now about the issues that persist; more weariness. The world is fairer, yes, but still not fair. Attitudes have evolved but are still hidebound. It's hard to regain the wonder of my childhood perspective.

The evening ends with my favorite rite—the draping of the so-called "Sacred Schmatta" (Yiddish for rag) around our shoulders—a chain of gauzy fabric, one piece tied crudely to the next, wrapped around our group like one continuous tallit, or prayer shawl.

"Wait a second," Mom says, puzzled. "This doesn't look like the original schmatta."

"It's not," Nahama Broner concedes as she sighs patiently and then explains, evidently for the umpteenth time, that she donated the wilted original to Brandeis University, whose library houses all of her mother's papers.

"I can get it back on loan if we want it next year," Broner offers.

"I think this replacement-schmatta is beautiful," Raps says. So we put our arms around each other, enfolded by the substitute schmatta, and sing Landsberg's version of "Dayenu" with verses such as this one:

If only Torah told the story
Of the women, gave them glory
If our mothers were remembered
Dayenu.

"Next year in Jerusalem" may mean this: Next year it's time for me and Robin to consider giving our daughters a tradition we didn't pass on, perhaps with a group of their peers. We could show them a ritual that dramatizes how often the story is incomplete, that women's "narrow places"—their "mitzrayim"—are not petty complaints, but urgent, persistent inequity; it's bolstering to be in a room of self-assured, introspective, unequivocally feminist women. It changes the conversation; it's a different kind of family.

The Seder Sisters include these words in their Haggadah as the evening comes to an end:

We end with grace
We greet the night
And the following dawn
In the bosom of friends
And a Seder of our own.

Rabbi Jacqueline Koch Ellenson
ON PASSOVER

What does it mean to have your heart open to another person who might be going through a difficult time? We translate this sense of mitzrayim, of Egypt, of this crowded space, squeezing under whatever is weighing us down, confining us. The seder is really about: What does it mean to appropriate all the pain in the world? What role do I have to play in alleviating it? Everyone at the seder has to do something. It's a great microcosm of participation. You cannot sit back in life, or at my seder. What needs to be fixed? What brokenness can motivate me?

Rabbi Joy Levitt
ON YOM HASHOAH

There's a way in which this act of naming the victims of the Holocaust feels like it is simply *kavod hamet*—the honor of the dead. That these people lived—had hopes and dreams and suffered and died. And they shouldn't be forgotten. And there's nobody to say their names in many, many cases. By reading the names, you give yourself an opportunity to sit with the tragedy of this. And the loss. And I think also the sense of responsibility to them—not only to remember, but to live. So on some level, it asks us to put aside the trivial concerns of our lives. I find—I know this sounds odd—but there's an uplifting quality to it. We recite mourner's Kaddish at 6 P.M. the next day. We don't do any liturgy . . . there isn't any prescribed liturgy because we didn't want to get into any of the issues that divide us as clergy. . . . All the issues that divide us weren't important. All we wanted to do was honor the names of these people.

"What I find interesting is that most of the must-do holidays are family-based. But Yom HaShoah is not about celebration, it's not about family, and it's not about us.

18

YOM HASHOAH

"We Did More Than Survive"

4.15.15

ACH STUDENT WALKS onstage holding the hand of the survivor whose biography he or she will recount. It is an unspoken promise from the child to the elder: I will tell your story. We are holding on— not just to history, but to you.

I am at the JCC in Manhattan at a performance called Witness Theater on the eve of Yom HaShoah, Holocaust Remembrance Day. Ten kids from two schools—Abraham Joshua Heschel and Trinity— have partnered with seven Holocaust survivors to dramatize their stories after months of interviews.

The seven narratives are each introduced with a brief, but shattering, slideshow: families smiling on boat trips, benches, front stoops, dressed in soft overcoats, painted in lipstick, holding babies aloft—all blissfully ignorant of the fate that awaits them.

An elegant woman on the stage named Betty, French-born and diminutive in her old age, has her story reenacted by a New York teenager in leggings, repeating the words Betty used when she beseeched her mother at five years old: "I want you to hide with me. I beg you."

The family threw their belongings into a truck to escape the Nazis. "We had to act like we were furniture in there," Betty recalls. No movement allowed. No sound. When she started audibly sucking her thumb, her family crossly silenced her. She was placed in a convent to keep her safe and missed her family terribly.

Another story is narrated: Natalie says no one in her town survived except her family.

Then Leon: he watched his brother get shot in front of him, solely because he reached for some ice to drink off the ground.

What boggles the mind, as it always does, is every survivor's main message: do not define us by this chapter. It was awful, yes, but it's not all there is. We did more in our lives than survive.

The students take turns placing handwritten signs on the stage floor to underscore this declaration. Each card displays one word, which gets spoken aloud by their older counterparts:

WRITER

MUSICIAN

COMEDIAN

GRANDMOTHER

BUSINESSWOMAN

INNOVATOR

"We should look at the people they were when they went in," Menachem Z. Rosensaft tells me on the phone. I called him after he sent me a galley of his 2014 book, *God, Faith and Identity from the Ashes: Reflections of Children and Grandchildren of Holocaust Survivors.* These wrenching stories are not just paradigms of endurance, but of positivity: *they lived more.* His parents survived Auschwitz, and he teaches about the law of genocide and war-crime trials at the law schools of Columbia and Cornell. "You focus on the fact that they did not allow themselves to be dehumanized, that poetry was still written, even in the camps. You look at the physical and the spiritual resistance. People rescuing others. Sharing rations with one another. Even in the worst period, even in the most dire moments."

His mother, a dentist who lost not only her parents, but also her first husband and their five-year-old son, Benjamin, managed to keep

149 children alive during a typhoid epidemic and brutal winter. Rosensaft's father, who narrowly escaped death multiple times, emerged after liberation as the leader of the survivors of Bergen-Belsen, representing them in a displaced-persons camp. "You have to look at what happened afterward," says Rosensaft. "History doesn't end in 1945; it goes on."

Recovery and reinvention, he says, can be beacons for victims of more recent horrors, from Bosnia to Syria to Boko Haram. "Rather than turning away from humankind and giving up on life, if the survivors of the Holocaust, in the days, months, and years after their liberation decided to rebuild their lives, to build new families, learn new languages, and start anew—whether it be in the United States, Israel, or Canada—and if their children or grandchildren within their generations are at the top of their professions in their fields of endeavor, then that is an inspiration to victims of other genocides and atrocities."

I ask Rosensaft whether he's perturbed by the idea that Holocaust remembrance gets just one official day. "There are going to be people who check the box. But even that is better than not doing anything at all. I view Yom HaShoah as an important reminder of what we have to do the rest of the year," Rosensaft says. "We stand and think back and say a communal Kaddish. But afterward, I would have to say, 'What are we going to do with those thoughts we had? What are we going to do tomorrow?'"

What is my answer? It's yet another referendum on personal paralysis: I care profoundly, but I don't act. I think about the Holocaust often, but I don't teach its hard history to those who I think may not have been taught. I don't revisit the survivors' memoirs that were painful the first time. I don't apply the war's lessons to helping refugees of today. I mourn without acting.

When I started researching Yom HaShoah, I assumed that, despite our people's penchant for dispute, this holiday would be uncontroversial. Who could argue that The Six Million don't deserve a separate day of remembrance? But argue Jews did. When Israel decided in 1948 to pick a date for memorial, it wasn't simple. Zionists who had been part of the underground Nazi resistance during the war wanted Yom HaShoah to fall on the anniversary of the Warsaw ghetto uprising—April 19—so that it would honor Jews' *strength*, not just their execution. Orthodox Israelis said it was wrong to create a day of mourning so close to Passover, a time that is supposed to be joyful. Some said Yom HaShoah should be folded into the *existing*, solemn day of remembrance, Tisha B'Av, which falls in the summer and marks the Temple's destruction and all our persecutions. Today, many ultra-Orthodox Jews still hold that view.

In 1953, after two years of argument in the Knesset, President David Ben-Gurion found a middle ground: Yom HaShoah would fall on the 27th of Nissan—not too close to Passover, but not on Tisha B'Av either. In Israel, every year on Yom HaShoah at 10 A.M. the air raid sirens wail with chilling volume and everything stops—traffic, commerce, conversations. It's an arresting portrait (which I've only witnessed on YouTube): the world halts for two minutes of frozen tribute. Dr. Yehuda Kurtzer, president of the Shalom Hartman Institute of North America, likens it to "a modern take on the shofar blowing; it reorients you." I find it totally affecting, not because I've been to Israel so many times (only twice), but because it's breathtaking to watch a nation stop for memory.

Though Yom HaShoah is a creation of the Israeli government, it is marked around the world, often with events that include a survivor's story. When I was looking for Manhattan commemorations, I came across the "Witness Theater" project and the "Reading and Hearing of the Names"—conceived by B'nai Jeshurun in 1995 and expanded in 1998 by the JCC in Manhattan. The JCC now coordinates every synagogue on the Upper West Side, across denominations, to read names of Holocaust victims from ten in the evening to seven the next morning. It continues the next day at the JCC building itself, from 9:00 A.M. to 7:00 P.M.

"What's stunning," says Rabbi Joy Levitt, the JCC's executive director, "is that I've been doing this for seventeen years, and we're not even a fraction of the way through the names we gathered from Yad

Vashem [the official Holocaust museum in Jerusalem], which obviously don't include all six million." The names are organized by country. "I remember that it took us four years just to read through the Jews of Belgium," she notes.

I struggle, as I'm sure every person has, to confront the truth without becoming unhinged by it, to make myself a student of this horror because it seems like the least I can do. But mostly, I end up feeling the weight of inadequacy: What does learning and lamentation really accomplish? Is it not somewhat self-serving to show up, hear names, and go home to bed, just to ease my impotence?

I answer myself: you don't matter; *they* do. Your task is to help remind the world that they were here. So at least I can read some names aloud. I decide to go.

I ask Levitt, who has been a reader every year for almost two decades, what the experience feels like. "Two things have struck me especially," she answers. "I'm sometimes suddenly aware that what I'm reading are the names of one entire family. You can't be a hundred percent sure, but you have the feeling, partly because we see the ages of the people who've died. That's overwhelming." This pulls me up short—the realization that those names could have been my family's if we'd lived then; it could have been all of us, consecutively itemized on a page tonight.

"The second thing that produces a lot of anxiety for me," Levitt continues, "is that the names are really hard to pronounce. You're talking about Russian names, Hungarian, Polish—languages that we are not that familiar with and where the spellings aren't Americanized. When I was a congregational rabbi, one of the things that mattered most to me when I would do a funeral is to make sure I got the name right. I would go over and over it before the eulogy. It felt to me so critical to pronounce someone's name accurately. And in the room, if you get it wrong, it feels so . . . disrespectful in a very profound way. But it's really hard to get these names right. And I ask myself, is it better to try and do the best you can? Or have we just botched it? I've decided that it's better to try. And that the intention of getting it right has to get me through it."

I ask her to respond to those who might contend that reading name after name for hours and hours is a morbid exercise that can *lose* meaning rather than heighten it. "It doesn't feel morbid, actually," Levitt counters. "It feels deeply respectful. And it connects us. It is a way of saying 'This is our family too.'"

There is always a JCC staff member present while the names are spoken, even in the wee hours of the morning when there are only two or three others in the sanctuary. It reminds me of *shemira*, the Jewish ritual of watching over a dead body from the time of death until burial, and I'm moved by that idea, that we stand sentinel for each other.

But this naming of the names has not become widespread, powerful as it is. Many rabbis tell me that because Yom HaShoah has no liturgy, blessings, or agreed-upon ceremony, the modern holiday has yet to take root, remaining precarious in the sense that it could ultimately fall away.

"Nothing in Jewish history is remembered without ritual," Rabbi Avi Weiss wrote in the *Huffington Post* in 2014. (Weiss is considered a founding father of "Open Orthodoxy"—a progressive approach to Orthodox Judaism.) "If Shoah memory is not ritualized, the Shoah will be relegated to a footnote in Jewish history."

In 2012, he created a Yom HaShoah Haggadah called "The Third Seder," in which the Holocaust gets its own ritualized dramatization, just as we are supposed to revisit the Exodus story on Passover. Weiss writes: "It's based on the Haggadah's dictum: *bechol dor va'dor chayav adam lirot et atzmo* . . . 'In every generation we must tell the story as if it happened to us.'"

He explains what can take place during this invented saeder: "We reenact the Shoah," he says. "Numbers are stamped on our arms, symbolizing physical destruction; the Hebrew alphabet, aleph bet, is burned, symbolizing spiritual devastation; children separate from their parents and walk to a roped-off area, symbolizing the million and a half children murdered during the Shoah."

To those who would say that it's trivializing to step into the shoes of survivors, Weiss counters that it keeps their stories exigent and vivid. "Unless all of us recite and reenact the narrative as if we were there, the Shoah will be forgotten," he said.

It's hard for me to imagine stamping numbers on my arms or separating from my kids to try to identify with the Holocaust. Maybe if Rabbi Weiss was in my living room, I could hazard this, because he has a reassuring, sagacious manner and feels like everyone's grandfather. But I flinch at the idea of letting families navigate reenactment on our own. The potential for mockery seems perilous.

But Weiss is not the only eminent rabbi who believes that, if we don't find ways to own Yom HaShoah more boldly, it won't hold. Dr. Yehuda Kurtzer ventures into what he knows is delicate territory. "I've been trying to push for ways to make Yom HaShoah look a little more like Pesach," he says, "where we are a little less concerned about the actual details of the perpetration of the Holocaust and much more interested in becoming narrators and participants in this drama, where we can see ourselves as having come out of Auschwitz."

We should really see ourselves as survivors?

"It's a very hard thing to talk about publicly, because the generation of survivors is still around and it's great chutzpah to say to people, 'I'm going to now reenact your story while you're still alive.' So I'm cautious about it. I think it may only make sense in twenty to thirty years, when you no longer have a generation of survivors around. But at a certain point, we are going to have to make a switch as a people, from thinking about this as an *historical* day to thinking about it as a *Jewish* day. I don't think we've really done it."

I grasp his point: if we depend on survivors to tell the story, the story won't outlast the survivors. And it may just be true that only when the survivors are all gone—sadly, in the not-too-distant future—will every Jew begin to personalize this history and holiday.

"At the risk of a very dangerous analogy," Kurtzer says, "the Israelites don't retell the Exodus from Egypt until they go into the Promised Land, when the whole generation of those who came out of Egypt *aren't there anymore*. I think something like that needs to happen with the Shoah, where we start telling the story as if it's our story."

But it still seems to me sacrilege for us to become the tellers ourselves. We can, and should, relate the grim events, but who are we to relive them?

"It may be too soon," Kurtzer concedes, "and it may feel a little bit too raw to do that; but I think we're sitting right now on the cusp of a generation that's going to have to decide to commit to that story."

Whether or not I'll be committed to observing Yom HaShoah every year, I am committed to helping protect and perpetuate this story. Many rabbis emphasize that the Holocaust can't be the organizing principle of our Judaism, and it isn't mine. But it is, to me, just as essential a narrative for Jews as escaping slavery. And just as we retell the Exodus every year, it seems clear that we should also retell the Shoah.

The BJ sanctuary at 10:15 P.M. is darkened and hushed. I walk in and take a seat. There is just a smattering of people at 10 P.M.; I recognize only the clergy.

BJ member Myriam Abramowicz, a filmmaker and daughter of survivors who conceived of this ritual, orchestrates it with brisk authority. I watch her unobtrusively guiding the line of volunteers waiting to read the lists. Every participating shul is given a half-hour slot to read aloud by the flickering light of six candles, one for each million lost.

It is my turn at the table with the large book in front of me, and Myriam points to the place to start, as she did with every volunteer, just as the rabbi or cantor points to the right place in the Torah scroll on Shabbat morning.

I feel the weight and sanctity of this task, but panic when I encounter the font size.

"I'm sorry. I can't see it," I say to no one in particular, walking hurriedly back to the seats. I'm disappointed. Ashamed. Though I'm not the only one who has trouble with the small print (the man ahead of me also demurred when he couldn't make out the ink), I feel like I've failed at my slight contribution to memory.

Miryam sees that some of us have struggled, and brings over another book with larger lettering. But, by that point, I am back in my chair and decide it would be selfish to return to the line. Everything feels sensitive to me in that sanctuary—fragile, sorrowful. I do not want to misstep.

So I just sit and listen: to name after name after name—all from Lithuania, which lost 90 percent of its Jewish population, one of the largest swaths of devastation.

Anya . . . Sacha . . . Ingrida . . . Bernard . . . Esther. . . .

I can't help but think about the last time I was in BJ's sanctuary; it was the antithesis of this scene, the raucous celebration of Simchat Torah in October, when giddy hordes danced with the Torah scrolls to music playing without pause, also late into the night. However obvious, it is still beautiful to me that our tradition holds the two extremes in every holiday cycle of the year: boundless joy and bottomless grief.

"Shoah" literally means "catastrophe" and "whirlwind." A whirlwind can't be pinned down. A catastrophe can't be compressed. For understandable reasons, the Holocaust has become untouchable, impossible to synopsize or adequately revisit. I was aware, going into Yom HaShoah, of all the critiques around commemoration: the history's Hollywoodization, the commercialization of Anne Frank, the anger at the notion that twenty-four hours could ever do it justice. But this modern holiday exists, and though I failed it, I marked it. I hope, at least, that's something.

Rabbi Yitz Greenberg
ON YOM HASHOAH

Yom HaShoah ended up in a week in Nissan—supposed to be a month of joy—despite the opposition of traditional Jews who said this is a violation of tradition. They understood that the joy of Nissan *should* be violated, or put another way, as I say it, it should be wounded. In some way, you are acknowledging that victory, joy, and celebration have been wounded by such a disaster. On the other hand, a week later comes Israel Independence Day, and to me there could be no more remarkable statement than the Jewish religion's belief that love is stronger than death. It also implies that life is stronger than death. The way the Jewish people have proven that has been in its history.

Whenever people face catastrophe, they wrestle with this question: Are the good guys or the bad guys going to win? Judaism insists that the good guys are going to win in the end. That's our message. Don't give in when bad guys win. Don't give in to catastrophe.

Rabbi Elliot Cosgrove
ON YOM HA'ATZMAUT

As a liberal, egalitarian pluralistic rabbi, I certainly have concerns about whether the Judaism I preach and practice is recognized in Israel. About whether or not Israel is going to be able to thread the needle of being a Jewish and democratic state into the generation to come. These are growing pains of a young state. The condition of the contemporary diaspora Jew is an unprecedented condition in Jewish history—to pray for, to live in the company of a modern state of Israel but not live there, is a state of affairs that our forebears couldn't imagine. So we in the diaspora are trying to figure out what that means. To love, care for, and engage with Israel, but at the same time not actually live there? That's a struggle.

The State of Israel teaches that we can grab ahold of a historic opportunity to author our own narrative as a people. We haven't yet had the opportunity to mythologize the events of the twentieth century, the creation of the State of Israel. I'm fully confident, with the passage of time, we will. The generation following the Exodus wasn't attuned to the miracle of the Exodus that they themselves experienced. We celebrate Passover now, but I imagine the intergenerational dialogue between the children and grandchildren of Moses's generation, saying, "These kids just don't get what we went through when we crossed the sea." So this is not new. I think it's incumbent among contemporary religious leadership to do exactly to the events of the twentieth century what our forebears did to the Passover story.

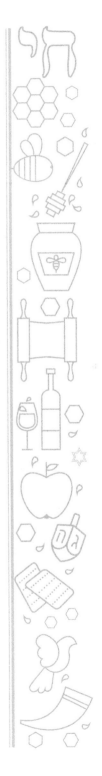

19

YOM HAZIKARON & YOM HA'ATZMAUT

For the Fallen and the Free—
Israel's Memorial & Independence Days

4.22.15 and 4.23.15

S AN Diego native Marla Bennett died at age twenty-four in a school cafeteria in Jerusalem.

She was killed in 2002 in a terrorist bombing by Hamas at Hebrew University, where she was pursuing an advanced degree in Judaic Studies. Nine people died, including five Americans. Nearly a hundred were injured.

"The year that followed was one of mourning, of crying out in agony, of grasping for ghosts," writes Michael Simon, who was Bennett's serious boyfriend when she died, "a year of searching for Marla, though she could not be found."

I contact Simon because I know he's known loss and this day is all about the lost. Now the Hillel Director at Northwestern University, Simon personalizes Yom HaZikaron—Israel's Memorial Day for fallen soldiers and victims of terror, which was created in 1963 and, this year, lands on Wednesday, April 22. I met Simon back in 2005, when I spoke at Harvard Hillel, where he was then the director, and he told me then about Marla while he was driving me back to the train station. He clearly couldn't help talking about her, and I won't forget how the story spilled out to a stranger: terrible and urgent. So when I learned this year that Yom HaZikaron is not only about dead IDF soldiers but about noncombatants, too—bystanders of terror—I call Simon. And Marla's story becomes my personal Polaroid for this holiday, since I know no war casualties myself.

"Marla's name is up on the wall on Har Herzl," Simon tells me, referring to Mount Herzl—also known as Har HaZikaron (Mount of Remembrance). "There's a wall with a couple thousand names. And it sadly continues to add more."

Names and names, again. One week ago, I was hearing the names of the Holocaust dead. Jews keep adding and reading names. The lost are consistently brought back into the room.

This time it's those who died for a country that became every Jew's automatic, international refuge. This is a holiday for Israel's fighters, whether they chose to wear the uniform or were accidental soldiers such as Marla Bennett.

Yom HaZikaron honors those who died *in* Israel *for* Israel, the tiny country that might have saved all those Jews whom we just honored on Yom HaShoah, the same nation that was forged before there was any concept of a Holocaust, when the Jewish land was a miracle of cultivation, innovation, pluck, and possibility. This is a holiday that salutes a nation I want defended.

So many have written about Israel's sunlight. The way it hits the Jerusalem stone and terraced hills. During Central's family trip in 2012, I saw what the poets wax lyrical about, the light's particular gold. I didn't expect to feel connected to the country right away. Looking back on that ten-day trip—the ruggedness of the landscape, the boisterousness of our tour bus, the rarity of having my clergy (Rubinstein and Buchdahl) escorting us, adding depth and devoutness—I realize now that ours was, in many ways, an itinerary for Yom HaZikaron—for memorial. Masada, where hundreds of Jews reportedly took their own lives rather than be killed by the Roman army; Yad Vashem, which harrowingly chronicles the Holocaust; Kinneret Cemetery, where my kids watched Rabbi Rubinstein stand by the headstones of Zionist pioneers and the grave of Naomi Shermer, the songwriter whose songs include "Al Kol Eleh," which brought our congregation to tears when Rabbi Buchdahl sang it on Yom Kippur. Our tour guide also called attention to the resting place of Rachel Bluwstein, considered a "founding mother" of Modern Hebrew poetry, born in 1890. Her poem "My Dead" captures an idea that glimmers on this holiday: Israel carries its lost, and so should we.

> They alone are left me, they are with me still, / In whom death's sharp knife has nothing left to kill. / At the turn of highways, when the sun is low, / They come round in silence, going where I go.

They go where I go. This holiday reminds me that the dead go with us. That's a lesson for this entire year: we are shaped by those who have fallen. Whether it be Gedaliah or my father-in-law, Milt. We carry them all.

Though Bennett's death devastated Simon, he managed to build a new, full life in its aftermath. He married Claire Sufrin, whom he met in Jerusalem four years later, and who now also works at Northwestern, as a professor of Jewish Studies. They have adorable children who smile in pictures on Facebook and likely haven't been told of the weight their father bears.

But his grief on this holiday goes beyond Marla. Just before Simon met Sufrin, he lost one of the students for whom he'd been a camp counselor in Israel. Yotam Gilboa was a twenty-one-year-old IDF soldier when he was killed in Lebanon in July 2006. "So I feel very connected to Yom HaZikaron," Simon says quietly in our phone call. "Because of those experiences, you get a tiny taste of what it's like. . . . I'm not Israeli, but I think I've had a taste. People I loved were killed. This is the price that is unfortunately necessary to enable there to be a state."

Simon highlights the coupling that these holidays drive home: nation-building and mourning. To build a state is to lose people. Israel's Memorial Day will be followed the next day by Independence Day.

Commemoration is followed by celebration. Yom HaZikaron by Yom Ha'Atzmaut.

Jerusalem-based journalist Judy Lash Balint in 2013 wrote of the about-face between holidays as they're observed in Israel: "As the congregations pour out onto the street, it's as if a cork has been released from a bottle—all the pent-up feelings from the difficult day of remembrance give way to celebration of our continued existence in this land."

Simon says it's not just the sharp turn from grief to pride; the two are inextricable. "Israel cannot have one without the other—Yom Ha'atzmaut without Yom HaZikaron," Simon says. "The State of Israel doesn't exist in a vacuum; it's not just celebration."

"Not just celebration," indeed. Israel is too complicated, especially in this moment when world criticism has reached a crescendo, when the Obama-Netanyahu relationship is strained, when there are internal tensions between the Israeli Orthodox and the secular. It's hard to ignore concerns that Israel is losing its Democratic ideals, about rising anti-Semitism in Europe, about the widening cleft between Jews and Arabs, more gaping this year thanks to the summer 2014 war in Gaza and friction on campuses such as Simon's.

I thought my holiday tour could dodge the quagmire of Israeli politics, but that's impossible when one approaches these modern milestones; Yom HaZikaron honors the IDF kids (I consider nineteen-year-olds to be kids, since my son is nearly that age) who made the greatest sacrifice in the prime of their lives; it brings back horrific terrorist attacks, which summon Orthodox ambulance workers to painstakingly collect body parts and spilled blood so that victims' families can conduct proper Jewish burials. Yom Ha'atzmaut honors the historic birth of an improbable state, the necessary and unnecessary bloodshed to create and protect that nation, the need for safe harbor, the spotlight on humane governance, the responsibilities that come with survival and sovereignty.

Many of Simon's Hillel students struggle with these holidays. "What's been more personally intense right now," says Simon, "more than my own story, is watching our students grappling with the question of, 'How do we properly embrace Israel without triumphalism, without exposing ourselves to being criticized for celebrating Israel without thoughtfulness about the challenges Israel faces or the things Israel does?' When you pair Independence Day with Yom HaZikaron, Memorial Day, even the story itself isn't just, 'Yay, it's a miracle we are here,' but, 'Here's the price that was paid not only to create the state, but that continues to be paid.'"

In February 2015, after impassioned debate and a close vote, Northwestern's student government passed a resolution asking the university to divest from six corporations that, according to the resolution's sponsors, violate Palestinians' human rights. The vote was largely symbolic, but it highlighted the fault lines between Jewish students and minority groups on campus whom Simon once considered close partners.

"You had some of our Hillel students saying, 'Wait a minute, why did we lose our natural allies?'" says Simon. "The African-American students with whom we've done Black Freedom Seders for the past ten years, the Latino group with whom we did a 'bat mitzvahñeria' the last two years—that's a combined bat mitzvah and quinceañeria program that brought the two groups together culturally."

I can't help but personalize his campus update, as my son is going off to Northwestern in the fall of 2015. I don't worry so much about Ben's identity being shaken by controversy, but I do worry that it's become almost politically incorrect to celebrate Israel's founding at all.

"I'm so glad our students are reflective about how to celebrate Yom Ha'atzmaut sensitively," says Simon; "but on the other hand, the idea that before we do anything, we have to worry about how we're perceived, that we're unsure whether we can have an Israel celebration—I wouldn't say it's chilling, but I would say it's concerning."

Simon tells me that one way he plans to observe the holiday is by participating in a public reading of Israel's Declaration of Independence. I like that idea. It's not active, but it's focusing, as if to remind us of the original point. *Remember what this state was built to become—to stand for.* It's embarrassing to realize that I never read the 1948 language before.

"THE STATE OF ISRAEL . . . will be based on freedom, justice, and peace as envisaged by the prophets of Israel; it will ensure complete equality of social and political rights to all its inhabitants irrespective of religion, race, or sex; it will guarantee freedom of religion, conscience, language, education, and culture. . . ."

It stirs the way the American Declaration stirs: because of its indisputable aspirations. The words make me imagine the back-room discussions of Israel's parents, how they must have debated the language for a nation's character. What kind of society are we building? Who should we be? I can't begin to parse whether we are indeed what the founders envisioned. Or whether I even see myself in the "we" I just used; am I Israel, too? Is Israel mine? I don't feel the ownership that many do; I haven't been there enough, I didn't work on a kibbutz or visit long enough to pick a favorite café or be able to explain the Knesset factions. But Israel does feel essential to me. Ineffably and existentially vital. And yes, miraculous, despite its shortcomings. And I've come to realize that the country represents me, whether I want it to or not. It's a signifier for Jews in the world, and I'm one of them. So I need to pay attention to this small-but-powerful place. And to the words that shaped and continue to shape it.

That's all I've come up with for this holiday in terms of what to do: read the blueprint. I plan to discuss this document with my teenage son and daughter when they get home from school on Thursday, even if it annoys them. And on April 22, 2015, the eve of Independence Day, I'll attend the "Community Celebration" at Park Avenue Synagogue, a gathering of Upper East Side rabbis and congregations, organized by the Jewish National Fund; it is clearly a concerted effort to make Yom Ha'atzmaut sing and make it stick. These modern holidays may just be too modern for us; we have no history or connection with either one. No routine. Yom HaZikaron and Ha'atzmaut still feel forced in America.

"I think these holidays are both failures in American Jewish life," says another Hillel veteran, UCLA'S Rabbi Chaim Seidler-Feller, who lectures in sociology and Near Eastern languages and cultures. "These holidays haven't reached or achieved that sense of sanctification. And one of the reasons for that is that there's no home ritual associated with either one of them. There's no Jewish holiday that can survive without a table."

He's right. I'm having trouble knowing how to mark these modern holidays without a meal. And he's duly pessimistic about how these table-less holidays will ever really resound in the United States. "There is an experience—a lived experience—that makes those days more immediate for Israelis. . . . It's a cycle from destruction to rebirth, and it's alive for Israelis in ways that are a bit distant for younger American Jews."

What makes it less distant is Marla Bennett. One person. Who should still be on this earth. Gone almost thirteen years as I write this.

In her essay, published just before her death by the *Jewish Journal of San Diego*, she described her new life in Jerusalem: "Just a month after I arrived, the current 'intifada' began. . . . I am extremely cautious about where I go and when; I avoid crowded areas and alter my routine when I feel at all threatened. But I also feel energized by the opportunity to support Israel during a difficult period. . . . Life here is magical."

On the eve of Yom Ha'atzmaut, Israel's Independence Day, I'm sitting under a cascade of blue and white balloons, Israel's colors, as they rain down from the balcony at Park Avenue Synagogue and cantors sing a medley of Israeli anthems, including "Jerusalem of Gold" and "Al Kol Eileh." Representatives from Jewish organizations each read sixty-seven words about Israel in honor of its sixty-seventh year. Black-and-white newsreels are shown, featuring Israel's prime minister, David Ben-Gurion, as he signs Israel's seminal Declaration of Independence. His description of the scene before he left home for the signing ceremony is moving.

"*The Jews of Palestine . . . were dancing because they were about to realize what was one of the most remarkable and inspiring achievements in human history: a people which had been exiled from its homeland two thousand*

years before, which had endured countless pogroms, expulsions, and persecu-
tions, but which had refused to relinquish its identity—which had, on the
contrary, substantially strengthened that identity; a people which only a few
years before had been the victim of mankind's largest single act of mass mur-
der, killing a third of the world's Jews, that people was returning home as
sovereign citizens in their own independent state."

Elliot Cosgrove, Park Avenue's popular Senior Rabbi, tells me how strongly he feels that all three modern holidays—Holocaust Remembrance Day, Israel's Memorial Day, and Independence Day—deserve more prominence. "This week is not just another week in the Jewish calendar," he says. "It frames contemporary Jewish identity." Thus, despite the hazards of discussing Israel publicly, he'll never stop. "For me not to speak about Israel from the pulpit would be akin to me not talking about Shabbat or kashrut or any aspect of Jewish life and living," he says. "That said, of course, like every congregational rabbi, I'm the rabbi to the red state and the blue state Jews. But I don't see that as an impediment, I see that as an opportunity: How does one construct a message about Israel which is unflinching in its support of the state but has eyes wide open to the challenges and pitfalls facing our moment in time?"

Despite my own Israel brain-fatigue, the experience of watching eleven rabbis, from varying threads of worship, reading aloud the Declaration of Independence isn't complicated. It's powerful. Watching the cantors sing Israel's national anthem is also uncomplicated. Their voices fill the sanctuary, led by Park Avenue's effective senior cantor, the Israeli-born Azi Schwartz, who himself served in the IDF.

"Our hope is not yet lost, / The hope of two thousand years, / To be a free people in our land. . . ."

Those words of "Hatikvah," which were written as a poem in 1886—before there was a state—seem, like the blue and white balloons that fell earlier, somehow innocent: unfreighted, optimistic, wholly unlike the public discourse of today.

"Yom Ha'atzmaut has raised issues for people for numbers of years," says Seidler-Feller, "but I must say, the State of Israel has a sense of restraint and perspective. The country abandoned the militaristic state parades they used to do with their hardware. That's a statement. Independence Day is not about fighting. It's not about victory. It's about values. It's about what we've achieved. Birthdays are days for taking stock."

20

LAG B'OMER
R-E-S-P-E-C-T
5.6.15

T HIS IS THE holiday that could finally stump me. I've barely heard of the Omer, other than the phrase "Counting the Omer," though I never knew what we were counting.

Now I see the Omer is the forty-nine days from the second day of Passover to the eve of Shavuot (which is the holiday that marks the giving of the Torah).

We're also counting the forty-nine days from the start of the barley harvest, when people would bring a sheaf of the newly harvested grain to the Temple to thank God. An "omer" is a sheaf (some say a certain measure) of grain. This holiday is the thirty-third day of the forty-nine. Lag B'Omer, translated literally, means: thirty-third day of the Omer.

That's all I got.

So with that blank slate, I delve into the backstory and stumble into meaning along the way. If I've learned anything this year, it's that resonance affixes itself to a holiday depending on what's happening in your life. Yom Kippur took on a strange poignancy because Ben was applying to college. Hanukkah candles flickered differently because we were losing Milt. The Fast of Esther became a referendum on whether I had the nerve to sign on for the shul presidency. What will emerge as Lag B'Omer's news peg? Robin and I just celebrated a "significant" birthday. My close friend Michael is marrying his longtime partner, Daniel, in a Jewish ceremony on the day the Omer ends. Two days later, Molly will join thirty-five fellow tenth-graders for Central's confirmation service—the ceremony that signifies the next step for a teenage Jew.

I'm not sure where I'll find the holiday hook, but then it appears; what at first had seemed like forced pertinence becomes pertinent, at least to me.

But first the legend that underpins the holiday: in the second century, 24,000 students who studied with the famed Rabbi Akiva (venerated because he learned Torah late in life, yet mastered it) were killed by a vicious plague.

What sin made Akiva's students deserve such a wipeout? "They did not treat each other with respect." That's the sole explanation in the Talmud.

Really? That's it? I mean, disrespect is bad, but a capital offense? I'm intrigued. Before investigating any further, I pause to appreciate the idea that Judaism might take mutual respect *that* seriously. The website Kabbalah.info sums it up without mitigation: "Kabbalists saw [the students'] plague as a result of their growing egoism, which led them to unfounded hatred. This was the opposite of their teacher's rule, 'Love thy friend as thyself.'"

They ignored their teacher's golden rule and died for it.

But what do 24,000 dead Akiva students have to do with Lag B'Omer? Answer: the holiday marks the *end* of the plague that killed them, and also heralds the *yartzheit* (death anniversary) of Rabbi Shimon Bar Yochai, one of Akiva's new crop of students, a group that turned out some of the greatest rabbis of the next generation.

The fact that Shimon Bar Yochai, or "Rashbi," as he's known, was taken on as a new student must, in some part, be due to his respect for fellow Jews. The nice guy did not suffer the same fate as his selfish predecessors. That's a moral many would hold up today.

And then, by chance, I'm asked to write a blessing for Michael and Daniel's wedding. A blessing for laughter. The grooms have asked seven close friends to compose seven homemade blessings to be recited before their vows—one for creativity, one for honesty, one for adventure, etc. Their wedding lands on the last day of the Omer—on Shavuot, when weddings are technically not supposed to take place because it constitutes mixing one joy with another, which is forbidden on any *Yom Tov*—biblical holiday.

But my friends' nonconformity feels fitting: they will stand under the huppah on Shavuot when Orthodox weddings are verboten; they are two men taking vows when gay marriage was recently unthinkable and remains unsanctioned by Orthodox Judaism. They are defying traditions, yet also embracing them. And they represent, for me, the kind of respect that's often missing: for individual choices. For difference. For one another. That's my Lag B'Omer spark, as far-flung as it may seem.

And in odd symmetry, just a week before this holiday, gay marriage is debated before the Supreme Court in a landmark case, *Obergefell v. Hodges*. As I scroll through Facebook's proverbial town square, a Reform rabbi has posted a brusque document I've never seen before: the 2011 *Declaration on the Torah Approach to Homosexuality*, which says gay children are victims of "emotional wounds" and should receive psychological help to eschew sin and return to God. It was signed by more than a hundred Orthodox rabbis, including several esteemed faculty at New York's Yeshiva University.

"We emphatically reject the notion that a homosexually inclined person cannot overcome his or her inclination and desire. Behaviors are changeable. The Torah does not forbid something which is impossible to avoid. Abandoning people to lifelong loneliness and despair by denying all hope of overcoming and healing their same-sex attraction is heartlessly cruel."

It is this document, in my view, that reads as "heartlessly cruel," echoing exactly the ancient error of Akiva's students: profound disrespect, forgetting Akiva's teaching to "*love thy friend as thyself.*"

I learn that this statement was written in reaction to a much more compassionate one in 2010—the "Statement of Principles," considered at the time to be a major step for the Orthodox community, signed by a different list of a hundred-plus Orthodox rabbis:

All human beings are created in the image of God and deserve to be treated with dignity and respect (kevod haberiyot). . . . Embarrassing, harassing, or demeaning someone with a homosexual orientation or same-sex attraction is a violation of Torah prohibitions that embody the deepest values of Judaism.

But it fell short of full tolerance:

Halakhah [Jewish law] *sees heterosexual marriage as the ideal model and sole legitimate outlet for human sexual expression. . . . Halakhic Judaism views all male and female same-sex sexual interactions as prohibited. . . . But it is critical to emphasize that halakhah only prohibits homosexual acts; it does not prohibit orientation or feelings of same-sex attraction, and nothing in the Torah devalues the human beings who struggle with them.*

For this wondering Jew—trying always to find the current idea in the ancient story, these two statements exemplify modern tensions around respect.

The rules of Lag B'Omer require us to suspend marriages and all happy occasions starting on Passover until the thirty-third day of the Omer. No joy is allowed during that time because we are supposedly in mourning for Akiva's students. That extended "shiva" lifts on Lag B'Omer. All picnics, live music, haircuts, and weddings may recommence on this holiday.

But when that Torah Declaration appears on my Facebook stream just four days before nuptials can resume, I can't help but think about the prejudices still ingrained and the gay marriages still prohibited. Some might say the sin of disrespect is doomed to repeat itself.

I compose my blessing for Michael and Daniel: "May you laugh in that particular way you laugh together—not just the chuckles but the doubled-over, not-breathing variety. May you remember—especially when there are hurdles, how easily you make each other smile, how uniquely you let each other be your silliest selves, how your sons make you beam. . . ."

Marriage is on my brain, true, but it's also in the holiday's DNA. I follow the crumbs that Rashbi left. I have to trace the wedding trail, and hope I don't lose you:

The anniversary of Rashbi's death, celebrated on Lag B'Omer, is called a *Hillula*, which means "wedding celebration." That's because Rashbi announced that when he died, he would *marry God*. More specifically: he'd wed the *feminine* aspect of God—the "shekhinah."

The emphasis on God's feminine nature, a radical idea when it was introduced in the Middle Ages, first gets explored in detail in the Zohar, the mystical Torah commentary that is the chief text of Kabbalism—Jewish mysticism. Rashbi, one of Akiva's students, is said to be the Zohar's composer, but the byline belongs to a rabbi named Moses de Leon in thirteenth-century Spain, whom I'm not going to go into because he would be one too many characters to keep straight. Since Rashbi is the primary rabbinic figure who appears in the Zohar, heading a group of fellow rabbi-mystics, the myth endures that he's the author, and that he revealed its "deepest" secrets on the day he died, the day he wed God.

To understand the Zohar (which I don't), I turn to the expert: Kabbalah scholar Daniel Matt, based in Berkeley, California, who has devoted eighteen years to translating the Zohar from the Aramaic to the English, with elucidating commentary and a ton of patience. He is currently completing the ninth volume of his series, *The Zohar: Pritzker Edition.*

"Rashbi sees his own death as his union with the shekhinah," Matt explains in scholarly, calming tones. "He said, 'I see God is coming and the souls of the righteous are coming and they're all coming here to participate in my hillula.'"

Rashbi's marrying God means the righteous can, too. It appears that "the righteous"—those who do good deeds, follow the commandments (mitzvot), and live ethically—are the ones who get to walk down the symbolic aisle with God. "By performing the mitzvot," says Matt, "we stimulate the divine union."

Put plainly: if you're good, you get to marry God, too.

I protest to Matt on the phone: Does God, masculine or feminine, really *need* us in marriage or partnership?

Yes. To borrow from *Jerry Maguire*, we complete God. Says Matt, "The Zohar's notion is that God cannot be whole or manifested in the world without human ethical behavior—living virtuously. That's one of its main teachings."

It reminds me of the Passover discussion about Elijah, the prophet—how he needs our participation to repair the world. We open the door at the end of the seder to symbolically usher in the Messianic time; Elijah can't achieve it without us. Similarly, in this holiday, God needs the righteous (i.e., Rashbi), those who understand mutual respect, to partner and complete creation.

But was Rashbi righteous? Rabbi Jill Jacobs, executive director of the Manhattan-based T'ruah, which organizes rabbis and cantors on behalf of human rights, tells me the story of Rashbi in the cave, which reveals a darker side of the hero of Lag B'Omer, Akiva's respectful student.

Here's the Talmudic legend (it's another detour, but worth it): Rashbi was dismissive of the accomplishments of the Roman government—the markets, the roads, and the bathhouses—stating that they were all done not for the sake of the people, but to serve the government's needs. For that outspokenness, Rashbi was sentenced to death. He and his son-in-law escaped to a cave for the next twelve years, studying Torah so intensively that when Rashbi emerged, he was judgmental of any Jew who wasn't studying just as hard.

He punished the farmers whom he observed working the fields instead of hitting the books, vaporizing them with his mere gaze. God disapproved of that. "God chastised him," Jill Jacobs recounts, "saying to Bar Yohai, 'Are you out to destroy the world? Go back in your cave.' So Rashbi has to go back for another year until he's able to deal with human beings. For me, that's a reminder that it's not just about living this perfect, wholly religious life that is separated from humanity, but that we actually have to be able to live *with* humanity, and engage with the human world. That's actually what God wants from us. Not just a life of Torah."

It's yet another lesson in respectful coexistence: a person should be deepened by Torah, not blinded by it. Rashbi may have been righteous in his piety, but he had to *learn* righteousness when it came to his fellow human beings. The Declaration on Homosexuality has a whiff of Rashbi's initial fiery gaze—so consumed with Torah that it overlooks humanity.

✡

As I mentioned, Lag B'Omer doesn't offer many rituals or prayers. In Israel, the Orthodox gather in the thousands to dance and light bonfires in Meron—thought to be Rashbi's gravesite. I can't justify a long flight to Israel to build bonfires. And I wouldn't feel right joining in the mirth anyway. The revelers will be marking Rashbi's hillula—his wedding—when others still cannot marry. They will be focusing on Rashbi's mystical union with God, rather than on those students who failed to show mutual respect and who commit a similar offense today. They will be lifting up a great teacher of Torah without acknowledging that, at one point, he took Torah too far.

Maybe it's overly convenient to connect all these threads for Lag B'Omer—the students' ancient sin and its current manifestation; the Zohar's message that only an ethical life leads to God's love; the Torah Declaration that appeared on Facebook—just before Lag B'Omer and my friends' gay wedding scheduled for Omer's end.

But Matt says this holiday invites our own interpretations. "One of the attractive things about Lag B'Omer is its undefined character," says Matt. "There's not really a clear specific reason for it. It's not mentioned in the Torah or Tanach or Talmud. . . . So it invites creativity."

That makes me feel a little better. Though I don't yet feel entitled to be "creative" about these holidays, I am open to where they might take me. And on this Lag B'Omer, I choose to focus on the Talmud's plain phrase about Akiva's students: *They did not treat each other with respect. And the world was desolate.* The world *is* desolate when people are intolerant or disrespectful of others.

I dissected my first Lag without an inkling of what was to come in terms of the election circus of 2015–16. But Lag B'Omer will, each year, be a yardstick for me of whether civility is in peril. And though I can't cry for Akiva's solipsistic and ill-mannered students, or admire the self-important Rashbi—who believed God chose *him* to marry, who dismissed humanity when he emerged bleary-eyed from the cave—I can hold on to the *ideal* of righteousness in a world where goodness is not at all a given.

Michael and Daniel's wedding is called for 5:30 P.M. in Prospect Park under the trees, where we all sit on backless benches, huddling because of the unusual spring cold. Dave keeps his arm around me to warm us both. Some of my college buddies are shivering alongside, all of us giddy to be celebrating this. The huppah finally appears with the couple walking under it. The four poles are held aloft by parents, siblings, and closest friends, a moving parasol over Michael and Daniel and their adorable little boys. I can't stop smiling at the sight of their foursome, not just because they're a handsome tableau in their smart suits and boutonnieres, but because they've chosen to cement a fifteen-year relationship with ceremony and witnesses, despite having already been a family for so long. Daniel holds the older son's hand; Michael carries the younger one in his arms.

The vows bring tears because they're so specifically loving. The reception afterwards is jubilant in an airy, beautiful hall in the park called the Picnic House, with blond wooden floors, white steel ceiling beams, a fireplace, and flowers festooning the long banquet tables. I eat a lot, dance hard, and toast the grooms with a spoof song that my friends and I wrote to the tune of "Summer Lovin'" from the musical *Grease*.

The whole night heralds more than mutual respect; it heralds much-deserved joy. The shiva for Akiva's students ended a little early this year.

Rabbi Brad Hirschfeld
ON LAG B'OMER

What caused 24,000 of Rabbi Akiva's disciples to behave so disrespectfully toward each other, as the Talmud describes, that they died? Not what was the sin which makes this punishment reasonable in the rabbinic mind, but what justified the behavior in the minds of those students? They didn't all die at once, after all, so what kept them at one another, persisting in the same hurtful and shaming behavior even as they were dying for doing so? What keeps any of us locked in such behavior even as we, and those we love, so often pay a heavy price for it?

It often comes down to valuing correctness over compassion. Correctness, truth, accuracy. Don't get me wrong; without them we are lost. But we are just as lost if they are all we have, or all we fight over, as is so often the case, especially when animated by deep faith and conviction, as the 24,000 surely were. Perhaps the path to balancing correctness and compassion can be found in prayer—not ours, but God's.

What does God pray? According to the Talmud (Ber. 7a): "Let it be my will that my loving kindness suppresses my anger and that I deal with my children beyond the letter of the law." Perhaps God's imagined prayer could be our lived lives. It's certainly hard to imagine those 24,000 dying had they believed as much. Imagine what believing it could do for us.

Rabbi Jill Jacobs
ON LAG B'OMER

The punishment for Rabbi Akiva's students is a bit of a warning . . . what God doesn't want from us. That we're so deep in what we think is our own truth that we can't engage with each other. There have to be relationships. It can't just be, "I know my truth and therefore I'm not going to engage." Akiva's students didn't behave respectfully to one another, and it was actually destroying the world.

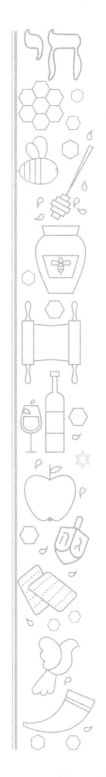

Rabbi Jonah Pesner
ON SHABBAT

The opposite of Egypt is Shabbat. When we say the Kiddush, we reference the Exodus from Egypt. To experience Shabbat is to experience the world as it should be. The world as it is is the world parched with oppression; it's the world of Egypt, it's the world of suffering. We have to work six days, some without respite, without fair wages, without breaks. And on the seventh day, we have the experience of Tikkun, we have the experience of wholeness. There is no work, there is equality and equanimity. And the agitation of that is that not all people have the experience of Shabbat. And even for those people who do, they often return to lives that are oppressed and full of suffering. So there is a kind of a moral injunction on Shabbat. We think of social justice as mostly about oppressed workers, but it also calls me to the urgency of brokenness that is so close.

21

ACTIVIST SHABBAT
Friday Night with the Kids

5.17.15

G OOD DEEDS.
With so many festivals and fasts oriented to healing the world, it seems entirely fitting to attend a Shabbat dinner run by recent college graduates who are devoting a year to fighting poverty.

"Avodah: The Jewish Service Corps" is a handpicked team of more than seventy young people in four cities—New York, Chicago, New Orleans, and D.C.—who have applied to spend a year working in the nonprofit world. Each member is assigned to a communal residence and matched with a job in one of fifty-seven organizations addressing hunger, homelessness, affordable housing, education, or domestic violence.

Each of the six so-called "houses" is considered a Jewish home, or "bayit." The "corps members" in the house decide how kosher to be and which holidays to celebrate. Relevant Jewish texts are taught by visiting faculty. Observance varies widely within each residence, but one principle does not: lifting people up.

"Three words in Deuteronomy," says Cheryl Cook, Avodah's executive director, "'*Tzedek, tzedek tirdof*: Justice, Justice, Shall You Pursue.'"

We're not just encouraged to pursue justice, we're *commanded*. Avodah answers that charge."

Have I answered that charge? What have I done to pursue justice? It's a complicated question for me because my mother led a life of activism and can easily point to the ways in which she pursued equality for women. I have long admired her and, in a sense, permitted myself some reflective *tzedek*: she made me appear more involved than I was. But what did I actually *do*, setting aside the angry letter I wrote to General Mills at age eight asking them to change their Wheaties cereal slogan from "He's ready for Wheaties. He knows he's a man," to something that included girls (they eventually did, though I can't claim credit), and besides working in high school for a short-lived organization called Future Generations for Nuclear Disarmament?

I take an honest inventory of what I've given back, setting aside the volunteer hours at my kids' school or our synagogue, which some might say should count, but admittedly supports institutions from which I benefit. Social justice, to me, means justice for strangers.

For the last six years, I've served 6:30 A.M. breakfast to the homeless most Thursdays at my synagogue's soup kitchen and participated in Central's Mitzvah Day, in which congregants fan out to various organizations for a number of hours. For two years, I taught memoir writing to formerly homeless men at the Doe Fund, whose board I then joined. I was once a mentor to a hardworking second-grader in a Manhattan Catholic school, and I've tutored at the Children's Storefront school in Harlem. I purchased blankets and helped organize food supplies for victims of Hurricane Sandy and was part of the shul's Community Organizing team for four years. I hosted a Fresh Air Fund kid for two summers and twice biked forty miles to raise money for Sanctuary for Families, which helps victims of domestic violence. But mostly I do tzedakah from my desk: writing checks to a lot of worthy organizations.

The list feels somewhat insufficient. It doesn't amount to hands-on "repairing the world," *tikkun olam*. So I look at the Avodah kids and think: "I should have done that. I could have given a year or more to improving the lives of others before starting my adult life." (And that thought is instantly followed by the realization that I'd be an anal, annoying roommate.)

All this is roiling in my mind when I head to visit the Washington Heights "bayit" on a Friday evening, which consists of three communal apartments in one walk-up brownstone, thirteen young people in all. The twelve members of the Brooklyn house have also come to this Community Shabbat. I can smell the cooking in the elevator.

The minute I walk into the apartment, I feel conspicuously middle-aged. Everyone is in their twenties, more casually dressed. The corps members chat with each other on sofas, scattered chairs, and the floor. There is a groaning bookcase, a batik wall hanging, and a string of small lightbulbs lending the room a twinkle. The sign posted near the fridge announces "This is a Kosher Kitchen."

I meet Kevin, who is working at the Crown Heights Community Mediation Center; Shoshana, who is working at the Bronx Jewish Community Council; Kayla, who is at the Red Hook Community Justice Center; Hannah, who works at Sanctuary for Families. (I promised I would use only first names.)

Eli is in charge of tonight's ritual and meal (everyone takes turns leading). A paralegal at NYLAG, the New York Legal Assistance Group, he wears a ponytail, square-top yarmulke, and rubber clogs with socks. He starts by asking each person to bring a family member into the room. It reminds me of the Feminist Seder when we were asked to invite "an invisible guest." Both Lynnie and Elana "bring" their grandmothers, whose first yartzheits fall during this particular week. I bring Molly, who first dragged me to Central's soup kitchen when she was ten, and where we've been serving breakfast most Thursdays ever since.

Eli then distributes a handout on conflict management, titled "Deep Dialogue: Saying What We Mean and Doing What We Say," by Professor Jay Rothman of Bar Ilan University in Israel. The essay suggests that "the art of peacemaking" is not to argue our own points, but to hear someone else's—to ask "Why do you care so much? Why does this matter to you so deeply?" I like the approach. It might be helpful to Jews who can't talk to each other about Israel anymore. Eli asks us to pair off to examine Rothman's essay, then to consider committing to truer listening, to being "a pursuer of peace," a "Rodeph Shalom."

As the noise level swells with competing conversations, I recall a recent exchange I had with Rabbi Adam Chalom, a Humanist rabbi in suburban Chicago, who pushed me to expand my definition of Shabbat observance. "If we remember that Shabbat was made *for* the Jewish people *by* the Jewish people, then it's not a matter of squeezing ourselves into some box labeled 'Shabbat,'" he told me. "It's a matter of defining what that box or space can be for us. A Sabbath meal, a Jewish novel, or Jewish study is as authentic as sitting in synagogue."

I know some would dispute his loose definition of a kosher Shabbat, but I also know how many more Jews would find his words inviting. You mean there's no one true way?

"It's based on our choices and our lifestyle," says Chalom. "And if you make different choices, the Yiddish phrase is 'Gey gezunderheyt'—go in good health. Would reading a Jewish poet or going to a Jewish movie on Shabbat count as a Jewish experience? I would say yes. Because it activates your Jewish identity."

Eli offers the Avodah group two options before dinner: to welcome the Sabbath through exercises in mindfulness, led by him, or through movement, led by Laurel in her apartment down the hall. I start in Eli's group, as he guides us through six brief activities pegged to the order of the prayers. During a "loving-kindness" meditation, Eli says, "We're channeling the feeling we get when we're hugging a loved one or a small child." I know that feeling from Ben and Molly. It's easy to channel, even among strangers.

We repeat a mantra—"May I be safe from harm. May I be happy. May I be healthy. May I live with ease"—a distillation of everything I need to believe is possible. I wish fiercely every week that my family will remain safe, happy, and healthy. That they live with ease. But this mantra is a huge ask. Do we really get to have safety *and* happiness *and* health, not to mention ease? I'm not so sure. All the more reason that we should be grateful when all four are present.

During "mindful walking," we put one step deliberately in front of the other across the small living room. Eli urges us not to speed up. As an incurably fast walker, this is excruciating for me, but I see the value in literally slowing things down like this, noticing how we move—or, in my case, charge—through our days. "We're working with this metaphor of putting Shabbat in the *being* mode," Eli says, "rather than the *doing* mode." Though Shabbat is always supposed to be a time for just *being*, it's nice to be in a roomful of people who are actually doing. These kids are living the Jewish values we hear so much about.

While I'm glacially placing one foot in front of the other, I can hear rap music a few doors down, where Laurel is leading four women through a series of exercises on yoga mats. Excusing myself from the mindful walking, I head down the hall to glimpse the mindful sweating. Taking in the unconventional scene, Chalom's admonition comes back to me: "The ultimate question is, 'What does Shabbat mean to you?' If you read the text of Shabbat, it's a Creationist holiday. In six days, the world was made; Creation stopped on the seventh. Well, the vast majority of Jews under the liberal spectrum are not Creationist. So there's an instant disconnect many people have with the language that's being used."

I see his point: if we don't buy the premise of Shabbat, Shabbat is mutable. It's up to us to redefine it, or to decide what aspects of it speak to us. And what if we don't believe the effusive words we pour about God on Shabbat? "Many Jews don't believe in a personally interventionist God, who either wants or needs all the praise," says Chalom. "So I think part of the challenge is that disconnect with what Shabbat means at its root. Is it a Creationist holiday commemorating the creation of the world and the creator of the world? Or is it a space for Jewish identity?"

Shabbat: a space in which to construct our own Jewish identity, a room each of us can fill with our own furniture. This Avodah clan has clearly made its own, undeniably spacious, Shabbat space. But identity questions have occasionally strained the bayit. Each house has to navigate its pluralism. "Some people wanted the house to be more observant; some worried it was *too* observant," says Lynnie from Southern California. Says another member: "We know that what we figure out inside these walls is just a microcosm of what we have to navigate outside."

Cook says the corps members are supported in handling these tensions, but never directed as to how to deal with them. "Being able to function within a diverse Jewish space is as important as anything they learn," she explains. "It's the real world."

There is one clear area of unanimity: Judaism's mandate not to stand idly by. These kids all share the mission to fix something; that's what they're doing here. And they're helping the helpless in a Jewish context. "I'm never going to be able to *un*-link Judaism and social justice again," says Lynnie.

Reuniting in Eli's apartment, the group recites the blessings over challah and wine. (The hot challah rolls from Trader Joe's are a revelation. Who knew?) Eli and Joey have whipped up six courses from two cookbooks—Syrian and Israeli, including lentil soup, cucumber salad, onion-and-feta salad, a potato-and-egg concoction, and a slow-cooked rice dish. As we eat, I ask these twentysomethings about their Avodah experience. "It's a demanding year," one tells me. "You're seeing hard cases, working long days, and then there are two educational programs per week with mandatory attendance." A young woman named Hannah says her favorite part is "Community Shabbats like this one."

Abraham Joshua Heschel said, "A religious person is one who suffers harm done to others . . . whose greatest strength is love and defiance of despair." Avodah's members meet Heschel's definition: they defy despair.

"We don't use the word 'compassion' very often," said Sarah from Rye Brook, New York. "We talk much more about justice. It's energizing to be around people who care about the same things." And sapping, too. "Sometimes," says Joey, "when we get home from these jobs, we need a break from the caring."

I ask him if his prevailing takeaway is that the world is unjust.

"Absolutely," he answers.

Is he optimistic that things will really get better for the populations they're helping?

"No."

His harsh candor actually makes me optimistic. Because Joey is doing the work anyway. All seventy-one current corps members *do the work anyway*—despite the daunting scope of poverty and its intractability. That seems to me holy labor, be it Chalom's definition or any other rabbi's. "If the angels of rescue are not on their way," Chalom says, "then we have to be the angels of rescue. *We* are the ones who have to take the raw material of the universe as we find it and make it better."

Make it better. That's Judaism's mandate in a nutshell, and every holiday brings it home.

Rabbi Ayelet Cohen
ON SHAVUOT

Moses warns the people to stay pure . . . be ready for the third day. On the third day, there was thunder and lightning. So the rabbis interpret these days of waiting as staying awake. This is the state they were in—this hyper-aware, but also very fragile, state. That's what we're trying to reenact on Shavuot.

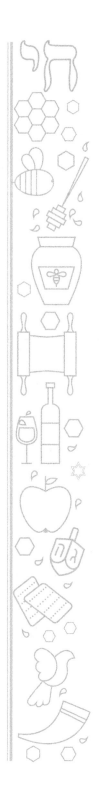

22

SLEEPLESS ON SHAVUOT

Let My People Learn

5.21.15

WAS NEVER GREAT at pulling all-nighters in college.

But I'm pulling one on Shavuot ("weeks"), which celebrates the completion of the "weeks" between Passover and Shavuot—when God gave the Torah to the Israelites on Mount Sinai.

I didn't grow up understanding how huge this Torah-giving moment was, how it marks, really, the beginning of Judaism. The Israelites were in a precarious state after decades of slavery in Egypt, and had barely escaped—with Pharaoh's army in hot pursuit. They had survived in the desert with little food and water, trusting Moses without knowing for sure that he could be trusted. They came to the foot of Sinai, were supposed to wake up early to receive the Torah, and then they actually *overslept.* According to rabbinic commentary, Moses had to wake the people, which is why we now mark Shavuot by staying up all night—to make sure we're up first thing in the morning.

In a cinematic crescendo, the Ten Commandments were proclaimed by God in a bracing crash of lightning and thunder. Shavuot represents the denouement—referred to as Revelation in our prayer books. Very soon after the thunder moment, we signed on, accepting the law and agreeing to live by it. This is when we became Jews, when we graduated from an enslaved people to an autonomous one. We had been at the mercy of others; finally we governed ourselves.

It helps to understand the weight of this symbolism before I start the observance itself. Especially because there aren't many Shavuot observances. It is celebrated over two days, with candles lit on both evenings. No work is performed and only dairy foods are eaten, since—according to one explanation—kosher laws were new on Mount Sinai and the Israelites hadn't yet kosherized (kashered) their cooking pots, so they played it safe by sticking to dairy. On this holiday, Jews go to synagogue the first day to hear the Ten Commandments, but the main event is the learning-binge the night before. It's the thing to do on the eve of receiving the Torah: stay up all night studying it. Or celebrating it, creatively.

So this coming Saturday, May 23, despite the temptation of traditional Memorial Day barbecues, I'll be heading to the JCC in Manhattan to take part in their jam-packed, 10 p.m.-to-5 a.m. smorgasbord of programming. There are seventy-five sessions on offer, including "Why Benjamin Netanyahu and Barack Obama Can't Get Along," led by the journalist Peter Beinart; "Midrash Through Dance," taught by Rabbi Mira Rivera, the full-time rabbi at Mount Sinai Hospital; "Opening Ourselves to Revelation through Meditation," with Sheldon Lewis, who teaches stress management at the Center for Women's Health; and "The Nepal Earthquake and the Ebola Outbreak: What We Know—and Fail to Learn—About the State of the World," with Ruth Messinger, the president of American Jewish World Service.

I'm already overwhelmed by the options—sometimes as many as twenty-one for each time slot—with categories including Text Study, Israel, Social Justice, Jewish Spirituality, Arts, Culture & Culinary, and Wellness.

For the 11:15 p.m.-to-12:15 a.m. segment, I'll be torn between "Line Dancing" and a session by my editor at the *Forward* newspaper, Jane Eisner: "All Who Leave: Shulem Deen on Exiting Hasidic Life." Post-midnight, I can't be sure if I'll feel like Jewish disco or Orthodox defection.

The 12:30 A.M. slot offers "The Future of Jewish Media" or "The Borscht Belt: Boot Camp for America's Comedians." I'm technically part of the media, so I should learn about its future. But I could probably use a laugh at twelve thirty in the morning. Or I could just drown my fatigue in alcohol at "A Taste of Schnapps."

At 4:15 A.M., the intrepid remaining souls will head to the roof to ring in the morning with a concert.

Master-organizer Rabbi Ayelet Cohen, the director of the Center for Jewish Living at the JCC, explains that the concept of this all-night Shavuot immersion, called a "Tikkun Leil Shavuot" (Rectification of the Night of Shavuot), started with the Kabbalists in the sixteenth century. But some trace it back to our old buddy from Lag B'Omer, Rabbi Shimon Bar Yochai (Rashbi), one of Akiva's few righteous students. He apparently would sit and study all night before Shavuot. (Reencountering a familiar figure like Rashbi makes me feel like I'm beginning to know my way around.)

The JCC's modern iteration of the "Tikkun" sprang from Dr. Ruth Calderon, an author and former Knesset member who, in 1996, founded the Alma College in Tel Aviv—a secular take on the yeshiva that calls itself a "Home for Hebrew Culture." "Ruth was here for a year," Cohen recalls, "and brought to us the idea that Jewish learning should be inviting and accessible to all Jews, regardless of whether they have a yeshiva background. She wanted every Jew to look at Jewish text and explore its intersection with the arts, to create immersive communities of study for people." Calderon's message epitomizes my Jewish Year. I'm a Jew unschooled in Judaism, looking for a way in.

Every space in the JCC building will be used Saturday night, from the *Beit Midrash* (house of study) to the cycling studio, from the kitchen to the roof. "In some ways it does feel like a reenactment of everybody gathered at Sinai," Cohen says, "the Jewish people in all of their complexity and diversity in one place getting ready to have this experience together."

But what about becoming too tired to enjoy it?

"An afternoon nap is a great idea," Cohen says. "And we have lots of coffee and cheesecake." Ah yes, I've heard about the surfeit of

Zabar's cheesecake, a nod to the holiday's dairy menu. "Our Tikkun this year has a learning session about lactose intolerance and how to manage Shavuot when you have issues with dairy," Cohen says.

The cheesecake theme seems as concocted as Shavuot itself. This is yet another example of a holiday whose meaning has morphed over time. Shavuot originated in the Bible as a harvest holiday, celebrated forty-nine days after Passover. It eventually became the moment the law was given on Mount Sinai, a dubious connection, according to Rabbi Michael Strassfeld. "We see a number of problems in associating it with the revelation at Sinai," Strassfeld writes in his invaluable book *The Jewish Holidays*. "The biblical references to Shavuot regard it only as the feast of harvest or the day of the first fruits. Nowhere in the Bible is any link made between Sinai and Shavuot. Indeed, even the biblical account of the Revelation at Sinai does not connect it with Shavuot."

So how did they get connected?

After the Second Temple was destroyed, Judaism moved away from Temple offerings—meat, grain, wine, and fruits—and began to accentuate the way in which the harvest holidays (Passover, Shavuot, Sukkot) are connected to historical events (Exodus, Sinai, desert wandering). The hurdle for the rabbis was that the Torah does not link Shavuot to any historical events. So they hitched it to the giving of the law at Mount Sinai.

I can see how there's a lot more staying power in the drama of Sinai, awaiting God's Commandments, particularly because those anticipating the law were told to stay awake. "There's a lot in our tradition about fasting and what that does to you—physically and spiritually to be in an altered state," Cohen explains. "So this is a sleep fast, and we should think about what that means."

I don't have to think about it; sleep-deprivation makes me as cranky as food-deprivation.

"We know we're not the same people after a night of no sleep," Cohen continues. "Our defenses are down. We're more vulnerable. We're less measured. It's a physical manifestation of the state of wilderness that the Israelites were in—where they had to receive Torah in a very vulnerable, raw, undefended state. Because that's the state you need to be in to really receive something wondrous. If we had all our usual defenses up, we wouldn't believe that revelation was possible."

Is revelation possible? Really, today?

I call Rabbi Irwin Kula, an author, popular speaker, and regular teacher at the JCC Tikkun (except this particular year, when he is speaking elsewhere). How would he explain to the vast majority of liberal Jews, who don't celebrate Shavuot, why it has urgency today? His reply: "I always ask the question, 'What do we hire a holiday to do for us?' In other words, Shavuot got invented because it was responding to a genuine, existential yearning that people had. So what's the yearning to which Shavuot is a response?" I like his answer. "It's the yearning to know what it is we're really supposed to do with our lives."

Shavuot brings us back to our contract with God and each other. What did we commit to at Sinai? So many rabbis talk about preordained purpose. It's not "What am I *going* to do with my life?" It's "What am I *supposed* to do with my life?" There's a "supposed to" for each of us; we just need to discover it. We're not bestowed with life solely to exist, but to act.

I hear again the Tevet message of helping in a time of need, the Passover message of helping Elijah bring the Messiah, the Avodah message to get involved where we can.

My own former senior rabbi, Peter Rubinstein of Central Synagogue, used to rouse our sense of obligation by reminding us that we were all at Sinai. If the Talmud contends that every Jew was there, that's a metaphor for us today: each of us receives this law, tradition, and history, and each of us must decide what to do with it. Standing at Sinai today means paying attention to what is heard at the foot of the mountain, after the lightning and thunder subside, when it's quiet. "The question is, 'What do you hear?'" Kula says. "If that's not a living question, Shavuot can't work for you."

I want it to work for me. Kula says the JCC Tikkun is a good place to start and has grown popular because people seek communal events that transcend denominations. "That's part of everyone standing at Sinai," he says. "It's not an individual experience. Everybody's there."

✡

I head to Sinai on the Saturday night of Memorial Day weekend, and 3,400 people are already in the JCC's various sessions and workshops. Let's be honest: New Yorkers do not do what they do not want to do. So the fact that I'm in the midst of such a big crowd on a holiday weekend tells me that a heck of a lot of people are here for more than free cheesecake (though I do have to admit, it's delicious).

I arrive late to the first segment of "Stay the Night," as the JCC mega-event is named, having rushed uptown from my friends' Brooklyn wedding (changing into more comfortable clothes in the taxi). When I walk into the warmly lit JCC lobby, there are people in jeans, sweatpants, sundresses, and yarmulkes. I join the hordes crowding into classrooms, gyms, dance studios, and the auditorium, all of us carrying the color-coded schedule available at the door. "Who says Jewish identity is in peril?" I think to myself. As Jewish parties go, this is a doozy. I feel affirmed in this throng, as if someone is whispering in my ear: "You're not wandering alone; look how many of us are with you."

I start my maiden voyage in a session on spirituality taught by Rabbi Josh Katzan of Congregation Habonim on the Upper West Side. Using the Leviticus text in which Aaron's sons make the fatal mistake of offering an "alien fire" to God (and then get summarily smitten), Katzan says these boys exemplify what happens when we get too caught up in our own spiritual fervor. "Our intense *feeling* can push us to do something without being cognizant of the impact on others," says Katzan.

I can remember too many examples of impulsivity that I regret—often involving college romances. I've also been swept up in the fervor of volunteer work without stepping back to assess whether it's really helping. Katzan says "feel-good" moments should not be "the center around which spirituality orbits." Holiness is found in how we react to others, Katzan says, more than in how moved we are personally. "I know it rattles the cage to say that," Katzan acknowledges. "But maybe spirituality is about the world we create, how we respond to the annoying neighbor or the earthquake in Nepal. How we *behave* says a lot more than how we *feel*."

This year has trained a spotlight on how I behave. It's also testing how much ritual can ever make me feel. I'm trying to get better at both.

There are fifteen minutes between segments, which allows time for chatting, picking the next teacher, and cheesecake fortification in the lobby. Though I recognize some people milling around, I have no friends in sight; I'm solo at Sinai. It's another metaphor for the year: I moved through it independently but never felt alone.

It's time to plunge into the quagmire of Israel and civility—or the lack of it—with a panel moderated by the sociologist Steven M. Cohen. I always like listening to Cohen, because he's smart and unvarnished. That's the dose of energy you need at midnight.

Maybe the room is too small, the hour too late (12:30 A.M. start time), or the air too stuffy, but the session's title becomes instantly self-fulfilling: "Too Toxic to Talk About." The panel features Kenneth Bob, president of Amenu, a Progressive Zionist organization; J. J. Goldberg, who writes about Israel's security issues for the *Forward*; and Shoshana Rosen, who directs programming for the twenties and thirties demographic at the JCC. Their presentations quickly devolve into audience shout-outs, criticism of the panel composition, petulant challenges, and prickly asides.

Rosen suggests that people raise their hands if they have something to say and asks us to notice how our hearts might be racing. She's right. Still, the clashes continue. I won't recap the remainder because it takes us down the rabbit hole of Mideast policy and Jewish angst. Suffice it to say that I leave the room exhausted by the impossibility of this particular conversation. (Not to mention, just plain exhausted.) But there is still more Holy Land thorniness to be

explored, so I head to the 1:45 A.M. lecture on West Bank settlements, given by Hagai El-Ad, the executive director of B'Tselem
("In the image of"), a Jerusalem-based organization that monitors
human-rights violations.

Because of the title—"Intractable Impermanence: 47 Years of
'Temporary' Occupation"—I expect this session to be virulently left-
wing. Far from it. El-Ad gives a complex, undogmatic primer on the
varying levels of Israeli control in the West Bank and its ramifica-
tions. "We are not a peace organization; we are a human-rights organization," he says. "We don't advocate for any one political solution.
Any solution that would uphold human rights is a solution we would
support." It sounds so straightforward, but of course nothing is simple
when it comes to Israel. El-Ad is not a flamethrower; his message
sounds eminently reasonable: concerns about Israel's security should
not justify human-rights abuses. Can't argue with that.

I raise my hand and ask him if he thinks anti-settlement zeal now
translates overwhelmingly to anti-Israel zeal. "There are three separate issues: anti-Israel feeling, anti-Semitism, and anti-occupation,"
he responds. "They get lumped together, but they're different. We at
B'Tselem are anti-occupation."

I leave, feeling depressed by the international rage directed at Israel. Those balloons of Yom Ha'atzmaut, Independence Day, have lost
some air in this session.

I need a break from the heavy stuff, so at 3 A.M. I head to "Midrash
Through Dance." Since Midrash is ancient Torah commentary, I can't
quite see how we're going to hoof it. The session is taught by Rabbi
Mira Rivera, whose personal history is more interesting to me than
her instructions to physicalize Ladino (Judeo-Spanish) words of
prayer. Rivera was born in the Philippines, grew up in America, and
became fluent in Spanish because of her immigrant grandmother,
who descended from Conversos—Jews who renounced their faith under pressure during the Spanish Inquisition.

When she describes, in graphic detail, how she used to watch the
family housekeeper slaughter, bleed, and denude a chicken according
to kosher rules, I think I might lose my cheesecake.

I feel somewhat restored when Rivera instructs us to stand up and stretch in the dance studio. But when we are asked to find a physical expression of the words of eighteenth-century rabbi Judah Leon Kalai ("Es razon de alavar al Dyo, alto i poderoso . . ."—"It is fitting to praise the God of greatness and of might"), I feel foolish and uncoordinated as I wave my arms and twirl, repeating the phrase over and over. It's nearly four in the morning, and I've officially hit the proverbial wall, so I sheepishly beat a retreat to the door.

Looking in on Israeli folk dancing in the gym, I see about fourteen people stepping, skipping, and hopping their way through some of the most complicated dance steps I've ever seen. No basic hora here; they're in another league.

I ask a bystander, "Are they *teaching* any dances tonight?" "Oh no," she replies, as if warning me to stay back. "These people go to class every week; they know the choreography cold."

Watching these expert steppers, I notice they aren't smiling. Each person moves through their routine with a cool nonchalance that calls to mind the 1969 film about a dance contest, *They Shoot Horses, Don't They?*—with dog-tired stalwarts struggling to remain upright on the dance floor. The dancers project the casual ease I've been looking for during my Jewish Year: Proficiency. Effortlessness. When it comes to my tradition, I want to know the steps.

"Stay the Night" ends in the morning—on the roof of the JCC with a final 4:15 A.M. concert. I cannot deny feeling like an Ironman Jew for having stayed the course.

As the *a cappella* group from Queens College, "Tizmoret," starts their fourth song, I wish I weren't so tired or so chilled in the night air. But I stay to listen, bouncing along with the music to stay warm. Finally, as I take the elevator down to the lobby, I feel full—energized by the Tikkun's bustle and by its testament to Jewish vibrancy. Look how many people came to study, question, argue, dance, sing, engage, and connect. (And look at how much cheesecake we ate.)

As I climb into bed at 5 A.M., my husband and kids are still sleeping and the sun is rising, painting the black sky a soft purple-blue. After such a marathon day, I need to rest my mind. But it is racing.

Rabbi Irwin Kula

ON SHAVUOT

The desire to all stand at Sinai—that yearning—is the yearning to really be a community. In America right now we have real fragmentation. Imagine if 500,000 people—Republicans and Democrats, conservatives and liberals, hawks and doves, religious and secular—all kinds of people could stand for an hour in front of the holy space, whatever you consider the holy space in America—the Lincoln Memorial, the Capitol building—and feel that we knew what it was like to be American—together. Imagine if every generation was there for the signing of the Declaration of Independence. And then, when we're really fighting and ugly to each other, somebody takes a step back and says, "Oh, right; we were there. We were there in Philadelphia that day. We were there." That would be the American version of Sinai. One minute standing together. And then an hour later we can start fighting again, because that's the Torah, too. That's the invitation of Sinai.

Dr. Elana Stein Hain

I'm not alone in saying this—it is said by prophet after prophet in the Jewish tradition: fasting should not be an end in and of itself. It's supposed to push us to something else—toward introspection, toward kindness, toward relationship with something greater than ourselves. It may be legally binding in the way that I understand tradition and in the way that I practice, but I don't pretend for a moment that I haven't missed an opportunity if it doesn't lead me to something good. . . . I think people want to view religion and identity as empowering and as a positive force in life. And I don't think physical comfort is necessarily always empowering. It might be a prerequisite for something, if used in the right way, just as discomfort can be useful; but I think often the story is that empowerment leads to blindness and privilege to a lack of self-reflection.

On the 17th of Tammuz, I am not going to be hungry the way the Jews were hungry during the siege of Jerusalem. Likewise, I may not feel a sense of urgency every time I fast. Nonetheless, fasting as giving up some of my privilege is always relevant. It need not be dramatic; it can be a rather simple attempt at experiencing what it means to need and not to have.

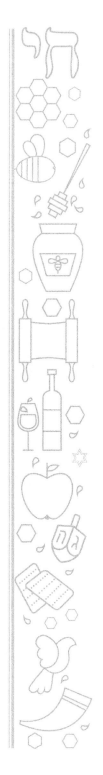

23

17TH OF TAMMUZ

Another Fast, Seriously?

7.1.15

AFTER THE UNSPEAKABLE joy and poignancy of Ben's high school graduation in June—where I couldn't quite believe that my first child was striding down the aisle in cap and gown—it's difficult to be mournful, on cue, the following month. Summer sadness seems oxymoronic. But it's required for the next holiday—the 17th of Tammuz (*Shivah Asar b'Tammuz*), which marks the breach of the walls of Jerusalem, before the Temple's final destruction three weeks later.

The summer has offered plenty of grief already. On June 17, 2015, nine black worshippers were killed in a Charleston church, where they had gathered for Bible study. Concurrent terrorist attacks in France, Tunisia, and Kuwait included families slaughtered on the beach and a decapitated head on a gatepost. Cancer returned to my close friend Julie, who has two children under six and now has a year at most to live.

And so, despite my general resistance to not eating (you must be weary of my fast-kvetching), it actually feels important to fulfill the demands of 17 Tammuz and take a day of self-denial this summer—July 5, immediately following America's Independence Day. (In a particularly bizarre coincidence of the calendar this year, two Jewish fast-days fall on two American holidays—10 Tevet on New Year's Day and 17 Tammuz on the day after July 4th—amplifying the contrast between my activities and what most people are doing.)

"The purpose of a fast is both to pray for salvation, but also to get rid of distraction and privilege and think about what we can do better in the world," says Dr. Elana Stein Hain, the director of Leadership Education at the Shalom Hartman Institute of North America, based in New York. Again, that double obligation: with every challenging fast comes the charge to make others' lives easier.

Stein Hain is right that fasts rid us of distraction; nothing focuses the mind like hunger. That temporary discomfort makes me keenly conscious of the deprivation regularly experienced around the world, the scourge of poverty and famine.

Stein Hain calls "magnificent" the suggestion she read a few years ago in an article by the Hebrew Bible professor David Lambert: that fasting in the Bible is like a hunger strike. "It's a way of a human being saying to God, 'Please change this, or I refuse to eat,'" she says. "It's a way of getting at injustice in the world."

What an idea: fasting as petition instead of penitence. Fasting to seek repair, not atonement.

The other four fasts this year—Tzom Gedaliah, Yom Kippur, the Tenth of Tevet, and the Fast of Esther—also made me think about suffering. But it's one thing to feel empathy. It's another to treat your fast as a plaintive appeal to God to pay attention.

I could make this fast a cry to stop all the Charlestons and Sandy Hooks. Or to beseech God to keep Julie alive for her small children. Her four-year-old has never known her healthy. But 17 Tammuz also teaches that you can't always fix it; the test is how you bear it.

In the Roman siege of Jerusalem, which this fast remembers, the Jews were barricaded in the city, cut off from food and water, dying slowly, inescapably, in full view of their captors. "They're in the moment where they've lost—because they know the walls have been breached," says Stein Hain. "But they can't mourn yet, because it's not over. Some people today know exactly what that feels like—to know how it's going to end and have no choice but to wait it out. That's what

I think 17 Tammuz is. It's the Jewish people nearing the end in Jerusalem. We were nearing the end and we had to wait it out."

When you know you can't possibly survive, each day is a victory. I will try to hold on to that perspective. Every additional day Julie gets will create memories for her children. She is in Stein Hain's liminal space, between the life you still have and the moment you'll lose it.

I'm carrying these disparate images in my head—an ancient people being starved to death and a close friend whom modern medicine can't save. They'll lead me to the same place on Sunday: a brief encounter with having less, to honor the people losing more.

Despite this bleak message, Stein Hain rejects the idea that Jews wallow in woe, insisting that ours is a hopeful, celebratory religion. "There is an ongoing debate about whether Jewish history is a sad tale with some intermittent joy, or a joyful tale with some intermittent sadness," she tells me. "Salo Baron, an American historian of Jewish ancestry, wrote that we've been working with the 'lachrymose' interpretation of Jewish history; that we're just downtrodden. But he rejected that conception."

I reject it, too: the sum of all these holidays has been buoyant. Despite the sobriety of atonement (Yom Kippur), warfare (Hanukkah, Yom HaZikaron), slavery (Passover), near-massacre (Purim), and annihilation (Yom HaShoah and the upcoming Tisha B'Av), the takeaway is joy.

"Most days, Jews are just living to the fullest, and on occasion we take note of the hard times," Stein Hain says. "That is such a testament to our tradition, that we want Jewish life to be normal and happy, but we have to be respectful of the many moments we experience that are *not* like that. So a few times a year we say, 'Let's pause.'"

We pause for the Temple's siege, breach, and destruction. For expiation. For appreciation. Every fast is a decelerator and a referendum on a glass half full.

"The goal of Jewish life is celebrating and emphasizing *life*," says Rabbi Steven Exler, who will soon succeed Avi Weiss as the rabbi of the Hebrew Institute of Riverdale in the Bronx. "But mourning and death are part of it, too, and three weeks out of the year—between this fast of Tammuz and the next fast, Tisha B'av—are geared toward experiencing collective national loss and entering that emotional religious space."

I'm finding it hard to enter three weeks of requiem in seventy-five-degree sunshine. I feel like the kid who's been kept indoors on the nicest day of the year. The Temple feels awfully remote on this holiday. Exler tries to help: "Even if it doesn't rattle or shake you to realize that there were centuries upon centuries of Jewish communities for whom this one place represented the presence of God in their lives—remember this was a place where mourners came, where bridegrooms came, it was the central hub of communal Jewish life," he says. "And the sense of that locus becoming vulnerable is an awareness that even the things we hold most sacred can be violated in this world. Even the most sacred things sometimes can be ruptured—their physical presence gone. So how do I go on?"

So many people do. They survive the end. Yom Kippur taught me that no life is guaranteed, Sukkot that no house is solid. Tammuz marks not just the shock of an ending but of its inevitability. Some people cannot be saved.

In that space—between certain loss and the unpredictable road that leads to it—there is struggle and suffering, but also strength and endurance. So we fast a fifth time, not only to honor the breach and the purgatory, but the people who, as Exler puts it, "go on."

Rabbi Judith Hauptman

ON TISHA B'AV

I used to think mourning for the destruction of a building—
because that is how Tisha B'Av is always presented—made
little sense. I could easily see mourning Jews killed in pogroms,
massacres, the Holocaust. But a building? Until 9/11; that
brought Tisha B'Av home to me. You can mourn a building. It
symbolized, as did the Temple in Jerusalem, the body politic. It
had a grand name. It was lost. If we celebrate history that ended
well for us, like Passover and Purim, we should also celebrate
history that ended badly. If one thinks about Tisha B'Av, it
forces introspection as a community, not as individuals—as
on Yom Kippur. To be a Jew means to be part of the Jewish
community. And that means to rejoice over successes and
mourn failures. It means to think about where we go from here
so that catastrophes don't befall us again. Celebrations are easy;
for whatever reason, people love taking stock and repenting,
asking for forgiveness. Tisha B'Av is a very hard sell.

Rabbi Steven Exler

ON TISHA B'AV

Tisha B'Av is when the decree was set that there would be forty
years of wandering in the wilderness and that the generation
that came out of Egypt wouldn't go into the land. So thinking
about it as a time of delayed redemption—that idea of delayed
fulfillment of promises—is at the heart of the day. This becomes
the time when we think about moments of brokenness. It's the
moment of breaking the glass under the huppah, expanded
out into a period of time. It's the sense that everything that we
think protects us ultimately falls away.

24

TISHA B'AV

Mourning History, Headlines, and Hatred

7.23.15

N O DEODORANT IN July? That's asking a lot. But Tisha B'Av demands it.

The twenty-five-hour fast marks the destruction of Jerusalem's two Temples (the first in 586 B.C.E. by the Babylonians, the second in 70 C.E. by the Romans), and also marks almost every other catastrophe that's befallen the Jews, including the sin of the Golden Calf when we built a false idol, the First Crusade in August 1096 when ten thousand Jews were killed, the 1290 expulsion from England, the 1306 expulsion from France, the 1492 expulsion from Spain, the 1941 approval of "the Final Solution," the 1942 deportation of Jews from the Warsaw Ghetto to Treblinka, the Holocaust as a whole, the 1994 bombing of a Jewish community center in Buenos Aires, you get the idea. A lot of pain in one basket.

Other religions fast—Christians during Lent, Muslims during Ramadan, Hindus, Buddhists, Mormons, Eastern Orthodox. Reasons include asceticism, contemplation, penance, purification, resistance to gluttony, spiritual improvement, closeness to God. Jews add memory. We fast to remember. Tisha B'Av marks the mother lode of memorial, exceeding Yom HaShoah and Yom HaZikaron.

We're supposed to abstain from food and drink, sex, leather shoes, studying Torah, greeting people, idle chatter, leisure activities, or "anointing" ourselves (meaning no perfume, deodorant, or sunblock). All of which adds up to a challenge at the height of summer.

This year, Tisha B'Av (translation: the ninth of the Hebrew month Av) falls on a Sunday, and is the longest fast besides Yom Kippur. But despite the momentousness of this remembrance, the holiday remains obscure, certainly not in the Top Ten. "Tisha B'Av doesn't come close," says Rabbi Judith Hauptman, a plainspoken, widely admired professor of Talmud at the Jewish Theological Seminary. "If you look at the most-observed holidays on a bar graph, Tisha B'Av doesn't get a quarter inch."

Nevertheless, Hauptman loves the music that is played on the eve of the holiday, and the power of the traditional reading—the book of Lamentations, whose first word, *"Eichah"* ("How?"), captures our inability to understand why God destroyed the Temple and let us suffer. The *Eichah* recitation had an eerie power for Hauptman when she heard it as a youngster at Jewish summer camp in the Poconos. The counselors went out on a floating dock at night and ignited the Hebrew letters of *Eichah* so that campers gathered on a hilltop could watch the word burn. "It was the most dramatic, beautiful, inspirational thing ever," Hauptman says. "And then they would get on the P.A. system and read these chapters from the book of Jeremiah, which were all about predictions of the destruction and so on. . . . It was like the most riveting ghost story. They really brought Tisha B'Av home to us. Not in a purely intellectual way, but in this emotional way."

I have no emotional tie to this holiday. Maybe because my childhood lacked that dramatic lake tableau (at my summer camp, I learned to tie-dye and weave on a loom), it's hard for me to find any hook.

Or maybe my detachment is because Tisha B'Av remembers the destruction of two ancient temples, and the Judaism I know and care about isn't based on a building, especially one that relied upon blood-soaked animal sacrifices as an expression of faith.

Or maybe I simply don't relish a sixth fast.

But then one idea *does* tug at my heart: when Rabbi Hauptman describes Tisha B'Av as an opportunity to grieve together. "This holiday is kind of a collective shiva," she says. "We're mourning for the past, and the many tragedies of the Jewish people. For solidarity."

A collective shiva. Judaism at its most unified. We cry on cue—it's required of us. Our tradition insists not just that we look at *past* pain, but present-day, too.

I think about the Paris kosher market in January 2015, when four hostages were killed just because they were buying groceries.

The Copenhagen shooting in the Great Synagogue on February 14, when a Jewish security guard was killed during a bat mitzvah celebration.

The same month, posters reading "A good Jew is a dead Jew" were found in Buenos Aires, "Jews to the gas" was painted on a community center in Tuscany, cars were spray-painted with swastikas in Montreal, "F*** the Jews" was written on the gates of a Jewish school in London.

The list is too long for this space. I'm not paranoid these days, but I'm rattled. The ground has shifted. Anger is less veiled.

"This has been a very bad year for the Jewish people," says Hauptman. "If there were to be any time when Tisha B'Av should strike home, it would be this year. We've had Jews killed just because they were Jews, swastikas painted, attacks of all sorts. So yes, the Jewish community has to come together as Jews. Just for solidarity."

On this holiday, therefore, I plan to focus on the places where there has been persecution—a word that shouldn't be used cavalierly, a word that has attached itself like a parasite to Jewish history. What I *won't* be doing Sunday, however, is focusing on myself. Hauptman says the holiday is not for reflecting upon sad events in one's own life. "When I hear a rabbi suggest that we all talk about our own personal tragedies on Tisha B'Av, it drives me berserk," she says. "We're pulling together as a Jewish community to mourn our common tragedies that befell us *as the Jewish people*. It's not about my personal journey from sadness to happiness. That's totally missing the point. We celebrate together and we mourn together. It's a lot harder to mourn together. I don't deny that."

It's a lot harder to mourn together. I saw that on Yom HaShoah, when we were supposed to pause communally to honor the victims of the Holocaust, but so few Jews in New York did anything. Many didn't know the holiday was even happening. Several told me that choosing one day to speak of the unspeakable felt insufficient or trivializing. Others said they wouldn't know where to begin.

I saw the same discomfort on Yom HaZikaron, Israel's Memorial Day, which most American Jews also skip or never learned. Until this year, I never knew it or observed it myself. Maybe that's the work of Tisha B'Av: to put communal sorrow on the calendar. To tell us to stop, intentionally, in the brightest possible sunlight, to remember the dark. I'm not sure if it works to sob on schedule. But Judaism doesn't give you the choice. It *requires* memory.

So on Sunday, I'll swear off the sunblock and do my share of mourning. I'll be honoring not just suffering, but survival. Because we weathered the Temples' destruction, the crusades, the pogroms, the Holocaust, the intifada, the kosher market, and all the scrawled hatred on the cars, schools, and walls. We've been hit and hit and kept walking. That's Tisha B'Av, too.

On the day of the holiday itself, since I choose to be in our Connecticut house with my family rather than in a New York synagogue, I rely on the geographically closest rabbi to guide me through the holiday: Rabbi Burt Visotzky, Midrash expert, who happens to have a home near mine. Burt was the first rabbi I interviewed for this voyage, and it seems fitting that he be my last.

I am well into my fast-funk when we sit down with the Lamentations text on a sofa. The rain has stopped, but the sky remains stubbornly gray. I ask Burt to explain why, when the Romans brought down the Second Temple, does *Eichah* suggest the Jews bear significant responsibility. When we ask "How?"—*Eichah*—*How, God, could you let our Temple burn?*, the answer apparently involves our own sin. The Talmud says we ripped each other apart instead of our enemy.

When we should have united to beat back the Roman army, we instead argued among ourselves, even killed each other. *Sinat chinam*—translated as "baseless hate"—was our downfall.

"God commands us to love one another," Burt explains. "So when we hate one another and then things fall apart, the rabbis say, 'Well, this is the punishment that God predicted for us.'"

The Talmud says: *But why was the second Sanctuary destroyed. . . ? Because therein prevailed hatred without cause. That teaches you that groundless hatred is considered as of even gravity with the three sins of idolatry, immorality, and bloodshed together.*

I get it: God destroys us when we destroy each other. We will pay for Jew against Jew.

Samuel G. Freedman's important book *Jew vs. Jew* (2000) exposed the modern, American iterations of "baseless hatred." His prologue invoked that ancient sin, which led to our exile and slaughter: "The Second Temple, Jews came to believe, was lost less to the Romans than to their own *sinat chinam*—pure hatred, groundless hatred."

Of course, *sinat chinam* meant something different in 70 C.E. than it does in 2015. But our current rabbis see the parallel and a warning: we are risking our proverbial edifices, our centers of Jewish life, when we go at each other.

Freedman reported contemporary civil wars through sharp stories: a zoning battle in a Cleveland suburb in response to an influx of Orthodox Jews; a dispute in Los Angeles over whether to introduce feminist language into the Amidah prayer—the core standing prayer; and a lawsuit against Yale brought by pious students who refused coed bathrooms. These are just a few of the flashpoints that can splinter a people.

I saw internecine strains come to a boil during the 2014 Gaza war. And during my entire Jewish year, as I've been attuned to the calendar, I've paid more attention to the roiled Jewish press, nasty Facebook posts, and Twitter feeds. *Sinat chinam* is alive and well.

"I'm afraid to look at my email in the morning," confesses Rabbi Judith Hauptman. "It's breaking my heart, what's happening today. Back in Temple times, there were Jews fighting over all these political factions. They were stabbing each other over political differences, possibly religious differences. And we're still fighting each other. Maybe not with swords."

Did God *instigate* the Romans' assault on the Second Temple, or simply do nothing to stop it? Burt answers the question with a question: "Is God's hand an active hand or a passive hand? That's not for me to decide."

The lesson that hatred corrodes is one that we evidently need to keep relearning. I try to believe in some halcyon view of Jewish unity—that we're one people and we have each other's backs; that we don't malign, fight, or undermine each other because we're too few (and battered) to risk more division. But then I see how much internal discord there has been throughout history— Jacob's theft of his twin's birthright; the nuances of Hanukkah, when observant Maccabees fought their Hellenized kin; I see how Orthodox Jews have chastised some Modern Orthodox for ordaining women, how angrily Jews have disagreed about Israel's settlements and its Arab citizens. Jews even disparage each other about who counts as a real Jew.

Earlier this summer, David Azoulay, Israel's religious-services minister, a member of the Knesset—Israeli's governing congress—said he doesn't consider Reform Jews to be really Jewish. I took that personally. My Reform congregation—six thousand strong—is, in my estimation, wholly legitimate. Moreover, the Reform movement happens to be the largest denomination in America, so Azoulay's condemnation impugns a lot of us. One could shrug off his blanket indictment as extremist; but when he claims that non-Orthodox Jews are "people who try and falsify" the Jewish religion, it smacks of *sinat chinam.*

Burt's own exasperation with Israeli divisiveness comes through as we talk. "We're commanded to love one another," he repeats. "*Ve'ahavta Lerei'acha kamocha.* Love your neighbor as yourself. We're commanded to love God. So why are we teaching hate? Why have we raised a generation of Israeli kids who can set fire to a bilingual school that teaches Hebrew and Arabic, and then, when they're sentenced at trial, hear them say it was worth it? Why are we raising a generation of kids in yeshivot [Jewish schools] who can throw bags of feces on people praying at the Wailing Wall because they're not Orthodox? I mean, how did this happen?

"And we're all equally guilty," he continues. "I've certainly been intemperate in my rage against politics that I don't care for, and I've probably said so too publicly. Instead of working to find ways to talk to one another, we find ways to shut one another out. That's really the tragedy of this holiday. If you want something to mourn for, that's it. We're reproducing what cost us the Second Temple. We're just wallowing in *sinat chinam*."

I know it sounds naïve, but I really can't fathom the acrimony; it feels fundamentally un-Jewish to me. And profoundly dispiriting. As I approach the end of a full Jewish year, I'm actually left with the opposite sensation: I have felt surprisingly supported, even by those rabbis who are miles away on the spectrum of observance. And I have drawn wisdom from countless different Jewish perspectives. As I reflect on what I'll remember most from my immersion, it is not *sinat chinam*—the rancor of my people. What will stick with me is the wide capacity to find meaning. Judaism perseveres because it still speaks to us, because it withstands our clashes and grows from them.

So, though I resist the Tisha B'Av message that God would punish our warfare—to the point of destroying the center of Jewish life—I see that this is perhaps just what God intended: the Temple needed to go in order for the tradition to spread beyond one location on the map. And indeed it has. Judaism is alive today despite our divisions and despite all the catastrophes subsumed in Tisha B'Av.

As I head into the next Jewish cycle—more privately this time around—I'm choosing to focus not on *sinat chinam* but on *klal yisrael*, the whole of Israel: a shared inheritance, and reverence for a calendar that has kept us intact.

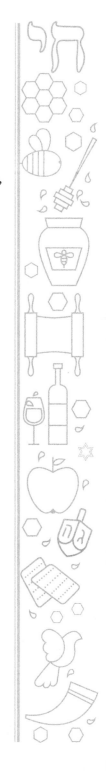

Rabbi Angela Buchdahl
ON SHABBAT

Judaism has so many prayers that require community. *Kaddish*: the idea that we don't mourn alone. *Barchu*: the call to prayer. You need a minyan — a quorum— again and again. And celebration: there is something about being in community that helps you multiply the joys that are present. In Shabbat services, people bring their energy, whatever it is, into that space, and there is a sense that joy is magnified. And those who walk in with a great deal of pain often find that just being among others dissipates it, even slightly. They do not feel as isolated, they sense that the congregation is carrying them in some way. For me, whatever kind of energy we're able to generate when we sing and pray together transports all of us present to a place that feels, at least a little bit, like what I think that taste of Shabbat is supposed to be: a taste of the world to come.

25

MY SHABBAT LANDING

Comforting Consistency

W HAT HAS MY Shabbat habit become, at the end of this year? A very simple, restoring routine. One that doesn't differ so visibly from where I set off, but has deepened immeasurably in the crossing.

By 5:50 P.M., I'm walking up the steep front stairs of Central Synagogue, even in the meanest weather, greeting the security guards at the door, making my way into the ornate sanctuary with its stenciled walls, massive columns, and high balconies, greeting the *shamashim* volunteers—the welcomers—who stand at the ready to distribute programs (the "order of service") as we wish each other "Shabbat Shalom."

Kabbalat Shabbat (Welcoming the Sabbath) is the spirited gathering on the eve of every Sabbath, a sequence of blessings, hymns, and psalms to usher in the week's holiest day. (In some Reform synagogues, such as ours, it can be the more widely attended service, compared to the next day's Shabbat morning service.)

I embrace the people I know on my way down the aisle, heading to my usual section on the left—there are no assigned seats, but we all end up gravitating toward the same rows. I didn't expect I would ever want this: the reliability of ritual. Familiar faces in pews. A Jewish home team.

By 6 P.M., I've found a seat, made sure my phone is off. Services always begin promptly. Sometimes my husband is with me; more likely he will arrive late from the office. There's a tenderness in our reunion here. Services end at seven fifteen, and those seventy-five minutes have become sacred time. I'm ruminative, unhurried. Nothing is asked of me. I'm surrounded by friends but not obligated to them. We're connected but on our own.

The rabbis and cantors enter together—not onto the bimah, but in front of it, on the level of the congregants—singing the first uplifting song, usually *"Hava Nashira"* ("We'll Sing Together") or *"Shir Hama'alot"* ("Song of Ascents"). The guitar, played by Rabbi Buchdahl, is never campfire-cheesy, rather an extra limb of her rabbinate. Orthodox synagogues forbid musical instruments (because "fixing" or tuning an instrument is considered "work," and because they see noise-making as counter to the restful Sabbath). But some Modern Orthodox shuls have reincorporated clapping and dancing, which was permitted in ancient times, later prohibited because it smacked of frivolity. German Reform congregations introduced organ music in the nineteenth century, and Shabbat music eventually evolved to where the songs of the late troubadour Debbie Friedman (who recorded mainly in the seventies and eighties) have become standard in services spanning denominations.

The rabbi acknowledges the visitors in our midst, asks the regulars to make sure those guests feel welcome, reminds us to turn off our phones to honor the peace of the Sabbath. We're asked to take a moment to introduce ourselves to someone sitting near us. Again, while this could seem forced, it feels called for; there's a fittingly Jewish commotion for a few minutes, welcoming the stranger, kibitzing.

I then watch the two Sabbath candles being illuminated on the bimah and join the blessing for the light, feeling thankful—even amazed—that we've reassembled again, despite so much turmoil in the world. That's a small miracle by itself, week after week.

When we sing *"L'cha Dodi, Likrat kallah"* ("Come, my beloved to meet the bride"), I recall how many times the wedding metaphor was invoked during this Jewish year: on Sukkot, on Simchat Torah, Passover, Lag B'Omer, Shavuot. We "married" the Torah, we betrothed ourselves to God—or to the female essence of God—depending on the holiday (and which rabbi was explaining the imagery). There have been spiritual nuptials all year.

Every Friday night is essentially a recommitment ceremony. I'm re-upping a certain vow, privately in my head, communally in public. On the last verse of that song, we all turn simultaneously—and without verbal prompting—to face the door (a traditional, collective invitation to the Sabbath bride to enter the sanctuary), bowing to our left, right, and center on the last line of the last stanza. That synchronicity conveys piety to me.

The musicians (all remarkable) feel by now like an extension of the clergy. The professional choir heightens every song. The musical director, David Strickland, nimble on the piano and organ, channels a kind of serenity, attuned to every turn in the liturgy. Music feels like consecration here.

I'm emotional during the *Hashkiveinu*, a prayer for protection. It conjures the shelter of the sukkah and the leitmotif of caring all year round. God will hear you on Yom Kippur. God will visit you in your sukkah, water your land on Hoshana Rabbah, stay with you on Shemini Atzeret. Judaism can't be outlawed (see Hanukkah), the earth will be defended (Tu B'Shvat), our people won't be exterminated (Purim) but will be delivered from bondage (Passover). Safe passage and safekeeping. *Hashkiveinu*.

With the full-throated *Shema*, we avow our faith and proclaim—without music or adornment—that we choose Judaism. We made this same avowal when we abstained from eating six times, when we put menorahs in our windows, when we shut down email on the Sabbath. So many times we telegraph our particularity.

During the prayer for the sick, the misheberach, I think about my cancer-stricken friend Julie. She brings back Ethan Tucker's teaching for *Tzom Asara B'Tevet*, fasting for those in pain, and Stein Hain's teaching for *Shivah Asar b'Tammuz*, surviving despite a certain end.

I count my blessings during the shehecheyanu, the prayer for gratitude. There are too many to list after this year, and so many junctures when the holidays demanded that accounting.

Whenever a new baby is blessed at the ark—squirming in a parent's arms or riveted by the rabbi's face—I'm overcome by the promise of this tiny new Jew. When the b'nai mitzvah kids come up to the podium to lead Kiddush, I see the continuum of our contract at Sinai.

I rise from my seat to honor my father-in-law during Kaddish, the mourner's prayer, along with others who have recently lost someone.

Central speaks to me, again and again. After all my wandering and wondering this year, I feel like Dorothy realizing "There's no place like home."

It always takes me a while to leave at the conclusion of Friday night services (Jews schmooze). Dave prods me deftly out the door to dinner. We go meet synagogue friends at a nearby restaurant or someone's home, where we recite the blessings together again. As the shiny challah is raised up, I feel lucky to be part of a gang that recites Kiddush without apology.

But the sweetest suppers are with our family foursome. I light the candles. Ben lifts the wine glass. Molly rips the challah. Dave joins every blessing, all of us singing in separate keys. We take a quiet moment to ourselves (I often cover my eyes as Mom did at our childhood table) to say a private word of appreciation. Shemini Atzeret taught me I'm entitled to that.

Dinner proceeds the way any family's does, with all of its comical ease. I'm at my most relaxed. The next day, Saturday morning, I won't usually be in services, unless it's for the bar or bat mitzvah of a close friend's child. I won't turn off all my devices the way I'd promised myself at the start of the year. But I'll take more walks with Dave than I used to. I'll be less "efficient" and more alert to the elemental luxuries of the Sabbath: another break, another breath, another chance to rest, revive, feel grateful. For the nuclear family that sustains me, the Central family that surprised me, and the larger Jewish family—found in a year of phone calls, coffee visits, prayers, pages, sermons, and sanctuaries—whom I found just in the nick of time.

Rabbi Peter J. Rubinstein
ON THE YEAR

The challenge actually continues every year, to *find why am I doing this? Why am I doing this?* These holidays, I think, were always meant to take us out of the mundane. And they keep you ethically alert. We're just untrained in taking responsibility for creating something sacred in our lives. We're always waiting for God to do that, or the rabbi. And yet, if you investigate the tradition, what I think it says, is that this is not up to anybody but you; create something sacred in your life.

Here's the irony: every time I think about people who insist, "The rule is," I want to say to them, *tradition wasn't always that rule.* Nowadays we look at authenticity, 'authentic' Judaism, and have certain models in our mind that didn't exist two hundred years ago. Three hundred years ago. "Tradition" is a loaded term. So I don't feel compelled by, *"You can't change this prayer,"* or *"How can you possibly do this differently?,"* or, *"You have to sing Kol Nidre only at the beginning of the service."* We have never been dormant. We have never been inactive.

The journey you took, Abby, was active. If our tradition isn't vital and changing, with full respect to what was before, then it's not alive. Our people, our liturgy, our holiday prayers have always been about the question: Do I feel the weight of it? I feel the weight of my ancestors—who actually created what was, in their age, forceful and powerful, and I think they would want us to be doing the same in our day.

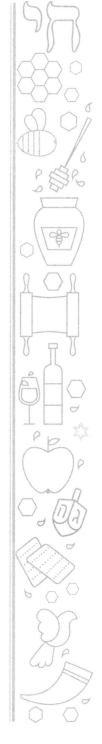

EPILOGUE
Where Did I End Up?

9.9.15

"**D**ID IT CHANGE YOU?"

That's what I was asked by people who knew I'd been living on Jewish time for the last twelve months.

The answer was yes.

And no.

Yes, because I now understand the tent poles of every holiday—ancient and modern, mournful and exultant.

No, because I'm in no hurry to fast six times again anytime soon.

Yes, because this year of mindfulness made me look harder at every priority, every relationship, every choice—in T. S. Eliot's words, the "coffee spoons" of a life.

No, because I still get restless in long synagogue services.

Yes, because I now see the point of many rituals I used to think were pointless.

No, because I still don't see the point of many rituals.

Yes, because I was taught and encouraged by so many rabbis and inspired by so many different paths to worship.

No, because after sampling various spiritual homes, I was happy (even relieved) to come back to my own.

After observing eighteen holidays (actually twenty, but eighteen is Jewishly neater, as explained in the intro) and writing twenty-five chapters (three about Shabbat) in which I quoted fifty-one rabbis, plus twenty non-clergy (writers, educators, etc.), I am moved, more than anything, by what our tradition imposes: moments of deliberate intermission; the demand to reach others in trouble; the rope pulling the ancient into the present. I felt strangely thrilled by the ongoing disagreements over phrases or sources, a constant reminder that this tradition is never finished, the opinions keep coming.

I've also just been moved by feeling moved. There were random flashes of emotion, when I felt privately captivated. The sound of the shofar in my own home. The trust of sharing Elul confessions with my friend Catherine. The focus required to fast when your family isn't. The pleading of the Selichot prayers. The sadness of the "Who shall live and who shall die?" liturgy. The warmer air of Sukkot in Los Angeles. The notion of hanging back with God on Shemini Atzeret. The high of dancing with strangers. The pride of seeing so many Jews milling among White House Christmas decorations. The idea that Tu B'Shvat is a chance to start over. The giddiness of staging the Esther story. Taking Passover into uncharted places. The unreadable list of Holocaust dead. The nod to fallen soldiers on Yom HaZikaron. The balloons on Yom Ha'atzmaut. The thousands eating cheesecake on Sukkot. The collective mourning that is Tisha B'Av.

I felt carried through the year, on a sort of insistent current that conveys all boats to the same port at the same time. That sense of being inseparable, interdependent. We all showed up together. We all slowed down together.

Though the year may not have been life-changing, it was decidedly mind-altering. Like when my eye doctor gives me option "1 or 2" as he sets my eyeglass prescription, I suddenly saw option 2. The Jewish schedule heightened the stakes, reminding me repeatedly how precarious life is, how impatient our tradition is with complacency, how obligated we are to rescue those with less, how lucky we are to have so much history, so much family, so much food.

I was moved by mundane, simple joys. The small stuff in the rest of my nonreligious life got sweeter. The way my daughter and son talk to each other when they don't know I can hear them. My husband's random text message, asking how my day is going. The fellowship of my college friends around a dinner table. The glimpse of my rabbi during Friday's Kaddish, locking eyes with a congregant who just lost his brother. The way something tastes after a fast. The raucous din of "Dayenu" coming from my cousins at the seder table.

I marked more. Paid attention. Lingered.

I understood why Judaism mandates not just eulogy but memory. Animate the story; it's not enough to retell it. We don't just *recall* Egypt or the Temples, we resuscitate our enemies: Pharaoh, Haman, Antiochus, the Babylonians, Romans, Nazis. We bring back our heroes, too: the Maccabees, Esther, Mordechai, Moses, Miriam, Rashbi, the Warsaw resistance fighters, Ben-Gurion. At Yom Kippur's Yizkor service, we summon lost relatives; on Yom HaShoah, we hear from survivors. We carry our dead.

I get this now, that memory is history, a corrective, a badge. Can I transmit that lesson to Ben and Molly while they're still living under our roof? A sense of the ancestors who came before us and why they matter? I now have a stronger grip on what's been transported for generations, despite the odds. No Jew starts from scratch.

I'm no longer the new mother choked up at my son's bris, afraid that I didn't know enough to teach him. I know more and I've passed on more. I've given (and continue to give) my kids Jewish scaffolding—incomplete, perhaps, but solid, more than I had stood on myself. Now I can only hope they will choose what I've chosen—an inquisitive Jewish life—not because I'm focused on continuity for its own sake, but because I know how invigorating this journey can be.

I've tried not to over-teach my kids while I was learning myself. To Ben and Molly's credit, they never recoiled (at least visibly) when I wanted to share a newfound discovery. But if they absorbed one thing above all this year, it was my excitement. I was often stressed, but entirely engaged. Maybe there's contagion in that by itself. At the very least, I know they know that being Jewish is really, really interesting.

Tradition has a point. And they'd say, without hesitation, that ours is a Jewish family.

Before I embarked on this expedition, I said I was "looking for drama" and for meaning. As the saying goes, be careful what you wish for. I never expected to lose my father-in-law, Milton, to watch him leave this world, to see the *Unetane Tokef* made real. I never expected to see my cancer-stricken friend Julie, a young mother, run out of medical options.

The holidays made me attuned to woe. The Jewish cycle compels us to notice the downcast and the stragglers: on Yom Kippur, Sukkot, Purim, Passover, and all six fasts.

Finally, I understood the chronological arc to the holidays and the themes that link them. I saw how the bleakness and fragility of Yom Kippur segues to the joy and fragility of Sukkot. How Hanukkah was a Sukkot redo. That four of the six fasts honor four stages of the Temples' destruction; why the Temple used to embody Judaism itself. The narrative tie between Passover, Shavuot, and Sukkot, and the desert that unites them.

And even though I fumbled at the most important holiday of all, Shabbat (I couldn't turn off all devices, no matter how many rabbis urged me to try), I experienced the day differently. I found my own Sabbath, with its own peace and sanctity. I applied the ethic of pausing to moments that deserved them. There was mindfulness in my mother-in-law Phyllis's first visit to us without her husband. And when I helped Ben pack for college, choking back tears. And when I observed Molly struggling as her brother left for the airport. I noted the kadosh—separation—between Phyllis as a coupled woman and a widowed one, between Ben's childhood and independence, between Molly's sibling normalcy, living next door to Ben and sharing daily banter, and now passing by his empty room on the way to hers. Judaism reminds us not to run from transitions, but to consecrate them.

Oddly enough, the *non*-holiday weeks were so fleeting and undemanding as to feel like holidays from the holidays. They pointed up how much structure is baked into this religion and how rare it is to be off-duty. At the same time, those rare stretches of purely secular life were heightened by the ceremonies on either side.

☆

When I finished the last fast, in the heat of the summer, and looked back on where I had been one year earlier, with all the holidays ahead of me, I felt both gratified and humbled. There were no trumpets, no shofar blasts, no cause for fanfare. For many Jews, marking all these holidays is simply living life. In a matter of weeks, we'd be starting the work of atonement all over again. But it felt important personally to have hit every mark on time, poignant to look back on all the reading and conversations that expanded my exploration. So many people helped, advised, spurred me on, or gave me a zetz (that's Yiddish for poke).

The final task of this book turned out to encapsulate my Jewish year. I gave the complete manuscript of this book, for fact-checking, to a rabbi whom I consider a walking encyclopedia of Jewish tradition, history, and liturgy, Dov Linzer, the Rosh HaYeshiva (essentially senior scholar) of Yeshivat Chovevei Torah (YCT), the Modern Orthodox seminary in Riverdale. Dov and I met in 2009 at a Jewish conference in Baltimore; we've stayed in touch, and I receive his erudite weekly Torah commentary in my inbox.

Our ensuing exchanges, over email and texts, was surprisingly delightful and quintessentially Jewish. His factual corrections were sometimes hairsplitting, sometimes sizable, playful, and scolding, but we were instantly engaged in a timeless endeavor. Page by page, we parsed language, rabbinic interpretations, rules, and new rulings on rules, in a way that not only quickened my brain but felt—I have to use the word—spiritual. As you know by now, that's how Judaism works for me: the learning sparks the feeling. My exchanges with Dov were expressions not just of education (my questions sometimes prompted his own), but of friendship. We were connecting over ancient things. Two Jews, who could not be further apart in terms of observance, lifestyle, and learnedness, finding common ground over nerdy questions such as who tithes on Tu B'Shvat and, when we're searching for chametz before Passover with a candle, feather, and spoon, is that ritual a recent addition—and what counts as "recent"?

Dov Text: The candle is from the Talmud, used because it produces fo-
cused light. I use a flashlight myself, because it isn't a fire hazard and lets
you do a better job. The feather, I just learned because you asked, was added
around the seventeenth century to get stuff out of the cracks. Spoon is nine-
teenth century, maybe a little earlier. It was added so that, if no chametz
was found during the search, something would be left from the act of search-
ing to burn the next morning when you're supposed to burn the last cha-
metz. Funny how these things become ritualized. So, it was earlier than I
thought. Although I still think that the ritualization of the spoon and
feather is relatively recent. Most people I know don't use them.

We both knew that, at the end of the day, there is no "right" answer
in Judaism—there are only more questions. But Dov challenged my
assumptions (example: nowhere in the Torah does it say Moses was
outraged before he killed the Egyptian, though it's implied), and he
cautioned against un-nuanced criticisms of Jewish behavior, such as
the suggestion that the Jews in Persia were purely motivated by revenge when they killed 75,000 at the end of the Purim story.

The verses make it clear that this killing was also preemptive—the proc-
lamation to kill all the Jews couldn't be cancelled, so the only way the Jews
could stop from being slaughtered was to arm themselves: see Esther 8:8 and
8:11. It is true that the Jews could have taken a more defensive approach; a
preemptive strike need not have been such a total slaughter. And it is true
that 9:2–5 makes it sound like it was primarily about revenge. Still, I
would nuance this point a bit.

As we neared my deadline on a Friday afternoon, I was cognizant
that Shabbat was approaching and Dov would be going offline at
dusk. I emailed him, "I'm rushing through your edits before sunset to
see if there's anything that will trip me up before I lose you."

"No problem," he wrote back. "I'm here."

"I'm here." That made me smile. It's what Moses said in response to
the voice from the burning bush: *"Hineni"*; "Here I am." It's what
Abraham said to God on Mount Moriah: "Here I am." This year I
reached for something without knowing exactly what it was. And so
many people said, "Here I am."

So back to the original question: "Did it change you?"

Yes. I understand now why Judaism's edifice has held Jews up for centuries, even without a building.

Yes. Clarifying a holiday makes me more likely to revisit it.

Yes. I felt part of something unshakable, unbreakable.

To be sure, there are a few caveats: my religion was amplified, but not my religiosity. I feel more prayerful now; but I don't think I'll pray more often. My Hebrew is still halting, despite the valiant efforts of my tutor.

But whatever my regrets, nearly every holiday magnified not just a personal gratitude but a larger one . . .

. . . That a people survived: the siege, the breach, the burning, slavery, crusades, pogroms, camps, ambushes, bus bombs, and Kosher market attacks.

. . . That we get another day, not just to live more, but to love fiercely.

. . . That we gather repeatedly, to pound our chests in unison, eat in makeshift huts, cavort with Torahs, light menorahs, break matzah, read names, study into the dawn.

And finally, to answer Rabbi Irwin Kula's compelling challenge— that we should ask what we "hire" the holidays to do for us—I have my answer now. A lot.

Leon Wieseltier's words come back to me again from our 2005 interview: "Sooner or later you will cherish something so much that you will seek to preserve it."

This year was my "sooner or later."

It was a watchful, demanding, food-filled, food-deprived, amazing year.

I'm not sure I'll repeat it, but I'm sure I won't forget it. Thank you for taking the trip with me.

ACKNOWLEDGMENTS

I AM BEYOND GRATEFUL to the remarkable Fig Tree Books team, led by publisher Fredric Price, who took a column and pushed me to develop it into a fresh new book, with meticulous care and a demanding-but-very-special book editor, Michelle Caplan—she's a gift to an author. Erika Dreifus is also a canny, tireless media editor and Miranda Pennington a patient production editor. Thank you.

I am indebted to the amazing *Forward* team, led by wonderful Editor-in-Chief Jane Eisner, who birthed and nurtured the original series in a way that was generous and bold. Jane made every piece better and brought every resource to bear. Publisher Sam Norich was a quiet-but-unflagging supporter and made me feel like part of the Forward family. Editor Dan Friedman's guidance was wry and wise. Thank you.

I relied upon (and drew strength from) all the rabbis and scholars who guided me with their interviews, books, sermons, articles and unstinting nudges. There were more conversations than I could include, but they all brought home the power and generosity of scholarship and insight. I am also grateful to so many friends who read these dispatches and kept me company, many more than can be thanked in this space, but here are a few of my relied-upon interviews and companions through it all:

Myriam Abramowicz, Rachel Ain, Anita Altman, Elana Arian, Nicole Auerbach, Andy Bachman, Tony Bayfield, Cori & Seth Berger, Catherine Birndorf, Jonathan Blake, Yosef Blau, Nahama Broner, Marcelo Bronstein, Bryan Brown, Erica Brown, Sharon Brous, Angela Buchdahl, Lauren Berkun, Maracia Caban, Julia

Cadrain, Adam Chalom, Anne Cohen, Ayelet Cohen, Michael Cohen, Steven M. Cohen, Susie Cohen, Elliot Cosgrove, Joshua Davidson, Miriam Pomerantz Dauber, Antoinette Delruelle, Marcia DeSanctis, Rachel Dretzin, Cindy & David Edelson, Susan Edelstein, Yaffa Epstein, David Ellenson, Jacqueline Koch Ellenson, Ruthie Ellenson, Steven Exler, Bruce Feiler, Ed Feinstein, Julian Fleisher, Matthew Gewirtz, Gary Ginsberg, Mo Glazman, Nancy Goodman, Arthur Green, Blu Greenberg, Yitz Greenberg, Lois Perelson-Gross, Marni Gutkin, Elana Stein Hain, Jill Hammer, Judith Hauptman, Shai Held, Carolyn Hessel, Ammiel Hirsch, Brad Hirschfield, Larry Hoffman, Daniel Hurewitz, Sara Hurwitz, David Ingber, Jill Jacobs, Rick Jacobs, Bruce Jacoby, Carol Jenkins, David Kalb, Barbara Kane, Josh Katzan, Elie Kaunfer, Sharon Kleinbaum, Shira Kline, Stephanie Kolin, Jennifer Krause, Itamar Kubovy, Dara Kubovy-Weiss, Miri Kubovy, Yehuda Kurtzer, Arthur Kurzweil, Amichai Lau-Lavie, Michele Landsberg, Lauren Bush Lauren, Sue Leonard, Naomi Less, Marion Lev-Cohen, Joy Levitt, Naomi Levy, Alan Lew, Asher Lopatin, Ari Lorge, Jamie Alter Lynton, Sara Luria, Joshua Malina, Roly Matalon, Daniel Matt, Jessica Kate Meyer, Julia Moskin, Daniel Nadelman, Alana Newhouse, Aaron Panken, Michael Paley, Barbara Penzer, Kathleen Peratis, Jonah Pesner, Holly Peterson, Lisa and Richard Plepler, Michael Price, Gena Raps, Michael Ravitch, Lilly Rivlin, Gary Rosenblatt, Menachem Rosensaft, Joseph Rosenstein, Norman Roth, Martine Rubenstein, Lisa Rubin, Peter J. Rubinstein, Ira Sachs, Joanna Samuels, Jonathan Sarna, Maurice Salth, David Saperstein, Sara Savage, Basya Schechter, Mindy Schachtman, Arthur Schneier, Azi Schwartz, Seth Schwartz, Chaim Seidler-Feller, Avi Shafran, Dani Shapiro, Judith Shulevitz, Michael Simon, Karen Sirota, Felicia Sol, Mychal Springer, Martyna Starosta, Joshua Steiner, Chaim Steinmetz, Adin Steinsaltz, Michael Strassfeld, Andy Straus, David Strickland, Alexandra Styron, Joseph Telushkin, Livia Thompson, Ethan Tucker, Burton Visotzky, Arthur Waskow, Deborah Waxman, Pamela Weinberg, Melissa Weintraub, Avi Weiss, Leon Wieseltier, Thea Wieseltier, and David Wolpe.

Special thanks . . .

. . . to Catherine Birndorf for being my Elul confessor, and
Jeremy Fielding for being my fast-chum.

. . . to Rabbi Dov Linzer for his invaluable, patient, and profi-
cient vetting (and genuine friendship).

. . . to A. J. Jacobs for setting the high bar and redefining
menschlichkeit.

. . . to Sivan Butler-Rotholz for extraordinary research, a
scholar's eye, steady judgment, and warmth.

. . . to Eric Alterman, for uncommon encouragement, shared
study-obsession, and introducing me to Sivan and to Fig Tree.

. . . to Carolyn Hessel, for starting me on my Jewish book path,
being a cheerleader and taskmaster, and insisting on a glossary.

. . . to David Kuhn, for being the toughest, wisest agent and a
constant friend.

. . . to Sarah Levitt, for being a gentler agent, but no less wise.

. . . to my twin and best friend, Robin, who edited every chapter twice, saved me in the eleventh hour, and whose gut I trust
the most.

. . . to my mother, Letty, who gave me my first Jewish home,
Jewish pride, and my first model of female Jewish leadership.
(Not to mention key edits in this book.)

. . . to my father, Bert, who in so many ways keeps my compass
and cared so much about this project.

. . . to my brother, David, who always picks me up when I'm
flagging.

My in-laws were wonderful and allowed me to share Milt in these
pages.

My fellow congregants at Central Synagogue were buoying and kind.

Rabbis Angela Buchdahl and Peter Rubinstein have my heart.

Most of all, to my children, Ben and Molly, who are my truest blessings. This Jewish Year made me rediscover everything they are and how much I need and love them.

And finally, to my husband, David Shapiro, my most honest reader, who knows me the best and keeps me steady and sane, even when I'm neither. I am so lucky for him.

APPENDIX 1

A JEWISH YEAR IN BULLET POINTS

M Y HEAD STILL spins with all the year's teachings, but recalling the flashpoints helps me to chart the sweep of the year:

1. During the period of **Elul**, the forty days of introspection leading to Yom Kippur, I won't forget the discipline of daily self-examination. It changed atonement because by the time I got there, I had already seen myself starkly; there was no shock in it. Which was better. It's better to prepare to be naked before you are. And the shofar blast that's required every day leading up to Rosh Hashanah was, to me, the sound of both history and resolve.

2. **Rosh Hashanah:** The *Unetaneh Tokef* prayer (the "Who will live and who will die" prayer) was suddenly prescient and blindingly factual. People died in every way on the list. By fire and by stoning. By water, sword, and plague.

3. **The Fast of Gedaliah:** Marking the assassination of the Jewish governor who was viewed as a collaborator by his fellow Jews left me cold (and annoyed that I had to fast just days before The Really Big Fast). But I'll remember the poignant suggestion that Gedaliah stands in for Yitzhak Rabin, another seismic Jew-on-Jew murder. And that we revisit intramural tension on Hanukkah and Tisha B'Av, too.

4. **Yom Kippur** made me wish that everyone knew it meant preparing for death, because then we'd waste less life. Who wouldn't make different choices if we knew this year was our last?

5. **Sukkot:** Spending it in Los Angeles made me see the harvest holiday less in terms of autumn corn husks and more in terms of the open air. As for its meaning, the holiday packed almost too many themes, but each one of them resounded: Impermanence. Vulnerability. Earth. Materialism. Wandering.

6. **Hoshana Rabbah:** The obscure seventh day of Sukkot, when the lulav and etrog are waved vigorously one last time, brought home the humblest necessity of rain. And who got the mystics' memo that *this* is actually the deadline for atonement, not the night of Yom Kippur? We had an additional eleven days—after the gates closed—to try to get a better verdict. I could have used the extra time.

7. **Shemini Atzeret:** The eighth day of Sukkot is the hardest holiday for Jews of all stripes to elucidate, because Sukkot is, by definition, seven days (so how can there be an eighth?), and because this holiday in Israel is conflated with Simchat Torah (the completion of the entire Torah reading for the year). I'll try to forget the confusion and remember its touching message: God wants us to tarry one day longer after hanging with us in the sukkah for a week.

8. **Simchat Torah:** Dancing with the Torah (and the hordes) is a rapture I'll nudge my friends to try with me each year. It's worth the humiliation. (Pre-gaming recommended.) Who cares if this holiday appears nowhere in the Torah? It was a great rabbinic invention, once the sages realized how psyched people were to finish one cycle of the entire story and start it all over again.

9. **Hanukkah:** I was disillusioned to learn the enemy was also us, that Hanukkah history entails Jews fighting Jews, not just oppressive Greeks. Okay, that's an oversimplification of a really complicated ancient dispute, but suffice it to say that the Maccabees weren't solely heroic, despite the fact that I dressed up as them at my childhood Hanukkah parties. I also loved this holiday's menorah metaphors: adding light or subtracting it. It came at the time when Milt was sick, and I saw the light leaving, and light remaining—his family keeping his memory ablaze.

10. **The Tenth of Tevet:** The third fast (marking the siege of Jerusalem) fell on New Year's Day, so I was hungry and hung over, not a great combination. That said, I was struck by Rabbi Blau's message to pay attention to the first signs of zealotry, and Rabbi Tucker's clarification that we don't have to fast if we're not currently persecuted. While the jury is out as to whether Jews are, there's zero doubt many are hurting. So we should be helping someone. And worrying less about eating (for a change).

11. **Tu B'Shvat:** Our tradition seems to know when we need a shot of joy after melancholy, not to mention an infusion of spring during relentless winter. The new year of the trees was a welcome reminder—in icy February—that

the earth is bountiful (albeit imperiled) and that our personalities resemble fruit. (Identify your personal pits and how they get in your way.)

12. **The Fast of Esther:** The fourth famishment (okay, a little hyperbole) came one day before Purim and made me revisit the moments when I've chickened out. Because Esther didn't.

13. **Purim:** The scotch tasting on Purim was a boozy way to end a fast, reminding me that Jews like their wassail. I tallied: the single malt of Simchat Torah, the four cups of wine on Tu B'Shvat, and the four cups of Manischewitz on Passover. But more importantly, Purim was a flashpoint of survival in the face of near-extermination: the anti-Shoah.

14. **Passover:** My family seder became, for me, the epitome of my holiday mission, a chance to share my discoveries with the people I hope find it contagious. I led the seder not as an evangelist but a beckoner, saying, please come this way with me so you can discover what I have—how fertile and germane the Exodus can be. One day later, I returned, unexpectedly and memorably, to my childhood's third seder, the Feminist iteration, and saw how revolutionary ritual can accrue its own history.

15. **Yom HaShoah:** I will remember the low light in a sparse sanctuary on this day of Holocaust Remembrance, as volunteer after volunteer strained to read endless names of the murdered, into the night. I'll remember that I couldn't see the list clearly enough to take part, despite reading glasses. The font was *that small*—to fit a list *that* large, family after family, country after country. The columns went on and on, and I felt guilty leaving to go to bed.

16. **Yom HaZikaron:** Of all modern holidays, this felt the most foreign. Israel's Memorial Day—the marking of Israel's fallen soldiers and victims of terrorism. I don't personally know any of the wars' casualties. I admire them deeply from afar. I worry there have been too many and there will be too many more. And I'll remember bomb victim Marla Bennett, who died eating lunch between classes.

17. **Yom Ha'atzmaut:** Israel Independence Day. There's no home custom for this patriotic holiday, which is probably why it's hardly observed in America. Seidler-Feller told me that "no Jewish holiday can survive without a table"; we need a meal to mark things. Maybe our holidays falter without feasts or fasts. Or maybe this celebration has just been hindered by intransigent politics—with some Jews worrying about too much Jewish triumphalism and others worrying there's not enough.

18. **Lag B'Omer:** The thirty-third of the forty-nine days we count between Passover (Egypt escape) and Shavuot (Torah bestowal), might have felt more like a technicality than a holiday, except I learned that the holiday is, in no small measure, about respect. And respect clearly hung in the balance just the week before, when coincidentally the U.S. Supreme Court heard arguments on gay marriage. That felt especially resonant to me on Lag B'Omer because two close gay friends were planning to marry on the forty-ninth day.

19. **Shavuot:** Though I now know that this celebration of receiving the law at Sinai was an invention of the rabbis, I love any excuse for an all-night party of Jewish learning. Call me a study-nerd, but the marathon was worth the fatigue, and the cheesecake worth the calories. And I won't forget Rabbi Kula's idea that Shavuot is the moment we were unfragmented, standing side by side, suspending disagreement. It represents "the yearning to know what it is we're really supposed to do with our lives."

20. **The 17th of Tammuz:** This fifth fast of the year (marking the breach of the walls of Jerusalem) was also badly timed for a semi-secular Jew who loves her secular holidays, too. Just as the January fast (Tenth of Tevet) followed New Year's Eve, this fast fell the day after July 4th. But one phone call with Stein Hain made the day suddenly matter. She identified a specific, sad gap between a sure death and the inescapable route to it. The Jews in ancient Jerusalem knew they were surrounded and sure to perish; but they held on. So did my father-in-law, as he faded in February. So is my friend Julie, staving off a cancer that will rob her of her motherhood. (Julie died seven months after I finished the year—in March 2016, when her children were seven and five.)

21. **Tisha B'Av:** The final holiday, the final fast. I was moved that I'd made it to the proverbial finish line. And awed to think that it would soon be starting all over again. I was annoyed to fast at the height of summer. But more annoyed by my annoyance: *Are you really going to complain about one day of discomfort, given all the suffering it marks?* Finally, I was disillusioned again by *sinat chinam*, baseless hatred, alert to how reliably internal hatred repeats itself, and yet uplifted by the support I received during this trek by so many Jews who approach tradition and ritual differently. I came away feeling more community than I did discord. So many helped me learn.

APPENDIX 2

INTERVIEWS

Rabbi Lauren Berkun, Director of Rabbinic and Synagogue Programs for the Shalom Hartman Institute of North America, Aventura, FL

Rabbi Jonathan Blake, Senior Rabbi, Westchester Reform Temple, Scarsdale, NY

Rabbi Yosef Blau, Faculty (Senior Mashgiach Ruchani), Yeshiva University, NYC

Rabbi Sharon Brous, Cofounder, IKAR, Los Angeles

Dr. Erica Brown, Director of Mayberg Center for Jewish Education and Leadership at George Washington University's Graduate School of Education and Human Development

Rabbi Angela Buchdahl, Senior Rabbi, Central Synagogue, NYC

Rabbi Adam Chalom, Rabbi, Kol Hadash Humanistic Congregation, Lincolnshire, IL

Rabbi Ayelet Cohen, Director of the Center for Jewish Living, JCC in Manhattan

Rabbi Michael Cohen, Director of Strategic Partnerships, Arava Institute for Environmental Studies, Israel

Rabbi Elliot Cosgrove, Senior Rabbi, Park Avenue Synagogue, NYC

Rabbi Joshua Davidson, Senior Rabbi, Congregation Emanu-El, NYC

Rabbi David Ellenson, Chancellor Emeritus of Hebrew Union College-Jewish Institute of Religion, NYC

Rabbi Jacqueline Koch Ellenson, Director of the Women's Rabbinic Network, NYC

Rabba Yaffa Epstein, Director of Education, North America for the Pardes Institute of Jewish Studies, Jerusalem

Rabbi Steven Exler, Senior Rabbi, Hebrew Institute of Riverdale, NY

Bruce Feiler, Author, *Walking the Bible: A Journey by Land Through the Five Books of Moses*

Rabbi Ed Feinstein, Senior Rabbi, Valley Beth Shalom, Encino, CA

Rabbi Art Green, Rector, Hebrew College, Boston

Rabbi Micah Greenstein, Senior Rabbi, Temple Israel, Memphis

Blu Greenberg, Founding President of JOFA, the Jewish Orthodox Feminist Allicance

Rabbi Irving Greenberg, Author, *The Jewish Way*, Cofounder, the National Jewish Center for Learning and Leadership (CLAL)

Dr. Elana Stein Hain, Director of Leadership Education at the Shalom Hartman Institute of North America, NYC

Rabbi Jill Hammer, Director of Spiritual Education at the Academy for Jewish Religion

Rabbi Judith Hauptman, Professor of Talmud and Rabbinic Culture, Jewish Theological Seminary, NYC

Rabbi Shai Held, Cofounder, Dean, and Chair in Jewish Thought at Mechon Hadar

Rabbi Ammiel Hirsch, Senior Rabbi, Stephen Wise Free Synagogue, NY

Rabbi Brad Hirschfeld, Faculty of the National Jewish Center for Learning and Leadership (CLAL)

Rabba Sara Hurwitz, Dean, Yeshivat Maharat, NYC

Rabbi David Ingber, Founder/Rabbi, Romemu, NYC

Rabbi Jill Jacobs, Executive Director T'ruah: The Rabbinic Call for Human Rights

Rabbi Rick Jacobs, President of the Union for Reform Judaism, NYC

Rabbi David Kalb, Rabbi of The Jewish Learning Center of New York

Rabbi Elie Kaunfer, Cofounder and Executive Director of Mechon Hadar, NYC

Rabbi Sharon Kleinbaum, Senior Rabbi, CBST (Congregation Beth Simchat Torah)

Rabbi Irwin Kula, Faculty of the National Jewish Center for Learning and Leadership (CLAL), NYC

Dr. Yehuda Kurtzer, President, Shalom Hartman Institute of North America, NYC

Arthur Kurzweil, Author, *Pebbles of Wisdom from Rabbi Adin Steinsaltz*

Rabbi Amichai Lau-Lavie, Founding Director of Storahtelling Inc and the Spiritual Leader of Lab/Shul

Rabbi Joy Levitt, Executive Director, JCC Manhattan, NYC

Rabbi Naomi Levy, Cofounder, Nashuva, Los Angeles

Rabbi Dov Linzer, Rabbinic Head (Rosh HaYeshiva), Yeshivat Chovevei Torah Rabbinical School

Rabbi Asher Lopatin, President, Yeshivat Chovevei Torah Rabbinical School

Rabbi Sara Luria, Founder and Executive Director, ImmerseNYC

Daniel Matt, Kabbalah Scholar and Professor at the Graduate Theological Union in Berkeley, CA

Rabbi Michael Paley, Scholar in Residence at the Jewish Resource Center of UJA-Federation of New York

Rabbi Jonah Pesner, Director of the Religious Action Center of Reform Judaism, Washington, D.C.

Rabbi Peter J. Rubinstein, Rabbi Emeritus, Central Synagogue, NY/92Y's Director of Jewish Community and the Bronfman Center for Jewish Life

Rabbi Joanna Samuels, Executive Director, Manny Cantor Center, NYC

Rabbi Maurice Salth, Rabbi, Central Synagogue, NYC

Seth Schwartz, Professor of Classical Jewish Civilization, Columbia University

Rabbi Chaim Seidler-Feller, Director Emeritus, Hillel at UCLA

Rabbi Avi Shafran, Director of Public Affairs, Agudath Israel of America, NYC

Judith Shulevitz, Author, *The Sabbath World: Glimpses of a Different Order of Time*

Michael Simon, Executive Director, Northwestern Hillel

Rabbi Mychal Springer, Director, Center for Pastoral Education of The Jewish Theological Seminary of America

Rabbi Chaim Steinmetz, Senior Rabbi, Kehilath Jeshurun, NYC

Rabbi Adin Steinsaltz, Translation and Commentary, The Steinsaltz Jerusalem Talmud

Rabbi Michael Strassfeld, Rabbi Emeritus, Society for the Advancement of Judasim, NYC

Rabbi Ethan Tucker, Cofounder and Rosh Yeshiva at Mechon Hadar

Rabbi Burton Visotzky, Professor of Midrash and Interreligious Studies at The Jewish Theological Seminary, NYC

Rabbi Arthur Waskow, Founder/Director, Shalom Center, Philadelphia, PA

Rabbi Avi Weiss, Founding Rabbi, Hebrew Institute of Riverdale/Founder, Yeshivat Chovevei Torah Rabbinical School

Rabbi David Wolpe, Senior Rabbi, Sinai Temple, Los Angeles

APPENDIX 3

BIBLIOGRAPHY

Aish.com. http://www.aish.com/.

Brown, Dr. Erica. *Spiritual Boredom: Rediscovering the Wonder of Judaism.* Woodstock, VT: Jewish Lights, 2009.

Feld, Rabbi Edward, ed. *Mahzor Lev Shalem.* New York: Rabbinical Assembly, 2010.

Foer, Jonathan Safran, ed, and Nathan Englander *New American Haggadah.* New York: Little, Brown and Company, 2014.

Frankl, Viktor E. *Man's Search for Meaning.* Boston: Beacon Press, 2006.

Freedman, Samuel G. *Jew vs. Jew: The Struggle for the Soul of American Jewry.* New York: Simon & Schuster, 2007.

Goldberg, Rabbi Edwin, Rabbi Janet Marder, Rabbi Sheldon Marder, and Rabbi Leon Morris, with Rabbi Elaine Zecher, Cantor Evan Kent, and Rabbi Peter Berg, eds. *Mishkan HaNefesh.* New York: CCAR Press, 2015.

Green, Arthur. *These Are the Words: A Vocabulary of Jewish Spiritual Life.* Woodstock, VT: Jewish Lights, 2012.

Greenberg, Rabbi Irving. *The Jewish Way: Living the Holidays.* New York: Touchstone, 2011.

Held, Shai. Abraham Joshua Heschel. *The Call of Transcendence.* Bloomington and Indianapolis: Indiana University Press, 2014.

Heschel, Abraham Joshua. *The Sabbath.* New York: Farrar, Straus and Giroux, 2005.

Hoffman, Rabbi Lawrence A., ed. *Who by Fire, Who by Water: Un'taneh Tokef (Prayers of Awe).* Woodstock, VT: Jewish Lights, 2010.

Judaism 101. http://www.jewfaq.org/index.shtml.

Kaunfer, Rabbi Elie. *Empowered Judaism: What Independent Minyanim Can Teach Us about Building Vibrant Jewish Communities.* Woodstock, VT: Jewish Lights, 2010.

Klagsbrun, Francine. *Jewish Days: A Book of Jewish Life and Culture Around the Year.* New York: Farrar, Straus and Giroux, 1996.

Kula, Rabbi Irwin. *Yearnings: Embracing the Sacred Messiness of Life.* New York: Hachette Books, 2006.

Kurtzer, Yehuda. *Shuva: The Future of the Jewish Past.* Waltham, MA: Brandeis University Press, 2012.

Kurzweil, Arthur. *On the Road with Rabbi Steinsaltz: 25 Years of Pre-Dawn Car Trips, Mind-Blowing Encounters, and Inspiring Conversations with a Man of Wisdom.* San Francisco: Jossey-Bass, 2006.

Levi, Primo. *Survival in Auschwitz.* New York: CreateSpace Independent Publishing Platform, 2013.

Levitt, Rabbi Joy, and Rabbi Michael Strassfeld. *A Night of Questions: A Passover Haggadah.* Elkins Park, PA: The Reconstructionist Press, 2000.

Lew, Alan. *This Is Real and You Are Completely Unprepared: The Days of Awe as a Journey of Transformation.* Boston, New York, and London: Little, Brown and Company, 2003.

Matt, Daniel. *The Zohar: Pritzker Edition.* (Vols. 1-9). Redwood City, CA: Stanford University Press, 2002-16.

MyJewishLearning.com. http://www.myjewishlearning.com/.

Nathan, Joan. *Jewish Cooking in America: Expanded Edition (Knopf Cooks American).* New York: Alfred A. Knopf, 1998.

Pogrebin, Abigail. *Stars of David: Prominent Jews Talk About Being Jewish.* New York: Broadway Books, 2005.

Rosensaft, Menchaem Z. *God, Faith & Identity from the Ashes: Reflections of Children and Grandchildren of Holocaust Survivors.* Woodstock, VT: Jewish Lights, 2014.

Rosenstein, Joseph. *Machzor Eit Ratzon.* Highland Park, NJ: Shiviti Publications, 2011.

Sacks, Rabbi Lord Jonathan. *The Jonathan Sacks Haggada.* Jerusalem: Koren Publishers Jerusalem, 2013.

Sacks, Rabbi Lord Jonathan. *To Heal a Fractured World: The Ethics of Responsibility.* New York: Schocken, 2007.

Shapiro, Mark Dov. *Gates of Shabbat: Shaarei Shabbat: A Guide for Observing Shabbat,* Revised Edition. New York: CCAR Press, 2016.

Shulevitz, Judith. *The Sabbath World: Glimpses of a Different Order of Time.* New York: Random House, 2010. Kindle edition.

Steinsaltz, Rabbi Adin, *The Essential Talmud.* New York: Basic Books, 2006.

Steinsaltz, Rabbi Adin and Arthur Kurzweil. *Pebbles of Wisdom from Rabbi Adin Steinsaltz, Edited and with Commentary by Arthur Kurzweil.* San Francisco: Jossey-Bass, 2009.

Strassfeld, Michael. *Jewish Holidays.* New York: William Morrow Paperbacks, 2011.

Telushkin, Rabbi Joseph. *Jewish Literacy Revised Ed.: The Most Important Things to Know About the Jewish Religion, Its People, and Its History.* New York: William Morrow, 2008.

Teutsch, David A. *A Guide to Jewish Practice: Volume 2—Shabbat and Holidays.* Wyncote, PA: Reconstructionist Rabbinical College Press, 2014.

Weiss, Rabbi Avi. *Haggadah for the Yom HaShoah Seder.* Hackensack, NJ: Jonas Pub, 2000.

West Coast Chabad Lubavitch. https://www.chabad.com/.

Wieseltier, Leon. *Kaddish.* New York: Alfred A. Knopf, 1998.

Wolfson, Dr. Ron. Shabbat: *The Family Guide to Preparing for and Celebrating the Sabbath.* Woodstock, VT: Jewish Lights, 2002.

Wolpe, David J. *Why Be Jewish?* New York: Henry Holt & Co., 1995.

APPENDIX 4

GLOSSARY

ADONAI: God.

AFIKOMEN: "Dessert," or "that which comes after." The piece of matzah set aside at the beginning of the Passover seder and which must be eaten at the end.

AGUDATH ISRAEL: An ultra-Orthodox communal organization.

AGUNAH: "Chained woman." This term refers to a woman who cannot re-marry according to halachah (Jewish law). It most often is used to refer more specifically, to a married woman whose husband refuses to issue her a gett—a halachic writ of divorce.

AGUNOT: Plural of agunah.

AL CHEIT: "For the sin." A confessional prayer that appears multiple times throughout the High Holy Day liturgy. The prayer consists of forty-four individual "al cheit," each one enumerating a different sin or category of sins for which we seek divine forgiveness.

AL KOL ELEH [Song Title]:   Literally, "For all These Things." Written by Is-raeli songwriter Naomi Shemer.

ALIYAH: "To go up." Can refer either to moving to Israel and becoming an Israeli citizen, or to being called up to the bimah to make the blessings over the reading of the Torah.

ARK: The structure that holds the Torah scrolls in a synagogue. The very first ark contained the two tablets on which were inscribed the Ten Command-ments. It resided in the innermost sanctum in the Tabernacle, a portable Tem-ple of sorts, and was carried by the Israelites through the desert.

ASHKENAZI JEWS: "German Jews." The Diaspora population that settled first in Germany, and then spread out to Central and Eastern Europe. Their vernacular was Yiddish, a German dialect with words from Hebrew and modern European languages.

ASSERET YIMEI TESHUVA (The Ten Days of Repentance):   The period beginning with Rosh Hashanah and ending with Yom Kippur, during which we are to ask forgiveness from those we have wronged and repent our sins before God.

ASSIYAH: "Making." In Kabbalah, it refers to the world of action, the lowest of the four worlds that make up the Kabbalistic tree of life and that are represented in the Tu B'Shvat seder.

ATZILUT: "Emanation." In Kabbalah, it refers to the world of the spirit, the highest of the four worlds that make up the Kabbalistic tree of life and that are represented in the Tu B'Shavat seder.

AVINU MALKEINU: Literally, "Our Father, Our King." A prayer from the liturgy of Yom Kippur and the Ten Days of Repentance, as well as the liturgy of fast days. It contains forty-three short supplications to God, each one beginning with the phrase *"Avinu Malkeinu."*

AVODAH: Work. In a religious context, this refers to service of God. It can also refer more specifically to acts of worship: bringing sacrifices or offering verbal prayers.

AYIN HARA: The evil eye.

AZAZEL: In the Torah, the place to which a sacrificial goat was exiled on Yom Kippur, carrying the sins of the people; most probably, a wilderness location. According to others, it is the name of a demon.

B'NAI MITZVAH: Plural form of bar mitzvah or bat mitzvah. Can refer to multiple bar and bat mitzvah ceremonies, or to people who have just undergone such a ceremony.

BAR MITZVAH: Literally "son of commandment." The coming-of-age ceremony for a boy, traditionally at age thirteen. Can also refer to the boy himself.

BAT MITZVAH: Literally "daughter of commandment." The coming-of-age ceremony for a girl, traditionally at age twelve. Can also refer to the girl herself.

BAYIT: Home.

BEDIKAT CHAMETZ: The ritual search for chametz—bread or anything leavened performed in the home the evening before Passover begins.

BEIT MIDRASH: House of Study. The room that is the center of a yeshiva or other institute of Torah learning, where people study, discuss, and debate traditional texts—most often Talmud—in study pairs, known as chavrutot (sing., chavruta).

BEITZAH: An egg. In the Passover context refers to the charred egg on the seder plate, symbolizing the peace-offering sacrifice, which was brought—together with the paschal (lamb) sacrifice—to the ancient Temple in Jerusalem on the day before Passover. The egg also symbolizes the cycle of the year.

BERIYAH: Literally, "creation." In Kabbalah, it refers to the world of intellect and imagination, the second of the four worlds that make up the Kabbalistic tree of life and that are represented in the Tu B'Shavat seder.

BIMAH: The platform or stage in the synagogue from which the Torah is read. It is also often where the prayer leader stands when leading prayers. It may be in the center or the front of the sanctuary.

BRIS: "Covenant." The circumcision ceremony for a baby boy, which occurs on the eighth day after birth.

CANTOR: The singer of liturgy; prayer leader.

CHABAD: A Hasidic movement, also known as Lubavitch Hasidim (the name Chabad is an acronym for chachmah, binah, vi'da'at, wisdom, understanding, and knowledge). It is one of the best known and most influential of Hasidic movements, and prioritizes outreach to unaffiliated and unengaged Jews throughout the world.

CHAG: A Jewish holiday, connoting a time of joy.

CHAG SAMEACH: "Happy Holiday!" A greeting offered on Jewish holidays.

CHAG URIM: Festival of Lights. Another term for Hanukkah.

CHAI: "Life." Also, the number 18, the numerical equivalent of the word's Hebrew letters. It is traditional to give tzedakah in denominations of chai (e.g., $18, $54, $180), to symbolize a wish or prayer for long life.

CHALLAH: The oblong braided bread that is traditionally eaten on Shabbat and Jewish holidays. A round challah is eaten on Rosh Hashanah to symbolize the cycle of the year.

CHAMETZ: Leaven products, such as leavened dough, bread, pasta, crackers, cookies, and pasteries. According to the Torah, chametz may not be eaten or owned during the week of Passover.

CHANUKKAH: See Hanukkah.

CHESED: Loving-kindness, the quality of giving something to another even if underserved, purely out of love. It is also one of the Thirteen Attributes of God.

CHESHBON HANEFESH: Accounting of, or for, the soul. The process of introspection and self-assessment. A spiritual practice for some pious individuals throughout the year, it is a practice that all are expected to engage in during the Hebrew month of Elul, leading up to Rosh HaShanah and Yom Kippur.

CHUTZPAH: Yiddish for audacity or temerity.

CONVERSOS: Latin for converts. Those Jews in Spain and Portugal, primarily in the fourteenth and fifteenth centuries, who converted to Catholicism to avoid persecution or expulsion.

DAYENU: "It would have been enough for us." The name of song sung during the Passover seder, the thrust of which is that it would have been enough for us if God had just taken us out of Egypt, but God did so much more.

DAYS OF AWE: The period from Rosh Hashanah through Yom Kippur, also known as the *asseret yimei teshuvah*, the Ten Days of Atonement. The term may also refer to Rosh Hashanah and Yom Kippur specifically.

DEUTERONOMY: Literally, "second law." The fifth of the five books of the Torah.

DREIDEL: The four-sided spinning top with Hebrew letters that children spin in a Hanukkah game. The letters, Nun, Gimel, Hay, and Shin, stand for "A Great Miracle Happened There." In Israel, the Shin is replaced with a Peh, to mean "A Great Miracle Happened Here."

EICHAH: "How?" This is the Hebrew name of the book of Lamentations. The book laments the destruction of Jerusalem, and expresses the inability to comprehend how God could have allowed the Second Temple to be destroyed by the Romans.

ELUL: Name of a Hebrew month, which usually spans August and September and is when repentance is supposed to begin in anticipation of Rosh Hashanah and Yom Kippur.

EREV: The day prior to the onset of Shabbat and Jewish holidays, which begin at nightfall. Erev Shabbat is Friday afternoon; Erev Pesach is the day before the evening of the Passover seder.

ESROG OR ETROG: A citrus fruit that looks like a lemon; it is taken and waved together with the lulav bundle on the holiday of Sukkot.

EXODUS: "Mass departure." The second of the five books of the Torah, which describes the escape (from Egypt) of the Israelites who were enslaved there.

GEDALIAH: The name of the ancient Judahite (Jewish) governor who was picked by the Babylonian king to rule over the remaining population in the province of Yehud (Judah) in the land of Israel after the destruction of the First Temple. He was assassinated by his fellow Jews.

GENESIS: "The beginning." The first book of the Torah.

GETT   a halachic writ of divorce.

"A GUTEN KVITEL:"   Yiddish for "a good note." This greeting is given on Hoshanah Rabbah, understood to be the final day of the period of repentance. It conveys the wish that one's verdict should be a good one, and that God has written the person into the Book of Life for another year.

HAGGADAH: "The telling." The text that is read and discussed during the Passover seder.

HAKADDISH HAKLALI: "The General Kaddish Day." The original name for a newly created holiday in 1949—attached to the fast of the Tenth of Tevet—to honor those who died in the Holocaust without leaving behind anyone to say the Mourner's Kaddish for them.

HAKAFAH: The circuit taken around the bimah with lulav and etrog every day during Sukkot, and with the Torah scrolls during Simchat Torah celebrations.

HALACHAH OR HALAKHAH: Jewish law or jurisprudence, based on the Talmud.

HAMAN: In the Purim story, Haman is the evil court adviser to King Ahasuerus who plotted to kill all the Jews in Persia.

HAMANTASCHEN: Literally, "Haman's pockets." The three-cornered cookies filled with poppy seeds or fruit preserves, traditionally eaten on Purim, often associated with Haman's hat or—in Israel—with his ears.

HANUKKAH OR CHANUKKAH: "Dedication." The eight-day holiday that marks the military victory of the Maccabees—the leaders of the Jewish rebel army—over the Seleucid (Syrian-Greek) armies in the land of Israel, restoring Jewish sovereignty to the region, and the retaking and rededication of the Temple, which occurred at that time. It also commemorates the miracle of the oil, where the one day's worth of oil that was used to light the menorah in the Temple miraculously lasted for eight days.

HANUKKIAH: The eight-branched Hanukkah menorah, or candelabrum, which is lit in the home on every night of Hanukkah.

HAROSET: The mixture of apple, honey, nuts, and wine—or other similar ingredients—eaten at Passover seder and said to symbolize the mortar used by Israelite slaves to build the Egyptian cities of Pithom and Raamses under Pharaoh.

HASHKIVEINU: "Shelter us." This is a prayer or song, recited daily in the evening prayer services, asking God to protect us.

HASIDISM: A Jewish movement or sect founded in the eighteenth century, emphasizing the religiosity of the masses and the importance of reverence for and submission to a rebbe, a single charismatic religious leader. Today, Hasidim are considered a subgroup within Ultra-Orthodox, or "Haredi," Judaism, and they are distinguished by distinctive forms of dress, social isolationism, and religious conservatism.

HATIKVAH: "The hope." The name of Israel's national anthem.

HAZERET: The bitter vegetable on the seder plate, symbolizing the bitterness of slavery. The hazeret is to some degree the same as the maror, and many families do not have hazeret on their seder plates because they decide the maror is sufficient.

HAZZAN: A cantor or musical prayer leader for Jewish services.

HILLULA: Wedding celebration.

HINENI: Literally, "Here I am." The response of many figures in the Bible when God calls to them.

HOSHANA RABBAH: "Great Supplication" or "Great Praise." The name of the seventh day of Sukkot, celebrated with its own synagogue services, including seven circuits around the bimah with the lulav and etrog, and supplications to God for a prosperous year.

HUPPAH (OR CHUPPAH):   The wedding canopy

IKAR: The name of the spiritual community based on engagement, ritual and spiritual practice, and social justice, founded by Rabbi Sharon Brous. In Hebrew, *ikar* means "essence."

KABBALAT SHABBAT: Welcoming the Sabbath. This is the traditional Friday night service that precedes the Sabbath.

KADDISH: A prayer of sanctification of God's name. There are a number of types of Kaddish, the Mourner's Kaddish being the most well known; the term often refers specifically to the Mourner's Kaddish for the dead.

KADOSH: Holy or held separate and apart.

KARPAS: A vegetable, such as parsley or celery, eaten at the Passover seder, symbolizing spring.

KASHER: To make kosher. Traditional Jews will "kasher the kitchen" before Passover—removing all bread and bread products, cleaning the oven, scouring all surfaces, and exchanging the dishes and silverware for special Passover ones.

KASHRUT: The rules of eating kosher, based on the laws that appear in the Torah and were expanded in the Talmud.

KAVANAH: Intention. Often, a thought shared or reflected upon before one performs a mitzvah or religious act, to focus us on the act and its significance.

KAVOD HAMET: The honor shown to the dead, which includes the care of the body before burial (shemirah), dressing the body in shrouds, and the burial of the body in the ground.

KETUBAH OR KETUVAH: The marriage contract at a Jewish wedding detailing the reciprocal obligations of the bride and the groom. Some contemporary versions will also contain expressions of love and commitment.

KIDDUSH: "Sanctification." The blessings recited over the wine on Shabbat at the outset of the meal, declaring the sanctity of the Sabbath day.

KIPPAH: A circular, rimless head-covering worn to show humility under God. Traditionally worn by Jewish males, it is now occasionally worn by girls and women as well. Also known as yarmulke.

KITTEL: The white coat worn often by rabbis or prayer leaders on Yom Kippur, by a groom under the chuppah, or by the person leading the seder. A kittel is also used as a burial shroud for a dead body.

KLAL YISRAEL: "The whole of Israel." The entire Jewish people.

KOL NIDRE: "All the Vows." The name of the prayer recited in the synagogue on the eve of Yom Kippur that annuls any vows that we might make in the coming year (or, according to others, that annuls vows that we have made in the past year). Also the name of the entire prayer service on the eve of Yom Kippur.

KOSHER: "Acceptable." Describes food that may be eaten according to the laws laid down in the Torah and developed in the Halakha (Jewish law). Can also be used to describe eating establishments which follow these rules, and cooking utensils, dishes and silverware which may be used according to these rules.

KVETCHING: Yiddish for complaining.

LAG B'OMER: Literally, "the thirty-third day of the Omer." This holiday occurs on the thirty-third day of the counting of the Omer, the forty-nine-day period stretching from Pesach (Passover) to Shavuot (when the Torah was given). It marks the day that a plague that had wiped out Rabbi Akiva's students had come to an end. In Kabbalistic tradition, it commemorates the anniversary of the death of Rabbi Shimon Bar Yocha (aka Rashbi), the putative author of the Zohar (the chief text of Jewish mysticism) who is said to have had a union with God at his death.

LATKES: Potato pancakes, traditionally eaten on Hanukkah.

LEVITICUS: "Priestly law." The third of the five books of the Torah.

LIMMUD NY: A three-day learning festival that happens annually in New York, for Jews of all backgrounds, patterned after the original Limmud, Limmud UK.

LITURGY: The text for worship.

LULAV: A closed frond of the date nut tree; it is taken and waved together with the etrog on the holiday of Sukkot.

MAARIV: Evening prayer, also referred to as Aravit.

MACCABEES: The Hebrew army, led by Judah the Maccabee, which routed the Seleucid (Syrian-Greek) armies in the land of Israel, restoring sovereignty and freedom of worship for the inhabitant Jewish population.

MACHER: "Maker." Yiddish for a big shot, a fixer, a mover and shaker.

MACHZOR: Holiday prayer book.

MAGGID: The storytelling section of the Passover seder, when the Exodus narrative is recounted aloud.

MALCHUYOT: "Sovereignty." Verses expressing divine sovereignty that are recited on Rosh Hashanah during Mussaf, one of the central prayers of the day.

MALKEINU: "Our king."

MAOZ TZUR: "Mighty Rock." A traditional Hanukkah song in Hebrew. The English language version of the song is known as "Rock of Ages."

MAROR: The bitter herb on the seder plate that conjures the bitterness of slavery to which the Israelites were subjected in ancient Egypt.

MATZAH OR MATZO: Bread that has been made without the dough having had a chance to rise. In ancient times, this was similar to a pita. In modern times, it is usually made as a flat, hard cracker-like bread. Matzah is eaten at the seder and during the eight days of Passover as a reminder of the ancient Israelites who were escaping slavery in Egypt and had no time to let their bread rise.

MECHITZAH: The gender-dividing wall or screen in an Orthodox synagogue. A balcony can serve the same function as a mechitza.

MECHON HADAR: Independent learning institute in Manhattan.

MEGILLAH: A scroll of parchment that has the biblical book of Esther inscribed on it. The megillah is traditionally read aloud on Purim.

MENORAH: A candelabrum. This often refers to the hanukkiah, the eight-branched Hanukkah candelabrum that is lit every night of Hanukkah.

MENUCHAH: Rest. A central theme of the Sabbath.

MESHUGAH: Yiddish for crazy or nuts.

MESHUGENAH: Yiddish for a person who is nuts.

MEZUZAH: "Doorpost." A piece of parchment with the biblical verses of the *Shema* (Deuteronomy 6:4-9 and 11:13-2) inscribed on it, which is affixed to the doorposts of a home.

MEZUZOT: Plural for mezuzah.

MIDDOT: Character traits.

MIDRASH: "Interpretation." A genre of rabbinic commentary on the Torah, often containing elaborations or interpretations of the biblical stories.

MIKVEH: A ritual bath, used to create a state of ritual purity.

MINCHAH: The Afternoon Prayer.

MINYAN: A quorum of ten, required for certain prayers, including the Mourner's Kaddish.

MISHEBERACH: "The one who blesses." A prayer for the sick made in the synagogue, primarily at the time of Torah reading.

MITZRAYIM: Egypt.

MITZVAH: Commandment or good deed.

MITZVOT: Plural of mitzvah.

MOHEL: The ritual officiant at a bris.

MOURNER'S KADDISH: The prayer of sanctification of God's name said for the dead, recited by mourners during the period of mourning, and on the anniversary of the death. A quorum of ten people is required for it to be said.

MUSSAF: An additional prayer added after Shacharit (morning prayer service) on Shabbat and holidays.

"NA'ASEH V'NISHMAH:"   "We will do and we will listen." This was said by the Israelites at the foot of Mount Sinai at the time of the receiving of the Torah.

NACHES: Yiddish for feelings of pride, typically the pride or joy one has from one's children.

NASHUVA: "We will return." Also the name of the spiritual community founded and led by Rabbi Naomi Levy in Los Angeles.

NEBUCHADENZZAR: The Babylonian king who led the conquest of Jerusalem and the destruction of the First Temple in 586 B.C.E.

NEILAH: "Locking." The additional service added at the end of Yom Kippur, to allow for one final chance of repentance and supplication as the Gates of Heaven are closing.

NIGGUN: A Jewish religious melody sung without words.

NIGGUNIM   plural of niggun.

NISSAN: The Hebrew month in which both Passover and Yom HaShoah fall. Nissan is supposed to be a month of joy.

NUMBERS: The fourth of the five books of the Torah.

OMER: Literally, "a sheaf." The offering of barley brought to the Temple on the second day of Passover to commemorate the start of the barley harvest. This also refers to the seven-week period of time that begins with the bringing of the Omer sacrifice and ends with the holiday of Shavuot, the Feast of Weeks, when two loaves of bread were brought to the Temple to honor the wheat harvest.

PARSHA OR PARASHA: The portion of the Torah that is read in the synagogue on a given week.

PASSOVER: The holiday that retells the Israelites, deliverance from slavery in Egypt

PESACH: "To pass over," or "to spare." Hebrew word for Passover.

PIRSUM HANESS: "Publicizing the miracle." In order to publicize the miracle of Hanukkah, the menorah is lit in the window so that it can be seen by passersby.

PITAM: The peg-like protrusion from the top of the etrog, not to be confused with the stem at the bottom of the etrog.

PURIM: Literally "lots." The holiday that marks the saving of the Jewish people by Queen Esther in ancient Persia. She foiled a plot by Haman, the king's adviser, to kill all the Jews. The date on which the Jews were to be destroyed was determined by the drawing of lots.

PURIM SPIEL: A Purim play, usually farcical, performed on Purim. Some reenact the Purim story while other spiels are only loosely connected or not connected at all to the story.

RABBI: A Jewish scholar, teacher, or religious leader.

RASHBI: Acronym for Rabbi Shimon Bar Yochai, one of the students of Rabbi Akiva and putative author of the Zohar. The anniversary of Rashbi's death is celebrated on Lag B'Omer.

RODEPH SHALOM: "Pursuer of peace." The name of many synagogues.

ROSH HASHANAH: "Head of the year." This holiday celebrates the Jewish New Year and the creation of the world.

RUGELACH: "Little twists." Horn-shaped rolled pastries filled with nuts, raisins, and the like; traditional Jewish sweets.

SABBATH OR SHABBAT: The weekly day of rest prescribed by the Hebrew Bible, beginning on Friday night at sunset and ending on Saturday night about one hour after sunset. Shabbat is traditionally marked by synagogue services on Friday nights and Saturday mornings, and an abstaining from work including writing, shopping, cooking, etc.

SCHACH: The roof of a sukkah.

SDEROT: The Israeli city closest to the Gaza strip, which has suffered Palestinian rocket and mortar attacks in recent years.

SEDER: "Order." The name of the service that takes place in the home on the first night of Passover.

SELICHOT: "Prayers of forgiveness." Penitential prayers recited before Rosh Hashanah and during the Days of Awe—between Rosh Hashanah and Yom Kippur.

SEPHARDI OR SEPHARDIC JEWS OR SEPHARDIM: The Diaspora population that settled primarily in Spain and Portugal on or around the year 1000, and its later descendants. One of the Sephardim's vernacular languages is Ladino, or Judeo-Spanish, which derives from Spanish, Hebrew, and Aramaic.

SEVENTEENTH OF TAMMUZ OR SHIVAH ASSAR B'TAMMUZ: The fast day that occurs on the seventeenth day of the Hebrew month of Tammuz—usually in June or July—and which recalls when the Romans breached the walls of the Second Temple in Jerusalem in 70 c.e.

SHABBAT: See Sabbath.

SHACHARIT: The morning prayer service.

SHALOM: Peace. Also "hello" or "good-bye." A traditional Jewish greeting.

SHAMASH: A sexton, a person who assists in the running of the synagogue and ensures that its needs are met. Also refers to the lighting candle used to light the other candles in the Hanukkah menorah.

SHAMASHIM: Plural of shamash.

SHANA TOVAH: "May you enjoy a good new year." Usually said on Rosh Hashanah.

SHAVUOT: "Weeks." This is the holiday that occurs seven weeks after Passover. In the Bible, it celebrates the beginning of the wheat harvest, and is generally understood to mark the day of the giving of the Torah on Mount Sinai.

SHEHECHIYANU: "That you have given us life." The blessing for new experiences, for joyous occasions, for seasonal mitzvot, and at the beginning of a Jewish holiday, expressing thanks to God for getting us to this moment.

SHEKHINAH: The feminine aspect of God.

SHEMA: "Hear." Also the name of the prayer recited twice daily that affirms Jews' fidelity to one God.

SHEMAD: Persecution or more literally "extermination" (often refers to periods when Judaism is outlawed and there have been attempts to make Jews convert).

SHEMINI ATZERET: "The cessation of the eighth day." The holiday occurring on the eighth day of Sukkot, often understood to signify the desire to stay a while longer with God before ending all the fall holidays.

SHEMIRAH: The Jewish ritual of watching over a dead body until burial; a form of kavod ha'met (the honor of the dead).

SHFOCH CHAMATCHA: "Pour out your wrath." A prayer recited at the end of the seder asking God to punish our enemies. Many people are opposed to the sentiment expressed in this prayer and choose not to say it.

SHIVA: The seven days of mourning and accepting visitors after a death in the family.

SHIVAH ASSAR B'TAMMUZ: See Seventeenth of Tammuz.

SHMATA: Yiddish for rag.

SHMURAH MATZAH: "Watched" matzah. Matzah that is made from grain that has been watched from the time of the cutting of the wheat to ensure that there was no contact with water prior to the time of baking.

SHOAH: Literally "catastrophe." The Holocaust.

SHOFAR: The ram's horn blown on Rosh Hashanah and during the month of Elul.

SHOFAROT: Verses that contain the theme of the blowing of the shofar, which are recited on Rosh Hashanah during Mussaf, one of the central prayers of the day.

SHOMER SHABBOS OR SHOMER SHABBAT: The term for one who observes the Sabbath according to the requirements of Halakha (Jewish law.)

SHTICK: Yiddish for a gimmick, comic routine, or type of performance associate with a particular person.

SHTUPPING: Yiddish for the act of sex.

SHUL: A synagogue.

SIMCHAT TORAH: "Rejoicing of the Torah." The holiday that occurs at the end of Sukkot and that marks the completion of the annual cycle of the reading of the Torah, when the last section of the Torah is read, followed immediately by a reading of the first section of the Torah, starting the cycle anew. It is a holiday of public rejoicing and dancing with Torah scrolls.

SINAT CHINAM: baseless hatred. The rabbis of the Talmud state that God permitted the Second Temple to be destroyed as punishment for the Jews' baseless hatred of each other, most likely referring to the infighting of Jewish sects during this period.

SUKKAH: The temporary booth that is built in honor of the holiday of Sukkot. We are supposed to eat in the sukkah during the seven days of this holiday.

SUKKOT: "Booths." The name of the seven-day autumn holiday that commemorates the fact that the Israelites dwelled in booths when they left Egypt and serves to remind us of our transience and fragility.

TA'ANIT: A fast day.

TA'ANIT ESTHER: The Fast of Esther. This occurs the day before Purim, and commemorates how Queen Esther asked her fellow Jews to fast with her as she prepared to go to appeal to her husband, King Ahasuerus, to ask him to stop Haman's plot to kill the Jews.

TALLIS OR TALLIT: A prayer shawl with tzitzit, fringes, hanging from each of its four corners.

TALMUD: "Study." The Talmud comprises the Mishna and the Gemara. It is the foundational text of the Oral Law, the Rabbinic rulings, interpretations, and discussions that define, apply, elaborate on, and expand upon the mitzvot in the Torah. It was composed between the second and sixth centuries, and is divided into six orders, and contains sixty-three tractates or books.

TANACH: An acronym for Torah, Neviim (Prophets), and Ketuvim (Writings). The word used for the entire Hebrew Bible.

TANTES: Yiddish for aunties.

TASHLICH: "Casting off." The service on Rosh Hashanah afternoon that takes place near a moving body of water and which symbolizes the ritual casting away of sins into the water.

TEFILAH: Prayer.

TEFILLIN: Phylacteries that are worn daily—except on Shabbat and holidays—by observant Jews during morning prayer services. They consist of two small black boxes, each of which holds four sections of the Torah—the two sections of the Shema as well as two others—written on parchment, and are attached to leather straps, which are used to bind the tefillin on the arm and on the head.

THE TENTH OF TEVET OR TZOM ASARA B'TEVET: The fast of the tenth of Tevet, the Hebrew month usually occurring in December and January. It marks the siege of Jerusalem by the Babylonian army led by Nebuchadnezzar leading up to the destruction of the Temple in 586 B.C.E.

TESHUVAH: "Repentance." The central theme during the period between Rosh Hashanah and Yom Kippur.

TEVET: One of the Hebrew months, usually occurring in December and January.

THE THIRTEEN ATTRIBUTES: The thirteen qualities of God that God revealed to Moses after the sin of the Golden Calf. According to Rabbinic legend, God told Moses that whenever Israel sinned, they need only say these thirteen attributes and they will be forgiven.

TIKKUN: "Repair." A term for a mystical repair of the shattered world. Can also refer to nighttime liturgical readings of mystical significance done on certain holidays.

TIKKUN LEIL SHAVUOT: "Rectification of the Night of Shavuot." Originally a liturgical reading of mystical significance to be said on the night of Shavuot, this term is now used to refer to the night of Torah learning that takes place on the eve of Shavuot, which celebrates the receiving of the Torah at Mount Sinai.

TISHA B'AV: "The Ninth of Av." The final fast day of the Jewish year, which falls at the end of summer during the Hebrew month of Av. This is the only fast, other than Yom Kippur, which begins the night before and lasts for a full twenty-five hours. Its purpose is to mourn all the tragedies that have befallen the Jews over the centuries, most specifically the destruction of both the First and Second Temples in Jerusalem.

TORAH: The five books of Moses consisting of: Genesis, Exodus, Leviticus, Numbers, Deuteronomy.

TU B'SHVAT: Literally, "the fifteenth of Shevat." A holiday occurring during the winter month of Shevat, which marks a new year for trees.

TZEDAKAH: The giving of money to the poor. Also used to refer to monetary donations to synagogues and religious causes.

TZEDEK: Justice

"TZEDEK, TZEDEK TIRDOF:"   "Justice, justice shall you pursue." (Deut. 16:20). This biblical quote serves for some as a primary mandate of the Torah, calling upon us to pursue social justice in the world.

TZOM: Fast.

TZOM GEDALIAH: Fast of Gedaliah. A fast day occurring the day after Rosh Hashanah and commemorating the assassination of Gedaliah, the governor of the Judean province, after the destruction of the Temple in 586 B.C.E.

UNETANE TOKEF: "Let us acknowledge the power [of the holiness of the day]." A central prayer on Rosh Hashanah and Yom Kippur in the Ashkenazic liturgy, underscoring how our fates for the coming year are to be written and sealed on these days. It is also known as the "Who shall live and who shall die" liturgy.

USHPIZIN: "Guests" in Aramaic. On Sukkot, there is a custom of inviting *ushpizin*—ancient guests, such as Abraham, Isaac, and Jacob—into the sukkah.

VA'ANACHNU KORIM: "We bend at the knees." This is part of the Aleinu prayer, which is recited daily and part of the Musaf prayer on Rosh Hashanah. When it is read on Rosh Hashanah, many congregations have the custom that everyone prostrates in prayer.

YA-ALEH: "Let rise." A penitential prayer sometimes sung during Kol Nidre services.

YAHRZEIT: The anniversary of a death.

YAMIM NORAIM: See Days of Awe.

YARMULKE: See kippah.

YECHIDAH: Literally "unit" or "single one." In Kabbalah, the essence of the soul. For some celebrants, it is the fifth world of the Tu B'Shvat seder.

YESHIVA: A school for Jewish learning; it can also refer specifically to a seminary for rabbinic education and training.

YETZIRAH: "Formation." In Kabbalah, it refers to the world of the emotion, the third of the four worlds that make up the Kabbalistic tree of life and that are represented in the Tu B'Shvat seder.

YIZKOR: "He shall remember." The prayer for relatives who have passed, recited in the synagogue on Yom Kippur and the final day of the holidays of Sukkot, Pesach, and Shavuot.

YOM HA'ATZMAUT: Israeli Independence Day.

YOM HASHOAH: "Day of the Holocaust." This is the modern holiday created to honor the victims of the Holocaust who were murdered by the Nazis between 1939–1945.

YOM HAZIKARON: Israeli Memorial Day, commemorating Israel's fallen soldiers and victims of terrorism.

YOM KIPPUR: "The Day of Atonement." The autumn holiday following Rosh Hashanah that marks the end of the Days of Awe. Widely considered the holiest day of the year, it is day devoted to fasting and prayer, when we confess our sins before God and ask forgiveness from the people we've hurt.

ZICHRONOT: "Remembrances." Verses expressing the theme of divine remembrance of humankind and the Jewish people that are recited on Rosh Hashanah during Mussaf, one of the central prayers of the day.

ZIONIST: The term for a founder of the State of Israel or one who believes in its continued existence and self-government.

Z'MAN SIMCHATEINU: Literally, "the season of our joy." This is another name for the holiday of Sukkot.

ZOHAR: The chief text of Jewish mysticism or Kabbalah.

Z'ROA: The lamb shank on the seder plate. It symbolizes the ancient lamb sacrifice made on Passover.

APPENDIX 5

WEB LINKS FOR THE BASICS

1. Jewish Holidays

A basic overview of Jewish holidays including a listing of the major holidays can be found on the "Judaism 101" website at http://www.jewfaq.org/holiday0. htm.

2. Denominations of Judaism

Denominations of Judaism practiced in the United States include the well-known Orthodox, Conservative, Reform, and Reconstruction movements; variations in practice occur within these groups. And, too, other, less well-known denominations are part of the mosaic of Jewish life. An overview of the denominations can be found at: http://www.myjewishlearning.com/article/the-jewish-denominations/#.

In addition, links to the following denominations will provide additional, in-depth information:

Orthodox: https://www.ou.org/
Conservative: http://www.uscj.org
Reform: http://www.urj.org/
Reconstruction: http://www.jewishrecon.org/
Jewish Renewal: https://aleph.org

3. Jewish Life Cycle events

Information on major life-cycle events such as bar and bat mitzvah, marriage, death, etc. can be found at: http://www.aish.com/jl/l/.

4. Basic Jewish beliefs

An introduction to the essential Jewish ideas and beliefs can be found at:

http://www.myjewishlearning.com
http://www.chabad.org/library/article_cdo/aid/109866/jewish/Jew-ish-Beliefs.htm

ABOUT THE AUTHOR

ABIGAIL POGREBIN's immersive exploration of the Jewish calendar began with her popular twelve-month series for the *Forward*. In *My Jewish Year: 18 Holidays, One Wondering Jew*, Pogrebin has expanded her investigation—infusing it with more of her personal story and exposing each ritual's deeper layers of meaning.

Pogrebin is also the author of *Stars of David: Prominent Jews Talk About Being Jewish*, in which she discussed Jewish identity with sixty-two celebrated public figures ranging from Justice Ruth Bader Ginsburg to Steven Spielberg, from Mike Wallace to Natalie Portman. Pogrebin's second book, *One and the Same*, about the challenges of twinship, is grounded in her own experience as half of an identical pair. Most recently, she published *Showstopper*, a best-selling Amazon Kindle Single that recalls her adventures as a sixteen-year-old cast member in the original Broadway production of Stephen Sondheim's flop-turned-cult-favorite, *Merrily We Roll Along*.

Pogrebin's articles have appeared in *Newsweek, New York Magazine*, the *Daily Beast, Tablet*, and many other publications. Pogrebin was formerly a producer for Ed Bradley and Mike Wallace at CBS News' *60 Minutes*, where she was nominated for an Emmy. Before that, she produced for broadcasting pioneers Fred Friendly, Bill Moyers, and Charlie Rose at PBS.

For seven years, Pogrebin has produced and moderated her own interview series at the JCC of Manhattan called *What Everyone's Talking About*. She is also a frequent speaker at synagogues and Jewish organizations around the country, Abigail Pogrebin lives in New York with her husband, David Shapiro, and their two teenage children.